STO

# ACPL ITEM

Y0-BVR-090

# DISCARDED

**DO NOT REMOVE
CARDS FROM POCKET**

# TOUCHING IS HEALING

# Touching Is Healing

Jules Older, Ph.D.

STEIN AND DAY/*Publishers*/New York

Parts of chapters twelve and thirteen first appeared in *Psychiatry*. A portion of chapter five appeared in *Child Abuse and Neglect*. Permission to reprint is gratefully acknowledged.

First published in 1982
Copyright © 1982 by Jules Older
All rights reserved
Designed by Louis A. Ditizio
Printed in the United States of America

STEIN AND DAY/*Publishers*
Scarborough House
Briarcliff Manor, N.Y. 10510

**Library of Congress Cataloging in Publication Data**

Older, Jules.
  Touching is healing.

  Bibliography: p.
  Includes index.
  1. Medical personnel and patient.   2. Touch—
Therapeutic use.   3. Touch—Psychological aspects.
4. Healing—Psychological aspects.   I. Title.
R727.3.037        615.8'22        81-40481
ISBN 0-8128-2837-2                AACR2

This book is dedicated to my parents,
Ruth and Morris Older,
and to my wife's parents,
Carroll and Phyllis Lawes

# CONTENTS

# AROHA*

Wherever in the world I've traveled, the idea of a book on touch and healing has been welcomed with enthusiasm. Many people—far too many to name here—have expressed their enthusiasm by encouragement, contributions of personal experiences, and active research assistance. Among that large number have been some whose assistance has been such that this book would be impoverished without it. Since their effort has crossed national borders, international datelines, and the equator, I gratefully acknowledge them in geographical order. Starting near the bottom of the globe and working in a roughly east-north-east direction, I wish to thank these people:

In Western Australia, Veronica White;

In the South Island of New Zealand, Jim Moody, Basil James, Ian St. George, the staff of the University of Otago Medical Library, and, for typing beyond the call of duty, Kathy White;

In the North Island, Denis O'Reilly and Bruce Gregory;

In Los Angeles, O. Ivar Lovaas;

In Miami, Lynn Carmichael;

In Baltimore, James Lynch, Richard Susel, and, for all manner of help, John Money;

In Boston, Dora Vazquez Older, both for research and translation from the Spanish, and Hobertha Wreagh;

In Burlington, Vermont, Bea Bookchin, Gary Eley, Julie McLane, Rick Nelson, Alistair Philip, Jan Strom, Louise Sunfeather, and, for translation from the Old French, Malcolm Daggett;

In Waterbury, Vermont, Kathy and David Black, who allowed me to witness the birth of their first child;

In Orleans, Vermont, the staff of the Jones Memorial Library;

In Brownington, Vermont, Marshall Hudson-Knapp, John Morley, and Marsha Cherington;

In London, Harold Bourne and Stanford Bourne;

And in Paris, Jill Bourdais de Charbonnière.

*Aroha means love. The best translation of this most important of Maori words is, "A love between my brothers and my sisters."

One friend's help has transcended geography and must be separately acknowledged. Whatever quality there is in the writing of this book has been greatly enhanced by the meticulous proofreading, intelligent criticism, and wise counsel of Gloria Parloff.

In all our travels my wife, Effin, has meant to me and to the book more than any words of mine can convey.

# TOUCHING
## IS
# HEALING

# Touching and Healing

This book is about using human touch as an agent of healing.

Three premises underlie the work. The first is that touch is an effective healing agent. This holds true not just in faith healing, where the laying on of hands has been practiced since ancient times, but in nursing, psychotherapy, counseling, and even surgery. Touch can be beneficially used by the family doctor as well as the chiropractor, by the behavioral psychologist as well as the masseuse.

The second premise is that touch is underutilized by healing practitioners from neurologists to social workers. If the first assumption is true, that touch is an effective healing agent, then it's reasonable to expect our healers to know how to make use of it. We take for granted that our internist is familiar with antibiotics; our pastor, with Scripture. Their touch knowledge should be no less developed. After all, the association between touching and healing goes back as far as recorded time, turning up wherever therapeutic accounts were kept. Healers touched their patients in ancient China, Egypt, and India. Early Maori healers touched in what is now New Zealand, early Christians in what is now Israel, and native Americans in what is now Arizona. The healing touch is used today in Swiss spas and by American osteopaths. These practices will be explored in later chapters as will the disastrous consequences of not being touched.

That touch can be therapeutic should come as no surprise to anyone familiar with patterns of human child-rearing, the social life of the great apes, or maternal licking in cats and rats. One cannot study mammalian behavior without concluding that physical contact is essential to emotional health, physical well-being, and even life itself. Evidence supporting this conclusion will be presented throughout the book. But without reading another page, you can find your own evidence to support or oppose the premise that therapeutic touch is underutilized by most practitioners. If you are yourself a practitioner, simply recall how often you effectively make use of hands-on contact as an agent of healing. If you are a patient, think of how many times you've been touched by your family doctor. By your therapist. By a cardiologist or internist. By the parish priest. Whatever your answer to these questions, there are psychologists, ophthalmologists, and clergy who do understand the therapeutic use of touch, and their accumulated wisdom has been gathered here.

The meanings of "touch" and "heal" are myriad. Webster's allocates nearly two full columns of closely set type to define touch, and the definitions range from "a brief or incidental stop on shore during a trip by water" to "an act of borrowing, swindling, or stealing." Neither has much to do with the subject of this book. Of more interest is: "to perceive or experience through the tactile sense," and "to examine by touching or feeling with the fingers; to lay hands upon." This book is concerned with the use of touch as a diagnostic tool and as an implement of healing.

Healing is another word of many meanings. It differs from touch in that nearly all its meanings fall within the scope of this book. "To make sound or whole; to cure of disease or affliction; to mend marital rifts; to restore to original purity or integrity; to make spiritually whole"—each will receive attention in the pages that follow.

*Steadman's Medical Dictionary* defines healing as "the process of a return to health"; it describes health as "the state of the organism when it functions optimally without evidence of disease or abnormality."[1] Such a broad definition is much to my liking, for it allows discussion to range far and free.

The healing process takes many forms and involves a variety of practitioners. Healing can mean restoring health or providing comfort. It can take the spectacular form of a miracle cure or the slow painstaking work of teaching an old woman with a broken hip to walk again. One can be healed after emotional trauma just as surely as after a skiing accident. Families need healing as much as individuals, and after the loss of a leader or defeat in war whole nations may need their spirit restored. The traditional healer was called a sha-man; the post-industrial age healer goes by many names. Doctor, nurse, physiotherapist, rabbi, social worker, psychotherapist—we train our healers in specialized schools and, upon graduation, grant them specialized titles and privileges.

What happens—or, more precisely, what doesn't happen—in these schools brings us to the third premise on which this book rests. It is this: Therapeutic touch has been ignored by the institutions that train health workers and generally neglected by the researchers who are in their employ.

Before going any further, let me acknowledge with gratitude two exceptions to this rule. In the last decade, American nursing pro-grams have given their students a solid background in the uses and meanings of touch between nurse and patient. This exception runs as true as the rule, a fact I take great delight in proving whenever I speak to a hospital group on the subject of touching and healing. I announce that I am going to predict how many in the room have had an adequate education in the healing use of touch, but before I do I indicate that I would like all the nurses present to raise their hand. I count the number who are still in their twenties and make that my prediction. I haven't missed yet.

The other exception also comes courtesy of the nursing profession. Their journals—and theirs alone—can be counted upon to print arti-cles on touch with any degree of regularity. Until very recently, the subject received but scant and irregular mention in either *Index Medicus* or *Psychological Abstracts*, the basic reference tools of med-icine and psychology. Furthermore, when examples of healing touch did appear in the literature, their significance was sometimes missed by the authors themselves. A case in point comes from the work of Jerome Frank. I choose it because its author is one of the very best observer-practitioners of the healing arts.

Jerome Frank is Professor Emeritus of Psychiatry at Johns Hop-kins Medical School and the author of *Persuasion and Healing*, a brilliant and now classic comparison of psychotherapy and other types of healing. The book discusses therapeutic techniques from abreaction to Zen, yet almost never comments on touch. In fact, one case is described in which touch seems to be the crucial element in the healing process, but the part it plays gets no mention. It was a case of *empacho*—soul loss—being treated by a Guatemalan healer. His treatment included "elaborate massage of the woman with whole

eggs." Later, "the healer massaged her vigorously and systematically with the eggs, then with one of his sandals." It was immediately
after this second massage that the patient "arose, put on her clothes,
lay down on the rustic platform bed, and was covered with blankets.
By this time she was thoroughly relaxed."[2]

Professor Frank discusses the case in detail, yet the one thing
overlooked is the healing touch. And if even this enlightened author-
practitioner-teacher manages to miss the importance of touch, his
colleagues certainly will.

And they do. The use of touch in treating the sick is a missing
element in the curricula of medical schools, graduate psychology
programs, and schools of social work throughout the English-
speaking world. In fact, the only mention of touch at a great many of
these institutions is a stern injunction not to do it. For many of the
teachers of today's healers, touch equals sex, and any talk about
touching patients is simply a coded way of advocating carnal, lasciv-
ious, unethical sex with patients. So to prevent s-e-x, avoid t-o-u-c-h.
And while that may or may not be an effective way of preventing
sexual contact between doctor and patient, what it does do is cut off
future practitioners from one of their potentially most useful therapeutic tools—human touch.

The cloak of the sex taboo has become the shroud of the healing
touch. It is probably the most important reason touch does not appear
in the medical school curriculum, why it is rarely mentioned in case
conferences, why there is no chapter devoted to its use in the psychotherapy *or* the general medicine text. And yet, as one author writing
for *non*-professionals said, "A nation which is able to distinguish the
fine points between offensive and defensive pass interference,
bogies, birdies, and par, a schuss and a slalom, a technical, a personal, and a player-control foul should certainly be able to make some
far more obvious distinctions between various sorts of body contact."[3]

Right.

> The purpose of this book is to make better touchers of our
> healers.

That statement of purpose is probably insufficient. We are living
in a time when every human endeavor—from training physicians to
making love—is expected to begin with a statement of objectives.

And I am willing to present mine. But first, it might be worthwhile to say a very few words about what this book is not.

It is not:

"Gee, touching is such a beautiful kind of thing, and if only we did more of it everybody would be a lot happier and get along better too. There's this tribe in Africa, or maybe it's the Philippines, anyway, they touch all the . . ."

It is not:

"Tactile sensations are carried primarily in the ventral spinal cord and will be referred to as spinothalamic throughout the text, whereas tactile information is transmitted through the dorsal cord and will be described as the lemniscal system. The former is protopathic; the latter, epicritic; however . . ."

Nor is it:

"This healing gift I seem to possess is really no credit to me. No, no—it's just the opposite. I am merely a channel through which God heals. For some reason unfathomable to mere mortals, God chose little me, a simple clinical psychologist, to do His . . ."

Here's that statement of objectives. This work sets itself the following tasks:

> to legitimize the use of touch as a healing agent;
> to describe the therapeutic uses of touch over a broad spectrum of the healing arts;
> to convey the skills of those who are gifted in the use of touch and the experiences of patients, touched and untouched;
> to discuss limitations and abuses of touch in the healing relationship;
> to generate a current of touch thought, experience, experiments, and research;
> to caress, massage, soothe, slap, pleasure, pressure, guide, poke, prod, stroke, scratch, tickle—my objective is to touch you.

# Touching and Birthing

## 2

I sing of skin, layered fine as baklava,
whose colors shame the dawn,
and once the scabbard upon which is writ
our only signature,
and the instrument by which we are thrilled,
protected,
and kept constant in our natural place.

Richard Selzer

Touch is as much a part of birth as it is of procreation.

And just as legal morality has repeatedly attempted to interfere with what sorts of touch take place in the bedroom, so has medical morality erected touch-barriers in the delivery room.

Birth is by nature a feast of physical contact. The newborn has been experiencing touch sensations since the sixth week after conception. Even at that stage the fetus—then less than one inch in height—responds to a stroking of the upper lip by turning its head and trunk. In fact, touch is the first of the senses to develop, and the uterine environment amounts to a continuous, head-to-foot massage that lasts for the better part of nine months. Desmond Morris has described the intrauterine sensations so lyrically, one suspects he remembers them with perfect clarity:

The entire skin surface of the unborn child is bathed in the warm uterine liquid of the mother. As the child grows and its swelling body presses harder against the mother's tissues, the soft embrace of the enveloping bag of the womb becomes gradually stronger, hugging tighter with each passing week. In addition, throughout the period the growing baby is subjected to the varying pressure of the rhythmic breathing of the maternal lungs, and to a gentle, regular swaying motion whenever the mother walks.[1]

From this apparent bliss of life within, the neonate emerges. The massage is over. After what is probably a harrowing journey down the birth canal, the newborn finds itself in the strange and harsh world outside. Until recently, this almost inevitably meant dazzlingly bright lights and a hearty slap on the back. Welcome aboard, kid. Now, with increasing awareness of the sensitivity of the infant and increasing concern about whiplash injuries from the traditional slap, many hospitals (and, of course, home deliveries) have softened the shock of entry.

But this new world is still a strange one to the newborn. The only thing familiar is the presence of mother. Her sounds and smell and feel are the infant's sole comfort, and that reassuring comfort is best experienced through skin-to-skin contact. For humans and other mammals, touch remains a great source of comfort throughout life. Birth is our first opportunity to enhance physical contact, but all too often we seize upon it as a chance to obstruct tactile comfort. The maternity hospital, as we will see, has developed into an anti-touch institution.

If physical contact is familiar and almost certainly comforting to the newborn, what about the mother? Does she have a physical need to hold, fondle, or embrace her infant? In the Behavioral Science course at Otago Medical School in New Zealand, there is an immutable rule that when the subject of birth is presented, women get their say before men, and mothers before doctors. Here, then, is the recollection of one mother on her need for touch at birth:

When Donna was born everything seemed just right. I'd had Stephen the year before, and this time I wasn't afraid. I wanted to really get into the whole experience. Reed was there with me, I didn't have any anesthetic, and the doctors and nurses were keen on the Lamaze method. But something was missing. After a really great, wide-awake delivery I was just dying to get my hands on my daughter. I was literally grasping, reaching out for her. But for what seemed like hours they didn't bring her to me. By the end of it I was really hyper—I was just crazy to touch and hold her. But she didn't come . . . didn't come. When they finally did bring her I couldn't wait for them to leave the room. As soon as we were alone I unwrapped her swaddling and took off my clothes. Then I just held her.

This "crazy," "hyper," "grasping" need to touch the new baby is not limited to one woman. It is not limited to humans. And, as this chapter will demonstrate, this desperate physical need serves a vital role in parenting and, indeed, in the preservation of the species.

To be a participant in touching and birthing, one must be present at the event. Yet until recently, one seminal figure in the transactions that preceded the birth was excluded from the scene in hospitals all over the world. Less than ten years ago a father's request to be present at the birth of his twins was greeted by the chief of obstetrics at a famous teaching hospital in New York with the words, "Over my dead body!" Less than five years ago any father who wanted to be present at the birth of his child in a famous teaching hospital in New Zealand was required by the chief of the nursing service to actually sign in as a patient.

Now that the old guard is stepping aside and fathers are gaining entry into the sanctuary of the delivery room, they are making the medical and nursing world realize just how important is their touch for the mother in labor and for building a relationship with their child, a relationship that starts with touch and that should begin as the baby's head emerges from the womb.      .

And it is not just fathers who are telling the story. Here is how one mother of twins described what her husband's presence meant to her. These are excerpts from her birth journal:

We got to the obstetrics floor where a nurse told me to come with her. [My husband] had to wait outside, but I was assured that he would be with me in a few minutes. Good thing. I didn't want him out of my sight. . . . The nurses were very nice, but I just couldn't feel as at ease with them as with him. I had to be polite to them. The contractions seemed endless. Just get through one and another was on its way. Having him with me during this time was so important. We did it together, and, for me, that's the only way I could have remembered the day as such a perfect one.

I had been on the delivery table for a few minutes when I realized he wasn't there. God, he couldn't miss it. I knew I could just keep panting until he came, no matter how long it took. I would not let the babies be born until he was there. I asked rather frantically to no one in particular, "Where is he?" And although I couldn't see him, he answered, "Right here." I felt great.

And there he was standing beside me, holding my hand. . . .

I knew perfectly well myself what the exercises should be, but my mind was completely blank. I do remember asking him how to do the transition breathing because I just couldn't remember. He did one exercise to show me how. It was so great to have him there. I depended on him totally. What a beautiful thing we did!

I can't claim a shred of scientific detachment about those words. They were written by my wife.

Touch is important in the birth process not just for the baby, the mother and father, but for the physician or midwife as well. Sad to say, they don't always know it. Witness my conversation with an obstetrician, a man with 25 years of clinical experience (or perhaps one experience repeated for 25 years). We were both on vacation and were introduced by a mutual friend. After the greetings I said, "I understand you're an obstetrician. I'd like to ask you a question."

His reply was instantaneous. "I charge double for vacation consultations."

O.K., thought I, maybe the guy is plagued with freebie patients every time he goes to a party.

"O.K.," said he, "What's the problem?" His voice said "Go Away."

"I don't have a problem; I have a question. But if this isn't a good time to ask it . . ."

"Ask it!" he snarled.

"I'm interested in touch and obstetrics—"

"Don't know anything about it. There's too much made of this natural childbirth business anyway. *My* patients never take the classes, and 99 percent of them don't need anesthetic. They listen to me—"

I broke in on what I foresaw as the beginning of a long, vitupera-
tive, and wholly unbelievable lecture. "Actually, I don't want to talk
about natural childbirth. I'm interested in the use of touch in
birthing."

"Never use it."

End of interview. Thanks a lot.

My first interview with a midwife on the subject made quite a
contrast. Her name is Jan Strom, and she practices in Vermont. I
met her housemate after a Grand Rounds I presented at the University of Vermont Medical School. She said Jan might have some
thoughts on touching and healing from a midwife's perspective, and
when we were introduced I asked if I might tape-record her ideas.
She answered that she didn't think she could say anything worth
recording, but if I wanted to turn on the machine she had no objec-
tions. I plugged it in, Jan took a deep breath, and began. She spoke
for a long time, neither hesitating nor correcting herself; there were
no long pauses and no tangents. When she finished, her housemate
and I looked at each other in amazement, and I prayed my recorder
had been working.

It had. The transcript, with almost no editing, is as follows.

First of all, touch is important in midwifery for its clinical
value. We teach our hands to ask questions and to listen for the
answer.

Early in pregnancy we do pelvimetry, which is assessing the
measurements of the bony pelvis by touch through the vagina.
This gives us a general idea if the pelvis is adequate to allow a
normal-sized baby to fit through. Later in pregnancy we'll be
trying to determine the positioning of the baby to some pretty
fine points, like, is the head up or down, where is the baby facing,
is the head engaged in the pelvis, how flexed is the head and what
size is the baby. The better a midwife has these hands-on skills,
the better her clinical judgment will be about the status of a
woman's pregnancy and what may or may not come up at the
birth. Touch is also important in determining the progress of
labor by doing internal vaginal exams. We'll explore the cervix,
feeling for how thinned out it gets and how open it's become.
We'll assess the level of the presenting part relative to the land-
marks of the pelvis. And we'll feel for the sutures and fontanels
on the baby's head to confirm our judgments on position and

attitude. So our ability to get the information our hands can give us is important.

At the same time I'm using my touch to gather objective information, there is a personal dialogue taking place between myself and the mother. The part of her I have my hands on will tell me if she's at ease with my touch or if there's something uncomfortable happening for her that I'd better pay attention to. The way I use my hands will tell *her* whether or not I'm respectful and caring toward her. Having this direct communication as a regular part of the prenatal routine is important both for her and myself in developing mutual trust.

I'm also aware that as I palpate a woman's abdomen for information about the baby, I'm also giving that baby messages person-to-person. I always give the baby a rub on the butt or the back just to say hello.

The best training I've had for learning to use my hands as a midwife was in studying massage. I'm also a professional masseuse. The sensitivity I've gained by working with massage has really helped me to develop my sense of touch.

I don't generally use rubber gloves when I catch babies. I feel strongly that I want my hands touching that woman and that baby. I trust what my hands tell me. When there's something between my hands and what I'm touching it masks the information that's available to me. While I *can* work with that, I prefer not to.

When a baby's just born, if there's any kind of problem—a baby that's not breathing immediately, a baby that has poor muscle tone—I would be maddened to have gloves on my hands. I feel it's important that my skin be on that baby's skin, that there's a physical communication between me and that baby.

I've had this happen a couple of times. Once, in particular, a baby was born with a cord complication that caused him to be moderately asphyxiated. When he was born he didn't breathe spontaneously, and he had no muscle tone. He was blue and limp, and I'd never felt any living body like that before. I worked on that baby with my hands for a couple of intense minutes before he started up, massaging energy pathways and stimulating reflex areas.

My experience with massage has made me aware of the feeling in my hands when I'm working with them consciously. I'm aware of a feeling of energy in them that isn't there at other times. When I'm catching a baby I want to have that energy totally available to that baby. I feel it's a way of sharing life energy, and I don't like the idea of having rubber there.

Because loving, empathetic touch is a tremendous source of comfort, it has a lot to offer during the labor of childbirth. I've taught workshops for couples who are pregnant, teaching massage for pregnancy and massage for labor. Like any other tool, a little practice with it makes a person more confident and more creative in using it. Massage skills are one of the things my partners and I bring with us to a birth. Not only will we use it ourselves to help a laboring woman, but we support other people there in using it too, to help the mother have her baby in the best way possible. Touch can increase the mother's physical comfort, and it offers a grounding point during her times of emotional stress. Touch—appropriate, compassionate touch—can help somebody to come back and be present in the experience they're having. We also make a point of offering shoulder massages to the mates during labor. They too are working very hard, putting out a lot physically and emotionally, and it's important to be caring for them too. Katra, Barbara, and I often do shoulder massages for each other, especially if we're at a long labor. It keeps us connected with each other, and, if one of us is tired, it's a way of clearing and renewing her energy.

When the baby's head is emerging is a time when it's really incredible to use touch to help the woman connect with the experience. I first learned about this from Nancy Mills, a California midwife. Often, this is the most difficult time for a woman in terms of her need for self-control. It's important that the head not be born too fast although the woman is having a very strong urge to push. We find that when we have a woman bring her hand down to feel the baby's head as it's coming out, it transforms her experience at that point. She becomes so connected with her body and her baby, so energized, that she's able to do anything we ask of her.

Some women don't let us bring their hand down, and that's too bad. But when we can, it's always incredible for the laboring woman. And we encourage the father to touch the baby then too, whether he wants to help catch the baby or not, because of the specialness of the connection at that time. There's only a few minutes when you can touch a baby while it's still partly inside. It really brings both parents close to the experience.

At home, most birthing women don't usually have any clothes on by the time their baby's born. I don't know what kind of relevance that has, but it certainly makes their skin available for touching.

We put the baby on mother's belly as soon as it's breathing. We feel that skin-to-skin contact is important for both of them in getting connected with each other and in starting to find some ease after the intensity of birth.

Everybody wants to touch the newborn. It's amazing. The hands just come up to baby from all around, bringing welcomes. And that's just what the baby needs.

Almost all the thoughts of this young midwife have been supported by the observations of others or confirmed by scientific study. We are going to examine a particularly important group of these studies, but first let us review her main points. They are as relevant for other forms of healing as they are for birthing.

1. Touch is an important means of gathering clinical information. For the midwife or obstetrician this includes information about the mother such as the size of her pelvis and the dilation of her cervix, and about the fetus, its size and position.
2. Touch is an important medium of communication. It tells the midwife about the emotional state of the mother, and this information may not be available through other forms of communication. The woman may deny being distrustful or be unaware that she is fearful. Thus touch can reveal important information that words conceal.

    Touch also tells the mother about the midwife and communicates messages about her skill, self-confidence, and caring.
3. Touch can help build trust.

    If the practitioner senses discomfort and brings it to the patient's awareness, this will be a bond between them. If the patient gets a sense of competence and caring from the practitioner, this too will add to feelings of trust.
4. Touch is an important—probably the most important—source of comfort.

    The comforting touch Jan described extended to mother,

father (often the neglected party at a birth), newborn, and midwife-colleagues.
5. Touch is a ground wire to reality.

The importance of the ability of physical contact to bring a person back into the experience of the moment also has major significance in treating madness. It will be explored more fully in a later chapter.

Jan also contends that effective touch can be learned, a contention which will be supported in this book's final chapter. In addition to these general observations, there are two that specifically relate to childbirth. The first is that there is a special time, those few moments when the head is emerging and the body is still in the womb, when touch is a particularly powerful connector between parents and child. The second is that the reaching out of hands toward the newborn is its welcome into the world. They both relate to a phenomenon intimately tied to birth practices, *parent-child bonding.*

Bonding is attachment, an attachment based more in instinct than conscious choice. No matter how attached you are to a Currier and Ives print, it is unlikely that you have bonded to it. But you can bond to an infant, and this is as fortunate for the preservation of the species as it is for the welfare of the child. The young human is dependent on the support and good will of its parents for longer than any other animal on the planet. Without bonding, parents might well just disappear after the first sleepless night, shrugging their shoulders in mutual agreement that raising a kid just isn't for them. Bonding is what keeps them on the job. It's what allows a squalling, colicky, beshatted baby to be fed, cleaned, and cooed over by exhausted, irritable—adoring—parents.

Touch is a vital component in establishing strong ties between parent and child, in humans and in other species. For many mammals its importance begins long before there is an infant to become attached to. For them, touch—self-touch—is a major part of the preparation for parturition and parenthood. Pregnant rats, for example, lick their abdominal and genital regions and intensify this form of self-touch as pregnancy progresses. When these rats are fitted with a collar that prevents licking, development of their mammary glands is retarded by 50 percent. Furthermore, the effects of prenatal collaring show up in behavior as well as physiology. The experimental rats—all of whom had their collars removed before delivery—were poor nursers, poor nest builders, and inadequate mothers.

After birth, touch is redirected to the young. In *Touching*, the book most responsible for generating new interest in the uses of touch, anthropologist Ashley Montagu reports that, along with other mammals, sheep use licking and maternal body orientation to stimulate lambs to nurse. As a result, licked lambs tend to increase weight earlier than unlicked ones.[2]

The female cat licks both herself and her newborn kittens during delivery, and the floor of the birth site as well. The licking follows a predetermined pattern that begins with the posterior of her own body, especially the vaginal area. This leads to licking the kitten's nose as it emerges, an excellent way of making sure it is clear for breathing. The cat's touching continues after the licking ceases. When all the kittens have emerged and the birth process is complete, the mother cat lies down, encloses the entire litter with her body, and rests in that position for about twelve hours. This encircling maximizes warmth and physical contact. It also presents her teats to her offspring. After the resting period, she again begins licking the kittens, now to stimulate nursing.

Marshall Klaus and John Kennell, the pediatrician-authors of *Maternal-infant Bonding* summarize mammalian practices as follows:

> All mammals prepare for the birth of their young, establish a birth site, and during parturition lick their bodies. After birth they display a profound interest in the protection of their young, ensuring their warmth, maintaining control over visitors, warding off intruders, keeping an eye on the young, and in some species retrieving those who stray. In addition, most mammalian mothers clean and arouse their infants by licking and grooming them.[3]

The fact is, many animals need touch, usually in the form of maternal licking, to survive the first few hours after birth. Licking of the young is common to all species except humans and the great apes, and one experiment, conducted during the 1940s, demonstrated just how vital to life it can be. At that time there was considerable interest in raising sterile—that is, germ-free—rats for laboratory use. When a scientist named Reyniers set up the necessary aseptic conditions and his rats gave birth, he thought he was on his way to success. The only possible source of contamination was from the mothers, and, by removing them from their young immediately after birth, he seemed to have even that problem . . . well, licked. But to his dismay, he found that although milk was freely available, the litters died. It was later discovered that the mother's licking was the missing ingredient, and only by providing a rough approximation of it using cotton swabs and applying them to the anal-genital region could scientists successfully raise the young.

Licking the nether regions may be partially rooted in the structure of the brain. As Money and Athanasiou have observed,

> In man's mammalian history, nature has ordained the approximation of the snout end and the tail end not only in connection with the odor of mating but also for delivery of the young. The representations in the brain are also in close proximity, in the amygdala (snout end) and septum (tail end). In some species, including the chimpanzee, the mother licks the baby clean at delivery and subsequently licks it clean when it soils itself.[4]

We have seen how the female rat uses self-touch as preparation for parenting; the human, too, prepares, but the process is usually thought of as completely nontactile. She dreams of the baby; she and her husband talk about the child's future and lie in bed thinking of the perfect name; her friends give her useful presents and the benefit of their maternal experience at a baby shower. The process incorporates the capacity of our species to think, our ability to use language, and our need for social interaction. But it may be that touch, too, has a part to play in preparing people for parenthood. Pregnancy is a time when there are sudden and urgent needs for back rubs from a spouse. Women's magazines encourage pregnant women to massage oils into the skin of the abdominal area to prevent stretch marks after the birth. Midwives encourage perineal massage for the last month of pregnancy to promote tissue elasticity at the time of delivery. Natural childbirth classes instruct on the use of light massage during labor and require its practice in the weeks that precede delivery. This adds up to a lot of touching during pregnancy; the question of whether these apparently unrelated activities help prepare a pregnant woman for parenthood is well deserving of further study.

The period immediately following birth is a time when physical contact is important in the bonding process. Klaus and Kennell call this the maternal sensitive period. As with imprinting fowl, what happens during this brief time may have long-lasting effects on family relationships and on the child's later development. (If Jan Strom's observation about the special touch time when the baby's head first shows is accurate, and if it applies to fathers as well as mothers, then the sensitive period begins just before birth and should be more accurately described as the parental sensitive period.)

Both clinical observations and experimental studies support the sensitive period hypothesis. The data hold up despite broad differences in subject groups, including their nationality. Studies have been conducted in Sweden, Israel, Brazil, Ecuador, and the United States. In no case have the results contradicted the hypothesis, and all significant results have pointed to the existence of a sensitive period. The studies were designed to vary the amount of early contact between mother and child to see what, if any, effects this would have on their relationship and on the child's development.

In the average American maternity hospital this contact has, until recently, been limited to a glimpse of each other at birth, a brief reunion at six to eight hours, and 20- to 30-minute feeding periods every four hours. Paternal contact time has been much, much less.

### Fathers

There is a long-standing hospital tradition of ostracizing fathers. If pregnant women are treated as though they were carrying a disease instead of a baby, their unfortunate husbands are regarded as the ones who gave it to them. Indeed, there were few hospitals that allowed men an active part in the birth process or even observer status at the birth of their children until the decade of the 1970s. Fewer still welcomed them. Yet research has shown that the most significant factor in paternal attachment is the father's attitude toward, and participation in, the birth of his child.

Social worker Gail Peterson and her colleagues observed fathers from the sixth month of their wives' pregnancies until the babies' six-month birthdays. They rated their subject's degree of attachment by the amount of interaction between him and the child, his reported feelings of closeness, his participation in child-rearing, and the pleasure both got from the relationship. The father's experience of the birth was consistently the best predictor of his later attachment, and, in the case of home births, it was the *only* significant predictor, accounting for all but three percent of the variance. Long labor and home delivery were associated with greater attachment; for those whose wives were anesthetized, disappointment was the most significant variable.

The importance of the birth experience—and the role played by touch—is illustrated in Peterson's example of a husband whose pre-natal attitude was rated as very low and whose emotional state throughout the pregnancy ranged from apathetic to sarcastic. He was reluctant to participate in the birth, but, since his wife insisted that it be at home, he felt he had no choice. What transpired came as a great surprise to the observers, and, no doubt, to him as well:

> After an initial period of severe discomfort for his wife, he became very concerned about her and supported her both physi-cally and emotionally by massaging her back and engaging in frequent touching and reassuring talking. . . . His disinterest (*sic*) and apathy were replaced by concern, amazement, and involvement. Following the birth of the baby he proceeded to cry and within 30 minutes held, rocked, and talked to his new son.[5]

The authors conclude that the experience of birth is a powerful catalyst for nurturing, not just for the mother but for her mate as well. They suggest that "... paternal attachment can be enhanced by provision of a birth environment that will help to overcome the father's inhibitions about being involved in the birth process along with the mother."[6]

Besides supporting that suggestion, I would like to add a thought of my own. In the birth environment, touch is at one and the same time an area of great inhibition and a powerful releaser of attach-ment. Paternal touch needs to be set free. Husbandly touch needs to be set free. This freedom will be achieved when birth workers—doctors, nurses, midwives—are trained to be comfortable with touch and when they are made aware of its importance. Only then can they encourage, support, and model the healing touch for both mother and father.

It should be said that the banishing of the father did not stem entirely from anti-male prejudice. True, there is an ancient tradition that birth is woman's business, and true, there is a medical tradition of secrecy and suspicion of outside observation; but another factor operates here as well. Along with limiting visiting hours and restricting visitors, the practice of keeping fathers away from their newborn child is a holdover from the pre-antibiotic era of hospital care. It is difficult today to conceive of a time—a not-too-distant time—when outbreaks of diarrhea would spread through a nursery like a California brush fire, or a time before that when women trembled at the thought of a hospital birth, knowing that many who went in never came out. The vestiges of those days are still alive and robust in the treatment of premature babies, and they are still alive—though weakened—in general maternity care. Whatever protection these practices might offer in terms of protection against microbes (and they probably offer none), their cost in terms of the relationship between a man and his child is too great to bear.

For the sake of this relationship, and for the great healing and helping a man can offer his mate during labor and birth, the time has come for all hospitals to welcome fathers to the event. Note, however, that "welcome" is not the same as "insist" or "demand." Not every father wants to be present, even when welcomed, and the choice is ultimately his own. Let us not in our enthusiasm for this generally beneficial change substitute a new orthodoxy for the old one.

Let us also encourage and welcome more research on paternal-infant bonding. That to which I would give highest priority would be on humans, not Norway rats. And I would particularly like to see well-designed studies on the role of touch in the birth process and in building father-child relationships.

### Mothers

In a most interesting study, mothers in an experimental group were handed their nude infants for an hour in bed during the first two hours after birth and for five extra hours a day during the next three days. The results as reported by Marshall Klaus and John Kennell were, at the very least, impressive. These extended-care mothers were found to:

1. behave more soothingly toward their infants at an interview one month after birth than did the control group mothers who had only the usual amount of contact allowed by the hospital;
2. fondle and make *en face* eye contact significantly more than the control mothers while feeding their babies a month after birth. *En face* is the position in which the mother's and baby's eyes meet fully in the same vertical plane of rotation;

3. spend more time assisting the doctor as he examined their babies one year after birth;
4. ask more questions and give fewer commands to their children two years after birth.

As for the children, the results are equally impressive. At *five years* of age those born to the early-contact group scored significantly higher on IQ tests and somewhat higher on two language tests than did the controls. No study to date has contradicted these findings, and most offer positive support for them. Klaus and Kennell conclude: "These findings suggest that just 16 extra hours of contact within the first three days of life affect maternal behavior for one year and possibly longer, and they offer support for the hypothesis of a maternal sensitive period soon after birth."[7]

A later study by Roberto Sosa and associates showed further effects of early skin-to-skin contact between mother and child. Guatemalan mothers were handed their unclothed infants immediately after birth and left alone with them in privacy for 45 minutes. The control group in this double-blind study was composed of mothers who were separated from their children according to standard hospital practice, usually about 12 hours after birth.

Again, the results were impressive. The early-contact children were breast fed significantly longer than the controls, and more of the early-contact mothers chose breast over bottle feeding. In addition, the early-contact children suffered fewer infections and received more affection from their mothers.[8]

Commenting on results like these, Betsy Lozoff and associates reached this conclusion: "There is now clear evidence . . . that certain maternity hospital practices interfere with breast feeding and early maternal affection. The routine postpartum separation of healthy mothers and infants appears to approach the limit of minimal contact below which disruptions occur for some mothers."

They continue: "For the mother and infant with a problem (prematurity, malformation, inexperience, emotional disturbance, social isolation), the relationship is even more susceptible to early disruption."[9]

If further research reaches similar conclusions, the case for a radical change in hospital practice will be made. But it is not necessary to wait for replication of results to initiate change. More and earlier contact between parent and child poses no health hazards and causes no dangerous side effects. Some hospitals have made some progress in this direction, and I know of not one whose staff has collapsed under the burden. As for the many more that are still resisting change, the words of Harvard pediatrician T. B. Brazelton should be sufficient to awaken them to the need:

> These studies serve to point out how punitive and interfering medical care systems in the United States are in birth and early attachment process. Anything which regains the priorities of the importance of the mother or of her baby or of their being together will enhance their self-esteem and, of course, the importance of their dyadic attachment.[10]

Ashley Montagu saw the same thing from an anthropologist's perspective. He wrote, "The two people who need each other at this time, more than they will at any other time in their lives, are separated from one another, prevented from continuing the development of a symbiotic relationship which is so critically necessary for the further development of both of them."[11]

### Babies

Touch is of utmost importance in binding mother to child, both at birth and in the days and months that follow. Klaus and Kennel consider the mother's desire to touch her baby as the primary behavioral system that bonds them together. But it is not just the mother who is equipped for physical contact. The human infant is born with a grasp reflex that is surprisingly strong, strong enough to support its own weight. This can be looked upon as a vestige of an ancestry that began in the trees, or it can be seen as a means of ensuring physical contact with the mother. Another touch-enhancer coming from the baby is its pleasure response when picked up, fondled, and held. Touch of this nature is the original comforter, the primary healer, the universal soother.

Still another form of attachment-enhancing behavior that originates in the infant is the sucking reflex. Sucking provides a great deal more than nutrition. It is an important source of comfort through touch. First there is the oral contact with whatever is being sucked, be it breast, thumb, or pacifier. Both humans and monkeys spend more time in nonnutritional sucking than they do in obtaining milk. Second, sucking for nutrition almost always results in close physical contact with whoever is doing the feeding. Thus, sucking brings the comfort and attachment that derive from body to body contact.

There is one further way in which touch draws together mother and baby. Earlier it was mentioned that, among other birth practices, some species of mammals retrieve their young. There is at least one authority—and he is an authority of considerable weight—who numbers human beings among those species. He is the English physician-scientist John Bowlby, and he is to attachment theory as Freud was to libido. Bowlby defines retrieving as parental behavior that brings the young to the nest or close to the mother. Rodent and carnivore mothers retrieve pups in their mouths while primates scoop them up with hands and arms. Besides strengthening the bond, retrieving serves a protective function and keeps the infant in close proximity to its mother. Retrieving comes into play when the child begins to crawl. But the groundwork has been laid long before, usually at birth. It is then that a woman first touches her child.[12]

## Touches

The way mothers touch their newborns for the first time follows a definite pattern, an ordered sequence that probably varies little from culture to culture. The pattern was first described by Reva Rubin, an American midwife whose observations were made in hospital maternity wards.

The pattern has three components: amount, direction, and rate.

Amount: The mother begins with small areas of contact and gradually moves to larger ones. Likewise, at first small areas of her own body are involved—almost always the fingertips—and later her hands, then arms, then trunk join in the contact.

Direction: The parts of her body involved in initial touch move steadily inward from the extremities.

Rate: How rapidly progression is made from small areas to large and from peripheral to central contact depends on several factors. Rubin lists three, and I would add a fourth. Hers are how the mother feels about herself in this role, how she perceives her child's response to her, and on the character of their relationship at the moment. I would add that the setting and the attitudes of those who populate it are of crucial importance, for they have a powerful and direct influence on the way the mother feels about herself, the baby's response, and the character of their relationship at the moment. And although Rubin does not include the setting factor as a determinant of rate of progress, she later acknowledges its importance by saying.

> Mothers who have had a very recent experience of appropriate and meaningful bodily touch from a ministering person, as during labor, delivery, or the postpartum period, use their own hands more effectively. . . . Conversely, if the mother's most recent experience of contact in relation to her own body has been of a remote and impersonal nature, she seems to stay longer at this stage in her own activities with the baby.[13]

This observation is of greatest significance to obstetricians, obstetrical nurses, and midwives. It says that the way a woman is touched during her time of birthing has a real effect on the way she touches her infant. We have already seen that the way she touches her infant seems to affect their relationship for at least a year and probably has an even more lasting effect on the child's intellectual growth. So the touch of the birth worker is important, much too important to leave to chance. How can we help the worker to develop a useful touch, a helping touch, a healing touch?

Touching skills can be and should be taught. Health practitioners can and should have developed some ease with touch, some supervised practice with it, before they graduate from their training program as certified healers. As the situation now stands, most of them—and this is particularly true of medical graduates—will have no formal training at all. Those who do know how to touch were either lucky enough to have been trained by a touch-skilled clinician or have developed their own skill outside the hospital walls. But since nearly all medical students in the English-speaking world are chosen primarily for their academic abilities, the odds are against a high proportion of either natural touchers or those who have had sufficient outside experience to develop touch skills.

It need not be this way. The obstetrician-in-training can learn reassuring touch. The nurse can develop information-gathering touch. The midwife can cultivate a communicating touch.

Reva Rubin says it beautifully:

> With unhampered growth, the beginning nurse and the beginning mother will develop their skills of information-gathering

through touch into a source of discriminating for diagnosis and into a vehicle of personally meaningful communication. They will be able to read and recognize, through touch, the amount of body heat produced by a local or general body task; the kinds of perspiration produced by physical or psychological work. They will discern skin textures and recognize change, favorable or unfavorable. They will recognize another's appeal for contact, controls, or guidance, and be able to provide appropriate dosages of touch for each of these. And since touch is always individualized, the interpersonal communications effected through touch will tend to be significant in a way that verbal language cannot achieve.[14]

# Bringing Touch to Birth

**3**

Fine, you say. Marvelous. So we need more touching at birth, Dr. Older. Thanks for telling us.

Have you been inside a hospital recently, Dr. Older? Try telling *them* that. Try telling them anything!

Touché. Yes, the hospital's resistance to change is legendary. There are hospitals so resistant that if a doctor has a dream in the night about changing something, he comes in and apologizes to his chief in the morning. I have seen more than one department where the professor or head nurse had to die or retire before anyone dared suggest altering ancient practices. Once, when I complained about a particularly nasty way of separating hurt children from their parents, I was matter-of-factly told, "We'll take care of it when the boss retires."

"And how long before that happy day?"

"Oh, three years. If he leaves when he says he will."

Yet change does come. Most maternity hospitals today are better places to give birth than they were ten years ago. As elsewhere in the hospital, medical students are showing more interest in patients and less in diagnosis as an art form. One class recently circulated a polite letter to the clinical staff of a large teaching hospital expressing appreciation for their general sensitivity and willingness to share their knowledge while at the same time expressing concern for lapses on the part of a few. The students suggested that all staff members make it a practice to introduce patients, not to talk about patients in the third person in front of them, and to ask women if they minded the students' presence at gynecological examinations.

All hell broke loose. There were threats of resignation. There were special staff meetings. The professor of pathology said it was a Communist plot. But the change came. The clinicians cleaned up their act, and patients throughout the hospital are better treated as a result.

Ordinary citizens, too, can have an effect, and even more so when they're organized. Groups of concerned parents and the La Leche League have nudged and prodded doctors and hospital administrators to stop separating sick children from their parents and to stop pushing formula instead of mother's milk. But hospital resistance to "outside" suggestions, no matter how sensible they are, has an automatic quality about it, rather like the response of a leg to a patella hammer. Such suggestions are often greeted with heavy sighs, raised eyebrows, references to "those people," and the fervently expressed wish that these non-doctors would "stay out of our business." But changes have come.

Whether you are a medical superintendent, a student nurse, or a concerned citizen, you have the power to initiate change in our health institutions. If your cause is a worthwhile one, and if you persevere, and if you're lucky, you will eventually create that change. Just don't ever expect to get any credit for it.

This book is about touching and healing, not about reforming hospitals. But without the ability to bring healing touch into practice, the theories and examples it presents are of no more than academic interest. That is why this chapter, using birth as an example, deals with the process of change. First we will look at normal birth and then at two special—and especially difficult—birthing situations: touching the premature baby and grieving the stillborn child.

We have seen that human touch can be enormously important at the time of birth. The husband's touch is important to his spouse. So is that of the doctor or midwife. The touch of both parents serves to welcome the infant into its new world, and their mutual contact builds a bond between parent and child that is long-lasting and beneficial to both. The next question is, how does one bring the benefits of touch into current birthing practice?

There are two possibilities. One is to take birth out of the hospital and into the home. The other is to make the hospital more like home.

A house is not a home, and a hospital is not even a house, but it can still be made into a place of security and familiarity, filled with workers who touch and encourage touching. Whether you are parent, doctor, nurse, or concerned citizen, you can help reshape the hospital by applying two principles.

(I exclude patients from the list of reshapers simply because most patients do not feel like doing anything but getting well and going home. They are too involved with coping with pain and fear, and they feel too vulnerable to their caretakers to risk upsetting them. Also, the way people who are sick or in pain think and feel is dramatically different from the way they operate under ordinary conditions. This has been beautifully described in Eric Cassell's *The Healer's Art*,[1] but you really only have to look as far as my friend Peter. Peter is a psychologist who specializes in studying physicians. Somehow, he has not learned to love the medical profession in the course of this association, and by the time Peter had to go into the hospital for some minor surgery he was well armed. He was not going to let the medics get away with anything. *He* was going to know *exactly* what procedures were to be used, *exactly* what side-effects might be expected, and *exactly* whatever else he might think of once he got there. After he came back to work, I said, "Well, Peter, did you give 'em hell?"

He looked a bit sheepish. "Jules, I had it all wrong. I went in prepared to demand full and realistic information, and as soon as I hit the bed I didn't want to know anything. All I wanted was to be taken care of."

So we will excuse patients from the change process—while they are patients.)

The two rules for initiating change in institutions are to be persistent and to be specific. What follows is a list of specific suggestions for improving the chances of helpful touching around the time of birth, and, with it, a brief description of the two books which have had the greatest impact on birthing procedures in recent times. Both are by French doctors, and both have increased the amount of positive touch available to mothers giving birth in a hospital.

Fernand Lamaze brought a system of mother-controlled childbirth out of the Soviet Union and, through his book *Painless Childbirth*, made it available to hospitals throughout Europe and North

America.[2] Instead of drugs, the Lamaze Method, as it has come to be called, uses relaxation exercises, breathing techniques, and light massage to control labor pain. The method is usually taught to husbands and wives, who attend classes as well as the birth together. My guess is that the specificity of the technique, such as when to switch from Stage I to Stage II Breathing, is less important than the comfort and security that derive from the presence of a loving, touching mate.

Indirect support for this guess comes from the research of an American professor of nursing, Karen Penny. Dr. Penny studied the way touch received during labor was remembered by women after they had given birth. Her main conclusion, incidentally, buttresses one of the tenets of this book, for nearly two-thirds of nonwhite women and more than nine-tenths of whites recalled the touching they received as positive and helpful. But it was her second conclusion that supports my guess about Lamaze; the most positively perceived touches were those given by the husbands.

On the basis of this evidence, Penny suggests, "Providing a chair for the husband next to the labor bed is one way to encourage touching behavior."[3] It is hard to credit that there are still hospitals that regard the mate as such a pariah that they will not provide him a seat, but, for those that do, my first specific suggestion is this: *Get him a chair!*

The other Frenchman is Frederick Leboyer, whose book, *Birth Without Violence*, attempted to observe birth through the eyes, ears, and skin of the baby emerging from the womb. It's obvious that there are inherent difficulties in such an exercise since the newborn cannot speak of its experiences, few adults can remember them, and those who say they can are usually suspected of self-delusion. Still, by whatever process he reached his conclusions, Leboyer altered his own obstetrical practice considerably. He dimmed the lights, dramatically lowered the noise level, gently massaged and bathed the newborn in a basin of warm water. Through his book, he disseminated his ideas internationally, and lovely, grainy photos of Leboyer's hands cradling a happy, floating infant have been reproduced many times in many countries.[4]

*Birth Without Violence* has had a real impact on light and noise levels in the delivery room, almost entirely as a result of a parent—not obstetrician—pressure. In fact there was widespread concern among obstetricians about the Leboyer method and dire predictions of disastrous consequences if it were to be adopted. Weekley wondered if darkness might do damage to the doctor's ability to deliver the baby's shoulders.[5] *Medical World News* hypothesized that the bath might heighten the risk of hypothermia.[6] I have found no evidence that any of this has come to pass; in fact, one study by Nancy Nelson and her associates at McMaster Medical School in Canada found no increased risks at all.[7]

But the question remains, what effect has all this on the child? Indirectly, I am sure it is for the good. The Leboyer birth encourages touch, promotes gentleness, and performs the miracle of bringing reverence and awe into the hospital delivery room. These are ideal conditions for a joyous birth experience for parents, and I am sure they greatly enhance the process of bonding with the new family member.

There is, though, one thing that bothers me; I cannot understand why Leboyer's arms are cradling and bathing a child who, at that moment, should be lying skin to skin and belly to belly with mother while father strokes and touches both of them. The Leboyer method is still a doctor-centered, not a family-centered, birth. I salute Leboyer for bringing touch, gentleness, and reverence back to birth. I do not think the rest of his ritual trappings are important.

The McMaster study supports this. Comparing a slightly modified Leboyer method with gentle, conventional delivery, they were able to find neither differences in infant behavior nor in maternal perceptions of the baby and the birth experience. It should be noted, however, that McMaster is probably the most advanced medical training facility in the world, and that what is "conventional" birth there is very different from many other hospitals. No perineal shaves, enemas, or analgesics are given; silver-nitrate drops in the eyes are delayed until an hour after birth, and, in Nelson's words, "In all respects, attention was paid in both groups to a gentle handling of the newborn and to facilitation of parent-infant interaction."[8]

Klaus and Kennell suggest that another way to ease hospital births is to arrange for labor and delivery to take place in the same room. My wife's written recollections certainly lend credence to that idea:

> I remember being wheeled from the labor room to the delivery room. I tried to look around to see where I was being taken since I didn't know where the delivery room was. I was panting all the way in. When we got to the delivery room I was asked to do what I

thought was the most incredible thing. The nurse told me to move from the labor room table to the delivery room table by myself! I felt like I weighed a ton, and I had no energy. It seemed impossible. Besides, wasn't it a service of the hospital to move its patients from one table to another?

Just as there should be a place for labor and delivery, so should there be a place for the newborn child, and that place is not in a bath, not on a scale, not anywhere but on its mother's breast. Then, unless the room is desperately needed for someone else, the family should be allowed to decide the appropriate length of time of this first contact. And, within the bounds of safe practice, they should be afforded the privacy befitting such an important occasion.

Baby must then be weighed, examined, and, to the extent necessary, cared for by the hospital staff. Mother may want to sleep. When they are ready for their next meeting, both the time and privacy should be arranged to allow the thorough maternal examination/ exploration that is in keeping with the pattern of our species. The baby should be nude, and the father's presence encouraged. Klaus and Kennell suggest a heat panel to maintain baby's temperature and to keep the parents cozy. I suggest a double bed.

From the point of view of making mother and child available for mutual touching, rooming-in is far superior to the traditional practice of the mother in a patient's room and the baby down the hall in the nursery. Rooming-in is now available in most hospitals and maternity homes.

The final suggestion regarding the hospital is that the staff should encourage physical contact with the child just as they encourage breast feeding or frequent bathing. It cannot be assumed that they know all about this themselves; rather, touching has to be part of the education of the birth worker and part of the routine of the hospital.

### Bringing the Birth Back Home

The other possibility is to take the normal birth out of the hospital and return it to the home. Studies of home births show that there is more holding of the child, more grooming by the mother, breast feeding within five or six minutes, and a striking mood elevation that involves both the parents and others who are present. Compared to the average hospital birth, the home birth is a tactile feast.

There are probably several reasons for this simultaneous increase in touch and uplifting of spirits. The familiarity of the home may be one, but perhaps more important is the meaning of home as opposed to the meaning of hospital. Home is your own territory. You are more likely to laugh out loud or throw a tantrum or wear an undershirt and drink beer out of the can at home than anyplace else. Hospital, on the other hand, is where you speak in whispers and act polite and hesitant and where there's always a distinctly unhomey and very unrelaxing smell permeating the air. Face it. If you are going to get naked and have a baby with all your friends watching, home is definitely the place to do it.

Another factor is the absence of anesthetic and, still another, the sort of help who will attend a home birth. If it is a doctor, he or she is an unusual one, almost certainly there against the wishes of medical colleagues. If it is a midwife, which is more likely, she is independent enough to go against medical preference and strong-willed enough to risk the wrath of the obstetrician's union. She is likely to be the sort of person who approves of touch and does not care much for anesthetics.

When home-birth parents reminisce about the birth experience, touch stands out as well-remembered blessing. Friends hug father. Father massages and caresses mother. Mother cannot take her hands off baby. When brother and sister are there, they get to hold the new family member and in their own way make room for her in their lives. And in the midst of hard labor, touch becomes the bedrock of healing and helping contact.

> Clifford would touch me precisely where I needed it, when I needed it, how long and at what pressure I needed it. It was like he was feeling everything I was feeling and we were one thing, too.[9]

Finally, there are some occasions when touch just saves the day. Here is a father's recollection of the home birth of his first child:

> I felt I was going to pass out. I didn't want to pass out because I would fall forward into the birthing fluids. I asked the closest person to hold my hand. I didn't pass out.[10]

### Touching the Premature Baby

A hundred years ago one popular view of children was that they were simply small adults. Ten years ago premature infants were treated as though they were smaller, frailer, full-term babies. Neither view was very helpful, and today—in most circles—children and preemies are recognized as different in needs and capacities from grownups and full-termers.

Premature infants are in the outside world when, by rights, they should be attached to an umbilical cord in the darkness of the womb. Preemies are not only smaller and frailer than full terms but also more likely to suffer from colic and respiratory disorders. Their senses work differently, too; they perceive the environment more through the skin than through eyes or ears.

Just as the premature child responds to the world different from its full-term sibling, so does the world respond to the preemie in a special way. One consequence of the early birth is that parents are likely to be slower to bond to the preemie than to the child born on schedule. There are very good reasons for this, the most important of which is that, at the same time they are longing to welcome the new infant into their hearts, they must be preparing for the possibility of its imminent death. This process, called anticipatory grief, is antithetical to bonding. It is, in fact, a strong pull in the opposite direction to the attraction of bonding.

There are other bonding inhibitors as well. The parents' feeling of failure for having produced what may seem like an imperfect baby is one. If "imperfect" sounds too harsh, ask yourself what the second question is after the announcement of birth. "Is it a boy or a girl?" is always followed by "How much did it weigh?" Any answer under seven pounds is said with a trace of embarrassment. Any under four pounds, with a slice of shame.

Another bond-deterrent is the feeling that this new and tiny being is so fragile, even breakable. It's no wonder that the early touch pattern is considerably slowed down when the infant is born prematurely. Mothers of preemies take much longer to progress from fingertip touch to whole hand and body caresses. It is hard to attach to a breakable reminder of failure who may die.

And yet there is much that can be done to help the baby survive *and* to help the parents risk loving their early arrival. A factor of supreme importance in both survival and bonding is touch. The child needs touch (and movement, as well) to calm its distressed life-support systems, and the parents need to have the child available to their touch so that their loving, protective feelings are allowed to grow.

Unfortunately, the premature nursery has traditionally been the no-touch center of the hospital; it has also been the impregnable fortress of no-parent land. It is protected from assault by touch-crazed mothers and fathers by the Glass Curtain.

In the traditional preemie unit, parents stood on one side of a double thickness of glass while busy nurses guarded warm metal boxes, supposedly containing infants, on the other. The parents were not allowed in, and, until they reached the magic five-pound mark, the infants were never allowed out. The main reason for this almost bond-proof arrangement was not misogyny or fear of fathers. It was fear of death. In the pre-antibiotic area, communicable, air-borne disease, usually in the form of diarrhea or respiratory infection, constituted a real danger to the life of the hospitalized premature infant. Then, during the 1950s and early 60s, hand-borne staphylococci presented a new threat to these young lives. It is understandable that the standard texts of this period urged strict isolation, exclusion of all visitors, and minimal handling. What is not so understandable is the ambivalence about these issues in texts written in the 70s when staph had long been safely managed, antibiotics were freely available, and the special bonding problems of premature birth were well understood.

For example, *Care of the High-Risk Neonate,* edited by Marshall Klaus and Avroy Fanaroff, was published in 1973. It contains an article by the two editors that advocates increased maternal contact, citing evidence that fondling and rocking both reduce crying and increase growth. They report a study that showed that "warm mothering" of preemies during early weeks produces better learners four months later. Yet another chapter on care of the high-risk infant, this one by Arnold Rudolph, is written as though this data did not exist. In his concluding "Recommendations for Care of the Newborn," Rudolph never once mentions the role of parents, the infant's need for sensory stimulation, or the benefits of touching and rocking. Rather, he advises that, "Newborn infants should be regarded as recovering patients," the infant should be placed not on the mother but "in a pre-warmed incubator," and, "All infants should remain in the transitional care nursery for at least six to eight hours or until stabilized."[12]

This ambivalence is even more evident in *Nonverbal Communication with Patients,* a book published in 1977. In the section on premature infants, the authors warn, "At first, the cardinal rules are to handle the 'preemie' as little as possible, to *minimize sensory stimulation.*"[3] But in the next paragraph they tell us:

> Health professionals, who have watched preemies grow, believe that there is a higher incidence among them of poor growth, lower intelligence, unwillingness to socialize, parental rejection, and child abuse. It suggests that these problems stem from the preemie's early *sensory deprivation* and separation from the parents. As a result, it is recognized by many professionals that the baby has a need to touch the mother's face, as well as to hear her voice from the earliest possible moment.[14]

Despite the ambivalence, which is considerably more marked in hospital practice than in the literature, the evidence is clear. Preemies need to be touched to aid physical and emotional growth. Parents need to touch to help them with the difficult task of establishing a bond with their premature child. And, most important, the presence of loving parents in the intensive care nursery does not pose a risk to the life and health of its inhabitants.

Sheldon Korones, author of *High-Risk Newborn Infants* writes, "Several studies have revealed that colonization rates and the incidence of infectious disease are not increased when parents are permitted entry into the nursery." Klaus and Kennel report that,

> If a small premature infant is either touched, rocked, fondled, or cuddled daily during his stay in the nursery, he has fewer apneic periods [temporary breathing interruptions to which preemies are prone], increased weight gain, a smaller number of stools, as well as an advance in some areas of higher central nervous system functioning, which persists for months after discharge from the hospital.[15]

An added bonus, both in savings to the parent and cost to the hospital, is that parental touching also reduces the time the infant needs to spend in the premature unit.

We are drawn to the inescapable conclusion that:

    (a) physical contact is a great healer and growth stimulator for the premature child,

(b) it strengthens the bond of attachment between child and parents, and

(c) those hospitals which haven't invited parents to step through the glass curtain should do so now.

Note that "invite" is very different from "permit." The parents' touch is *needed* here, yet the parents of the at-risk child may find it hard to give. The hospital, with its tremendous authority, can make that touch possible.

I firmly believe in this conclusion, and still I say it with trepidation. I fear that a zealous hospital staff, now having a new ruling to replace the old one, will disregard the individual differences in parents and apply these lessons with equal force to all. It has happened before. After the publication by Elizabeth Kübler-Ross of *On Death and Dying*,[16] many doctors simply switched from a policy of never telling any patients that they were dying to insisting that all patients be told, whether they wanted to know or not. I have seen a medical resident, schooled in the psychology of behaviorism, tell a mother who was comforting her burned and frightened four-year-old, "You're reinforcing her crying behavior."

The old commandment on preemies was, "Thou shalt not touch." I don't want to write the new commandment. Some parents have no difficulty getting involved right from the start. Others need a great deal of time before they can make even the first tentative touch. The critical bonding period that Klaus and Kennell postulate may be in the first moments after birth for some, the day baby leaves hospital for others. So for those whose training has left them incapable of performing their tasks without a commandment to follow, let it be this:

> Encourage touch by word and deed,
> Then let the parents choose.

### Touch and the Stillborn Child

As I picture you sitting there reading that parents are rebuffed by hospitals, that touch is underutilized by doctors, and that change is mightily resisted by much of institutionalized medicine, I imagine you lining up in two groups. If you are a parent or patient, you are cheering me on, gesticulating, and writing me a letter that supports my words with your own experience. If, on the other hand, you see this criticism as an attack—one more in a long series of attacks—on the art and science of medicine, you are wondering about my credentials, finding evidence of personal pathology in my words, and composing a letter to my boss.

If you are firmly committed to Group Two, then nothing I can say will change your mind, so get on with your letter. But if you're wavering, if you're a borderline case, let me try once more to persuade you. The example I will use is not from my own work, nor is it based on the reports of patients; rather, it is from the experience of a medically qualified British psychoanalyst, Dr. Stanford Bourne. Understand that Dr. Bourne is not an anti-psychiatry psychiatrist. He is neither young nor rebellious nor in any way on the medical fringe. Just the opposite; he is a highly respected, fairly orthodox, English medical specialist.

In the late 1960s Dr. Bourne's caseload included a number of parents of stillborns, children who had died during the last three months of pregnancy or during labor. It is not surprising that this should be so, for one out of every 100 births in England and Wales is a stillbirth, and this amounts to 8,000 a year in Great Britain.[17] By including those who died shortly after birth the figure is raised to 20,000.[18] So the problem is hardly a rare one.

From his work with these parents Bourne came to the somewhat startling conclusion that hospital staffs were dealing with the event of stillbirth in a way that was most psychologically damaging to the mother. Working on the implicit theory that what is not seen is not missed, the dead baby was whisked away from the mother and "disposed of." Tears were discouraged, and the standard prescription was for a stiff upper lip. Terribly British, this advice, and terribly destructive, for the grief that was stifled at the time of the event lingered in the mothers' souls like smoke in a windowless room, seeping into every corner, deadening the air. Depression, bitterness, and guilt hung over these women for years, sometimes for the rest of their lives. Their husbands and living children, and sometimes those yet unborn, suffered with them.

On the basis of what he learned from these troubled, often tortured families, Bourne prepared an article advocating change in hospital practice. He recommended that immediate expression of grief be encouraged, not suppressed. He said the dead baby should be brought to the mother who wished to see it, not spirited away into the bowels of the hospital disposal system. And above all, he insisted that the mother who wanted to should be able to touch, fondle, and hold her stillborn child, in order to say a tactile farewell.

In the preparation of the article Dr. Bourne searched the medical literature for previous work on reactions to stillbirth, then submitted his paper to the two most prestigious British medical journals, *Lancet* and *The British Journal of Medicine.* Both rejected it with the explanation that "enough had already been published on the subject." The tragic irony is that Bourne had already searched the literature and *had not turned up a single article in the English language* on the subject of reaction to stillbirth. After ten years more research, he had still uncovered only one reference, and that written on the other side of the Atlantic in 1962. Writing of these events in a letter that *was* printed in the *BMJ*, Dr. Bourne concluded,

> In considering whether or how to encourage parents to handle a stillborn baby and attend the funeral it is essential to grasp that here is a syndrome in which the compulsive, even overwhelming, aversion of professional attention is an integral part. This is not a moral proposition for existential philosophy but a clinical sign to be faced and recognized and studied, like ketosis on the breath of a diabetic.[19]

Now, more than a decade after Bourne's first article appeared (it was finally published in a general practitioner's journal),[20] hospitals in England and throughout the Commonwealth are adopting his suggestions, and most seem to be well pleased with the results. But for me, an American living in the Antipodes, there is a second irony involved, this one in the way the change came about.

For it was only after a British doctor published an article in a British journal, followed by other publications by other British doctors in other British journals, that New Zealand hospitals began to encourage mothers to hold their stillborns, to weep openly over them, and to attend their funerals. I think it wonderful that those New Zealand hospitals initiated this change after the article appeared in a British medical journal. But the irony stems from the fact that some New Zealand mothers have been practicing this form of good grief therapy for generations. Dr. Bourne was prescribing what Maoris (those New Zealanders whose origins lie in the Polynesian, not British, Isles) have always practiced. They knew the importance of a literally touching farewell, they recognized the need for a ceremony, they encouraged the free flow of tears. Ironically, the news had to come from the other end of the world when the whole time it was right there in the next bed.

The lesson to be learned is by no means limited to New Zealand. In many places (Canadians and Americans take note), the best starting-point for bringing human touch into health care is to watch what the people who were here when the Europeans arrived have always done.

The publication of the Bourne article opened the gates, and other articles began appearing, particularly in British journals, about the effects of stillbirth on families. Nearly all argued that touching the dead infant was of prime importance.

In 1976, Hugh Jolly, who bears the cross of forever being called the British Dr. Spock, spoke further of the hospital's responsibility in helping parents see and handle their dead baby. He drew the important distinction between "encourage" and "insist," concluding that, "This is not something which should be imposed on them . . ."[21] He then spoke of the unspeakable. What of the child who is physically deformed, missing parts, or so hideously misshapen as to bring a shudder to our soul? Surely the parents are better off not seeing, much less holding, this child.

No, says Jolly, whose statements are made from vast clinical experience, "Seeing and holding the dead baby should, if possible, include those who are born malformed. It is possible to show a malformed baby to parents using drapes in such a way that the horrific element is reduced, and, to a large extent, neutralized."[22]

In 1978 Jolly and a number of colleagues published a working draft of a clear, well-written pamphlet for the parents of stillborns. The pamphlet combines helpful advice, reassurance that others have gone through this before, and old fashioned sympathy in about equal measure. The healing effects of touch are included:

Should you see and hold your baby?

This is never an easy decision and even though it is painful it is worth thinking about. You and your husband have every right to see and hold your baby if you so wish. This may seem strange to some parents, although an obvious desire for others. The experience of holding your baby even though he is dead may make him a more real person to remember and in this way may help you and your husband."[23]

Borderline Group Two's, are you with me? Can you see the need for change? Do you see your role in bringing about change—what you can do to bring the healing touch to your practice, to your hospital? If neither Bourne's observations nor Jolly's advice has persuaded you, let me try one final tack. Let me close this chapter with the haunted words of a woman who did not get to touch her dead child. Let me speak to you through her.

I didn't get a chance to really touch him, to hold him like a mother. This is something a mother wants to do so much, to touch the baby. Even though she knows she can't pick it up, she wants to touch it. Sometimes I dream about him, and I can see him, and I wake up. I didn't really pick him up. But the dreams go that I'm picking him up and holding him, and I know I didn't do it. So I wake up because I wanted to so bad.[24]

# Touch Gone Wrong

## 4

Touch gone wrong. We have seen how important is the human touch at the time of birth. Touch is, if anything, even more crucial in human growth. This chapter will look at four problems associated with touching and growing. In it, and the chapter that follows, the ways touch can play a part in resolving these problems will be discussed. These chapters will show, once again, that touch has been neglected by health professionals, this time by those who write about the treatment of growth disorders. This chapter will also expose one genuine villain. Stay tuned.

### Interruptions to Touch

I'm beginning with the problem of interruptions to touch because it is by far the easiest to deal with and correct. The bulk of the problem is created by poor hospital practice and can be eliminated by changing that practice. Many hospitals around the world have already done so, and I know of none that has gone back to the old ways after trying the new.

The problem of interruption is similar to problems of hospital birth and premature nursery care; parents are physically isolated from their children at a time when their caring touch is most needed. The situation occurs when either parent or child is hospitalized and the institution's rules prevent contact between them. It is amazing that such rules still exist in so many hospitals since the damage

43

caused by them was hardly discovered yesterday. It has been documented for decades. Indeed, damage caused by separation has been not only documented, it has been demonstrated to all who have been willing to see by a dedicated pair of English researchers, James and Joyce Robertson. For three decades they have traveled the world showing their films of children in hospitals, and they still encounter resistance, defensiveness, and closed-mindedness among hospital doctors and administrators.

For instance, one New Zealand surgeon responded to the very cautious suggestion that mothers of children *under 2½ years* be allowed to accompany them to the hospital as follows:

> Mothers present in wards with their children create a nuisance and disrupt ward routine, particularly when a doctor wants to do his ward rounds. . . . In my book they are odd people who selfishly want the children to themselves.[1]

I regard the Robertsons as saints for being able, after three decades of encountering this sort of arrogant ignorance, to reply in a quiet, informative, unruffled way. I would have strangled him.

For a graphic, gut-twisting look at the effects of this ignorance, one has only to watch the film *John*, a film made by the Robertsons. The first scene takes the viewer into the home of a normal, loving, middle-class English family. A pregnant mother is playing with her 17-month-old son, John. They touch each other frequently and have an attachment that is obviously strong and healthy. We learn that while mother is in the hospital giving birth, John will spend the time at a residential nursery. They will be separated for ten days, the usual period for a stay in a maternity hospital in Great Britain. The nursery was suggested by the family's general practitioner since they have neither relatives nor close friends in the city (to which they have but recently moved), and John's father is forced to work, not stay home with his child, during that time. The nursery is a fully approved institution that is used for training health professionals.

The next scene and those to follow are shot in the nursery. We watch in growing horror as John's initial bewilderment changes to outrage, his outrage twists into anguish, the anguish sinks into depression, and the depression hardens into despair. In the course of a week, the worst has happened—he has grown resigned to the fate of abandonment. When the resignation sets in, his tears dry up, and lassitude takes the place of tantrums. This is a change of overwhelming tragedy in the life of a young child, and it is one that has been traditionally greeted with happy approval by institutions. They call it "settling in." (That surgeon who was so incensed about the nuisance mothers create when the doctor is making his rounds reckons that "a child would settle in well after about half a day away from his parents."[2])

When, on the tenth day, John's mother comes to retrieve him, he does not rush out to greet her. He ignores her. John refuses to be comforted by his mother or even to look at her. She struggles bravely to find a way to reconnect with him. She speaks softly to him and tries to break down his stiff withdrawal by a slow increase of body contact until she is cuddling him. Finally, he looks at her for the first time. But what a look it is! It is the look of one who has been betrayed, filled with distrust and hate. It is a look she has never seen before.

Anyone who sees *John* through touch-conscious eyes knows the role physical contact plays in the frantic attempts of a young child in a strange and frightening institution to find some comfort in the environment and to use it to hold himself together. John snuggles ferociously into the laps of the ever-changing nurses, and he clings desperately to a large teddy bear. But it is not enough; the damage has been done.

How, then, to undo it? The problem was caused by a misguided institution; it can be prevented by redesigning the institution or, better still, eliminating the need to institutionalize the child. It is a great deal cheaper and infinitely more humane to have trained people available who can watch a child like John in his own home, where he would be surrounded by that which is familiar. It is not just supposition that this is easier for a youngster to bear; the Robertsons demonstrated in a later film that a young girl staying with a neighbor suffered far less than children who are "placed," even for short periods of time.

But there are times when this is not possible, and still, much can be done. Instead of a bevy of rotating nurses, many hospitals and nurseries have successfully experimented with assigning one primary caretaker, whose job it is to be with a child or small group of children for the duration of a brief stay in the institution. One hug from a familiar set of arms is worth more than a dozen from strangers. And the arrangement is more satisfying for staff as well; it is more fulfilling to help and hold one small patient than to scatter your skills and love over half a dozen wards.

Another important change is to extend a welcome to visitors, to make it easy for them to pay a call, to let them know their presence is needed and appreciated. It is not always thus.

For example. In exploring alternatives to nurseries like the one that kept John, James and Joyce Robertson have used their own home to care for children whose parents were in the hospital. They were watching one little girl for what was intended to be a seven-day stay. But complications set in, and one week became three. As time passed, the child grew increasingly distraught over her mother's disappearance. She needed to see her mother. So, despite a hospital rule set in concrete against visits by children under any conditions, the Robertsons each took one of her little hands and marched her in. Through the heavy doors, down the polished corridors their footsteps echoed. They swung open the door to the mother's room and deposited her daughter on the bed for a joyous, hugging reunion. In hot pursuit was the head nurse who suddenly appeared behind them at the bedside. She rose to her full height and, in a voice indistinguishable from that of a sergeant major, barked, "Just look at her! That's why we have rules against child visitors. Will you just look at her? Look at what that child is doing!"

The Robertsons looked. Other than hugging her mother, now as much in fear as happiness, she was doing nothing. Puzzled, James turned to the menacing nurse. "What *is* she doing?" he asked.

"What's she doing? I'll tell you what she's doing. She's *sitting* on the *bed*! *That's* what she's *doing*!"

This incident took place in England, but resistance to allowing children and their parents to share hospital time is a worldwide phenomenon. One form this resistance takes is the absence of beds for parents in children's wards. Writing in 1972, Carol Hardgrove and Rosemary Dawson stated, "In 1968, only 28 of 5,000 general hospitals had facilities allowing parents to spend the night with their child; of 132 children's hospitals only 20 allowed rooming-in, and of these, 15 admitted only mothers from upper socioeconomic groups. The figures are little improved today."[3]

By now the situation has improved considerably, but it still has far to go. There are new hospitals being built today that still make no room in their plans for parents who wish to stay with their child. This must be changed. Just as the husband's touch is that which means the most to a woman in labor, so is the parent's touch the one most healing to the frightened child in a hospital.

As a long-term step, we must train our caregivers—in this case pediatricians, nurses, and nurse-aides—in the uses of physical contact for softening the blow that separation and institutionalization represents. They need to learn how to touch, how to improve the touch skills they already possess, to know the meanings of touch to the patient, and to recognize those times when touching is not appropriate. This has to be part of their formal training and not left to chance or instinct.

Another possibility is the recruiting of community volunteers—sometimes paid volunteers—to hold, rock, listen to, play with, reassure . . . to love the lost children of the hospital. Whoever was the first to recruit grandparents to fill this function deserves a prize for having the brilliance to bring together two age groups who are often separated but who need and can help each other.

The contribution elders can make to the growth of young children goes far beyond a relationship in the hospital. Anyone who has seen the kind of unconstrained loving that grandparents can give knows that this is true. Now, from a rather exotic source, comes some possible scientific support for these observations.

It comes from the Kikuyu of Africa. H. R. Leiderman and his colleagues were interested in this group because Kikuyu infants score above American norms in most tests of mental and motor functioning. They wanted to find out why. To do so, the team separated the group's cultural patterns into a number of discrete demographic factors. When these were analyzed, the only one that correlated significantly with advanced motor test scores was the number of people in the household who were over 40 years of age. On the basis of their observations, Leiderman's team concluded that the great amount of physical contact between these mature, adult caretakers and Kikuyu infants might lead to their precocious development.[4]

The positive effects of handling are not limited to humans. Psychologist Seymour Levine and a host of other researchers have found that the handling of infant rats has major and positive effects on their lives as adults. Not only are the handled rats calmer, less aggressive, and more approachable, but they are more resistant to infection, are better able to adapt to stress, and are *more precocious in both physical growth and motor coordination.*[5] This finding has given rise to a great deal of research effort of the type that only an academic psychologist can truly appreciate. Apparently unconcerned with the implications of the handling phenomenon in the raising of human beings, psychologists have set out with grim determination (and a fair amount of money) to discover what factor was *really* operating that made handled rats so much better off than their unhandled compatriots. This led to four hypotheses, each to be tested and retested. Was tactile stimulation the important factor? Stress? Maternal behavior? Or was it . . . hypothermia?

Ah, hypothermia. Those who really understand the mind of the academic psychologist know that the hypothermia hypothesis (which argues that the important thing is that the rats are cooled off when the handler removes them from their cage) is the one that's going to excite him. And so it has. But to no avail. Many articles, many hours, and many, many dollars later, P. A. Russell was forced to conclude, ". . . it seems unlikely, then, that the cooling hypothesis can be made to account for all the effects reported."[6] Alas.

For me, a subject more worthy of attention emerges from another of Levine's findings. After he divided the infant rats into the handled and non-handled groups, he added a new category by forming a third group. To this new group he administered mild but painful electric shock on a regular basis. To his surprise, the shocked rats did about as well as those that were handled and considerably better than those which received neither handling nor shock. One might conclude (or at least hypothesize) that any stimulation is better than none at all.

This resonates with the human condition. Those who work with young delinquents, drug addicts, and children who are driven to alcohol abuse say that if they cannot get positive attention, they will settle for negative. For some, it is better to be beaten than to be ignored. Which brings us back to touch gone wrong.

Serious though the consequences can be when touch is interrupted, they pale beside those that eventuate when touch is absent to begin with. A rat seems to be able to thrive when shocked or touched. With humans the rule is a little more complex. I think it goes like this:

> The hugged child will thrive.
> The hit child will survive.
> The untouched child will die.

Let me immediately acknowledge the exceptions. Variation within the human species is enormous. There are hugged children who do not thrive. Children who are not just hit but badly beaten sometimes don't survive. And there are children who make it despite everything an unjust world can throw at them. But these are exceptions. Most of the time the rule holds true.

The untouched child will die. An examination of touch gone wrong must begin here. Two other observations demand scrutiny as well. They are:

> The child not touched enough will not grow.
> The child touched in a disturbed way will suffer.

### The Untouched Child Will Die

Like the cat that needs the touch of its mother's tongue to survive the first few hours of kittenhood, so we humans depend on touch to survive. But there is a difference. Within a few hours after birth the kitten can make it on its own, but not so the human. The child well past infancy can die from lack of touch.

Some of the strongest evidence for this comes from foundling homes and orphanages. Throughout the nineteenth century and the first quarter of the twentieth, children raised in these institutions stood less than a fifty-fifty chance of reaching puberty. A German foundling home at the turn of the century had a mortality rate of over 70 percent for infants in their first year of life. A 1915 study of American orphanages revealed death rates of 32 to 75 percent by the end of the second year. In that year, Baltimore institutions were estimated to have at least a 90 percent mortality rate, and at New York's Randall's Island Hospital it was closer to 100 percent.[7]

The child-rearing experts of the time—always male, always medical, always authoritarian—laid down rules for parents and institutions alike to protect growing children from the twin evils of the day—germs and moral decay. Either might strike if the parent or caretaker's guard were lowered for even an instant.

Concern about "moral decay" long predated the germ theory, and religious leaders were the original protectors of morality. In fact, the Christian church often served as the anti-touch authority in the days before "scientific" authorities admonished parents about the evils of physical contact. The Dominican Giovanni Dominici addressed himself to this issue in the late fourteenth and early fifteenth centuries. James Ross, writing in Lloyd deMause's disturbing book, *The His-*

*tory of Childhood,* quotes the priest's advice to parents: From three years on a boy should ". . . be a stranger to being petted, embraced and kissed by you until after the twenty-fifth year. . . . Let not the mother nor the father, much less any other person, touch him."[8]

Medical experts carried on this tradition, but now backed with "scientific" rather than "divine" authority. Prominent among these experts was the influential American pediatrician, Emmett Holt. The expert who most influenced him was a German who lived from 1808 to 1861. His name was Daniel Gottlieb Moritz Schreber.

Schreber was a man of many parts: he was a physician, educator, author, and pre-eminent authority on child-rearing. Like many today, Dr. Schreber was one who thought his age and his nation suffered from softness, moral decay, and weakness. He dedicated his life to the eradication of these evils, instructing his fellow citizens through books and by example on the proper way to raise children. The building blocks of his improved society were to be discipline and obedience: from them would grow a structure of moral purity, uprightness (both physical and mental), freedom (the freedom to obey), health, strength, and self-discipline.

Schreber had five children. Of his three daughters we know little. But of his sons, on whom he tested and practiced his theories, we know a great deal.

Both went mad.

The elder son also committed suicide; he shot and killed himself at age 38. The younger, Daniel Paul Schreber, became first an eminent judge and then the most famous paranoid schizophrenic in the history of psychiatry.

Daniel Paul became psychotic in his forty-second year and spent half of the rest of his life in mental asylums. He died in one some 27 years later. When he was 61 he published a remarkable record of his madness (which he experienced as a holy time of direct contact with God) called *Memoirs of My Nervous Illness.* Freud used this document to support his theory of paranoia, and the book has been discussed and debated by psychiatrists ever since.

One of the most interesting analyses of the Schreber case is that of Morton Schatzman. In *Soul Murder* he links the son's delusions to the father's child-rearing methods. For instance, Schreber felt that little devils were compressing his head as though in a vice; he also felt as though his head were being pulled apart. This delusion becomes a bit easier to understand when one turns to his father's writings. He invented the *Kopfhalter*, a device that pulled the child's hair if he failed to hold his head straight. He also devised a head-encircling chin band, supposedly to ensure straight teeth. Like his many other tools of restraint and oppression, he tested them first on his own sons. These devices were very much in keeping with the doctor's chief tenet of child-rearing: "Suppress everything in the child . . ." He demanded "absolute obedience" before the first birthday, urging his readers to crush disobedience into total submission.

Dr. Schreber's notions almost certainly influenced Adolf Hitler; many of the views he expresses in *Mein Kampf* could easily have been spoken by the doctor himself. But Schreber's influence was not limited to Germany. *Medical Indoor Gymnastics*, one of his many books, has gone through nearly 40 editions in seven languages. He had a major effect on the practices and prescriptions of authoritarian physicians around the world. And, as we shall see, his views on touch were echoed by a leading American psychologist and child-rearing "expert" nearly 100 years after his death.

Like other authoritarian authorities, Schreber took a firm stand against unnecessary touching of children. And like the others, he exhorted mothers to refrain from this sort of contact *for the good of the child*. In 1858 he wrote:

> If the child is lifted from the bed and carried around each time he makes noises—without checking if there is really something wrong—and is calmed by gentleness of one kind or another, this may often lead to the appearance of the emotion of spite later in the life of the child. I wish mothers and nursemaids would recognize the importance of this point![9]

The expert advice of Schreber and those who followed was aimed at toughening-up, the shining opposite of degenerate mollycoddling. Good parents and the right sort of institutions did not mollycoddle. The experts cautioned them not to handle the child too much, not to rock her, not to pick him up when he cried, not to cuddle, comfort—not to s-p-o-i-l the little bugger. The children died, unspoiled.

Finally, the toll in children's lives overcame the moral force of orthodoxy. Other experts—also male, also medical, but considerably less authoritarian—rebelled against the teachings of their professors and brought a more maternal, less Prussian philosophy to child-care institutions. In New York, Dwight Chapin began boarding babies out rather than leaving them to fight the survival odds in an institution. Bostonian Fritz Talbot's conversion experience came in the Children's Clinic in Düsseldorf, whose director was Arthur Schlossmann:

> ... what piqued Dr. Talbot's curiosity was the sight of a fat old woman who was carrying a very measly baby on her hip. "Who's that?" inquired Dr. Talbot. "Oh, that," replied Schlossmann, "is Old Anna. When we have done everything we can medically for a baby and it is still not doing well, we turn it over to Old Anna, and she is always successful."[10]

When Bellevue Hospital adopted a policy that every child was to be picked up, held, and carried around several times a day, infant mortality rates on the pediatric wards dropped from over 30 percent to under 10 percent in one year."

The contributions of these pediatricians to the welfare of institutionalized children was enormous. But the most important figure in bringing lifesaving touch to the children of the asylum was not a pediatrician but a child psychiatrist and psychoanalyst, René Spitz.

Spitz compared two children's institutions.[12] One he called the Nursery; the other, the Foundling Home. Both provided their charges with well-prepared food, adequate clothing, and competent medical services. While both institutions were clean and well-staffed, in terms of both services and hygiene, the Foundling Home had the edge. Furthermore, its children were significantly brighter when they entered than were those of the Nursery, averaging IQs of 124 vs. 101.5.

But the Nursery had one thing that the Foundling Home lacked, and this one difference more than compensated for any material disadvantage. That thing was the presence of mothers or mother-substitutes, for the Nursery was in fact a prison nursery where convicted women who were either pregnant or mothers of infants served their time. Still, from a viewpoint of straight physical medicine, children should be expected to do well in either institution.

It did not work out that way. Despite the Foundling Home's emphasis on hygiene and precautions against the spread of contagious disease, its children were terribly susceptible to all manner of disorders. A measles epidemic wiped out 23 of 88 children under the age of 2½. Ear infections, eczema, and intestinal disturbance swept through the survivors. In the two years it took Spitz to complete his study, 34 out of 91 children died. Furthermore, it was clear that there was something about life in the institution that was causing these deaths. Whereas in the general population younger children are the most susceptible to disease, in the Foundling Home the older children (who had been institutionalized longest) suffered a higher mortality rate than the younger ones. Like Levine's untouched rats, their resistance to disease was sapped as a function of their time in the home.

Mental deterioration was just as striking. Lack of speech, incontinence, inability to walk or eat unaided characterized the 18-month to 2½-year-olds in the Foundling Home. Their development quotient dropped a horrendous 52 points in the course of a year in the institution. From an average of 124 on admission, they dropped to a meager 72 by year's end.

By contrast, the Nursery children, who averaged 101.5 on admission, actually gained a few points, scoring 105 a year later. At 10 months of age, they were full of energy and curiosity; all could walk with support, and some could walk unaided. There were no epidemics and not one death during the study.

What accounts for the vast difference in the fates of the children in these apparently similar institutions? We have seen that neither food nor medical services nor innate differences in the children explain it. There are two factors which do. One is the general lack of stimulation, of sensory input, in the Foundling Home. Not only were there few toys in evidence there, but the daily routine included hanging bed sheets over the foot and side railing of each cot, effectively placing the child within in a sensory deprivation chamber for much of the day. And while the information was not available in the 1940s when this study was undertaken, we now know that adults deprived of sensory input develop symptoms that range from loss of concentration to hallucinations. It is unlikely that the effects on children would be *less* severe.

But important as sensory deprivation may be, Spitz wisely discounted it as the significant source of the deterioration. The critical difference in the two institutions, he concluded, was the presence of mothers in the Nursery. In Spitz's words, "The presence of a mother or her substitute is sufficient to compensate for all other deprivations."[13]

And what was the significant maternal behavior that protected children from the wasting away of their counterparts in the Foundling Home? Granting that it is extremely difficult to tease out a single factor from the immense complexity of a mother and child relationship, in this case one can make a fairly safe bet. The women of the Nursery were, as prisoners, cut off from their mates, from customary sexual gratification, and from most compensating activities besides. There were few opportunities to fulfill ambition or achieve satisfaction. Their one channel for love, libido, rivalry, and life satisfaction was their babies.

Were there ever babies more loved than these? Held, cuddled, passed around for mutual admiration, fancied, dandled, adored, these children got a full dose of mother's touch, and they thrived. Those in the Foundling Home were denied loving contact for most of the day, and they wasted away.

The lesson for healers and helpers associated with institutions is too obvious to belabor. The child in an institution needs a mother's touch. When mother is not available, her closest approximation should be sought and used. This is a requirement of the highest priority—the child's survival depends on it.

### The Child Not Touched Enough Will Not Grow

Growth takes place in the emotional, intellectual, and physical spheres. Insufficient touching can retard growth in all three. The most dramatic to observe is physical retardation.

For most people it is a distinct shock to learn that lack of love can actually stunt growth. By stunting, I am not talking about an inch (although Arthur Janov's *Primal Scream* describes an adult patient who grew an inch after experiencing the blocked primal pain of his childhood).[14] Lack of love—and I believe this is especially true of physically expressed love—can produce physical dwarfs. In one extreme case reported by the Johns Hopkins team of John Money and June Werlwas, a love-deprived 4½-year-old achieved only the size of a 12-month baby.[15]

It is important to emphasize that love deprivation can encompass a host of behaviors. I am emphasizing lack of physical contact. Others include food deprivation, inactivity, neglect, enforced solitude, torture, and filth. All may be contributing factors to growth lag.

This failure to grow has accumulated many names, a sure sign of a disorder that still has more questions than answers attached to it. Among its suggested titles are: deprivation dwarfism, psychosocial dwarfism, maternal-deprivation syndrome, failure to thrive, hypo-somatotropic dwarfism, and reversible hyposomatotropism. Whatever the name, the condition is truly psychosomatic in origin, symptoms, and treatment, and this makes the criteria for diagnosis both specific and complex. The most common diagnostic signs of deprivation dwarfism include:

1. A significant slowing of statural growth and skeletal maturation some time after the first few months of life. The usual result is a height in the bottom three percentiles for the child's age, i.e., at least 97 percent of children of that age are taller.
2. Reversibility of the condition through environmental manipulation. Growth resumes when the child is removed from the home.
3. An insufficiency of pituitary secretion (called hypopituitarism) before the change of environment, but not after.
4. A history of a damaged or disrupted relationship between parents and child.
5. Apparently bizarre behavior on the part of the child. Typical behaviors include eating from garbage cans and drinking from toilets, indiscriminate eating alternating with self-starvation and vomiting, wetting and soiling, sleeplessness and night-roaming, indifference to pain (pain agnosia), and self-injury.
6. These symptoms disappear or diminish after the change of environment.
7. Retarded motor development and retarded intellectual development, which also disappear or diminish when the child is removed from the home.[16]

Although there is still a great deal unknown about this condition, ongoing studies at Johns Hopkins, Yale, and the University of Virginia have brought many of its strange aspects to light. It is now known that the growth hormone ACTH is not produced in sufficient quantities for normal development by a number of children who live in oppressive or loveless atmospheres. It is also clear that after only 24 hours away from such conditions (usually in a hospital), normal growth hormone response is recovered. During the time they are away from home, these children shoot upward in height and weight. This growth spurt is accompanied by improved sleep, eating, and behavior. Then, unless conditions at home have changed in their absence, when they go back, all their symptoms—including growth lag—return.

Researchers have long associated deprivation dwarfism with lack of body contact and tender loving care.[17] The disorder is clearly linked to the wasting away that Spitz described in the Foundling Home. That lack of physical contact is a major cause of these syndromes is given indirect support by Spitz's summary of other research into the fates of institutionalized children. He wrote, "The worst offenders were the best equipped and most hygienic institutions, which succeeded in sterilizing the surroundings of the child from germs but which at the same time sterilized the child's psyche."[18]

There is a second institutional connection to deprivation dwarfism, this one leading back to the premature baby nursery. Klaus and Kennell reviewed a number of studies of families in which the parents deprived their children of love and care, the sort of families which produce deprivation dwarfs. They discovered that, in a statistically significant number of such cases, the children were either premature or separated from their parents for a period of time, often because of an illness that required hospitalization. Prematurity and separation also marked those families in which children were battered or otherwise physically harmed by their parents.[19] We have already seen the anti-touch regulations enforced by hospital preemie units and the effects these may have on the bonding process. The deprived or battered child is one legacy of such a policy.

The thought of parents so depriving of love that their child fails to grow is enraging to some, piteous to others, horrifying to all. And there is no denying that many parents who so behave are themselves severely disturbed. But it is also important to acknowledge that a fervent, fanatic, vitriolic anti-love, anti-touch philosophy was the mainstay of American psychology for much of this century. At its heart (if that be the word) stood the founder of American behaviorism, John B. Watson.

Watson was not on the lunatic fringe of the psychology profession; he was at the villainous center of it. Greatly admired by the many colleagues who applauded his efforts to turn the art of psychology into a Real Science by dismissing all that is human from its domain, Watson was, and in many ways still is, a moving force in academic psychology in the United States and the world. He was also the author of what his publishers accurately called, "The Standard Book of Child Psychology."

The name of this book (which went through at least five large printings) was *Psychological Care of Infant and Child.*[20] The *Atlantic Monthly* called it "A godsend to parents!" *Parent's Magazine* said it should stand "on every intelligent mother's shelf." By any standards, popular or professional, the book was enormously successful. It was also monstrously destructive.

With Emmett Holt as his guiding light, Watson used all the scientific and academic prestige at his command to admonish mothers *NOT TO TOUCH THEIR CHILDREN!*

If I were reading that incredible statement instead of writing it, I know that I would simply not believe it. After all, how can anyone, much less a scientific psychologist, argue against what is probably the one most basic pattern of human—indeed, of mammalian—relationship? Could this arrogance, this abysmal ignorance, possibly be put to paper as serious advice to mothers?

Sadly, it could. Here are some direct quotes from Watson's book. The first dwells on the dire consequence of "extreme" maternal touch—spoiling:

> The mother knows the infant can smile and gurgle and chuckle with glee. She knows it can coo and hold out its chubby arms. What more touching and sweet, what more thrilling to a young mother! And the mother to get these thrills goes to extreme lengths. She picks the infant up, kisses and hugs it, rocks it, pets it and calls it "mother's little lamb," until the child is unhappy and miserable whenever away from actual physical contact with the mother. Then again as we face this intolerable situation of our own creating, we say the child is "spoiled." And spoiled most children are. Rarely does one see a normal child—a child that is comfortable—a child that adults can be comfortable around—a child more than nine months of age that is constantly happy.[21]

Watson's concept of what constitutes "extreme lengths" is as telling as his concept of a normal child.

Having pointed out the danger of maternal touch, the scientific psychologist then lays a surprisingly unscientific guilt-trip on the mother who might still be tempted to show love to her offspring:

A certain amount of affectionate response is socially necessary, but few parents realize how easily they can overtrain the child in this direction. It may tear the heart strings a bit, this thought of stopping the tender outward demonstration of your love for your children or of their love for you. But if you are convinced that this is best for the child, aren't you willing to stifle a few pangs? Mothers just don't know, when they kiss their children and pick them up and rock them, caress them and jiggle them upon their knee, that they are slowly building up a human being totally unable to cope with the world it must later live in.[22]

Now we know that hugging equals spoiling and that the mother who still yearns to touch her child is a woman who just will not stifle her desire. Next we learn what that desire really is:

She is starved for love—affection, as she prefers to call it. It is at bottom a sex-seeking response in her, else she would never kiss the child on the lips.[23]

Watson was neither the first nor the last to equate touch with sex, but his certainty that a mother kisses her child's lips to satisfy her own sexual starvation is just plain madness. But Watson knows what he says is true because he has proof. And what is the proof put forward by the founding father of scientific behavioral psychology? He raises the question: Does the kindly, affectionate—kissing—mother *succeed* in raising a kindly affectionate child? The question asked, Watson answers:

The fact I brought out before, that we rarely see a happy child, is proof to the contrary. The fact that our children are always crying and always whining shows the unhappy, unwholesome state they are in. Their digestion is interfered with and probably their whole glandular system is deranged.[24]

All the quoting is not merely to skewer the villain. It is to help rearrange perceptions of the parents who do not express love. Hard as it may be not to blame them, we must look first at the expert advice that *their* parents received. The effects of that advice are still with us.

The exact relationship between physical and intellectual growth lag is not yet known, but there is no doubt that lack of expressed love, of which physical contact plays a major part, leads to both. Intellectual dwarfing regularly accompanies physical dwarfing, and the effects of non-touching institutions on intellectual and emotional development are well-documented and devastating.

The first study of the causes of psychiatric damage to young children in institutions was conducted in 1933 in Austria by H. Durfee and K. Wolf. They found that there was no measurable impairment to children under three months of age, but those who had been institutionalized for more than eight months during their first year were so disturbed that they could not be tested.[25] Lauretta Bender and her colleagues found that three years in such an institution were enough to cause irreversible damage.[26] In 1945 Spitz described Foundling Home babies as showing "a complete restriction of psychic capacity by the end of the first year."[27] Commenting on the permanence of this restriction, he wrote, "This restriction of psychic capacity is not a temporary phenomenon. It is . . . a progressive process. How much this deterioration could have been arrested if the children were taken out of the institution at the end of the first year is an open question."[28]

In 1956 that question was largely answered. That was the year when adoption was made legal for the first time in the history of Lebanon. The new law had enormous consequences for children in orphanages, and fortunately social scientist Wayne Dennis was there to study and record them. Dennis went into a foundling home in which children were living under conditions of limited physical contact and severe social deprivation. The average IQ in the institution was just over 50, and most of the inmates would be classified as imbeciles or morons.

In *Children of the Crèche* Dennis describes the effects of the new adoption law. The first, and most dramatic, was that parents rushed to take advantage of it. Children who had been condemned to a certain fate of an institionalized childhood suddenly found themselves cherished members of real families. The next effect was on the intellectual capacity of the former inmates. For those adopted before their second birthdays, this change, too, was dramatic. After the children had been in their new environment for only a brief period, their IQs rose to normal levels. In most cases that meant a doubling of intelligence in a matter of months! But for those who had lived in the foundling home longer than two years, the results were not so happy. For every year spent in the institution they suffered a permanent loss of six months in mental age. Adoption could not make up for this loss; their intelligence was forever dwarfed.[29]

If growth is stunted and intelligence diminished by insufficient touch, emotional life is wizened and shrunk. Sensorially deprived children grow up with twisted or shriveled capacity to feel, to touch or be touched by other human beings. Some develop an actual physical aversion to touch. Others, like the Tin Man in *The Wizard of Oz*, become adults without hearts, those whom John Bowlby described as marked by lack of affection or feelings for anyone. While the name for such emotional dwarfs has varied through the ages, the current psychiatric diagnostic label is sociopathic personality disorder. Despite its scientific sound, the term is a confused one, often serving as little more than a diagnostic dumping ground for troublesome people who do not seem to fit other labels. Clearly, more research is needed, both about sociopaths and whether touch deprivation plays a part in their disturbance.

Research need not be right to be important. Good scientific studies raise new questions, and it is this, far more than a finding which is likely to prove ephemeral, that is of lasting value. Seemingly unrelated studies are like pieces of a jigsaw puzzle. One such puzzle is currently being put together about the effects of physical contact. Combining animal studies and cross-cultural data, the pieces are being fitted together in a way that is leading to a new theory as to the relationship between childhood touch and adult behavior. The work is being done by a neuropsychologist at the National Institutes of Health, James Prescott. The puzzle that he is piecing together is a major contribution to our understanding of touch gone wrong. His work is important though his conclusions may well prove incorrect.

Prescott believes there is a strong relationship between the amount of physical contact infants receive and the likelihood of their becoming violent adults. The less children are touched, the more likely they are to grow up violent.

To test his theory, Prescott began to examine societies around the world to see if a cultural, as well as individual, pattern could be established. He also examined research on monkeys to find out if other primates exhibited this inverse relationship between touch and violence. We will look at his findings in both areas after a highly condensed summary of the underlying theory.

Prescott's theory is, in essence, that sensory stimulation is a necessary ingredient for the normal development of the cerebellum. In his words, "Sensory stimulation is like a nutrient, and just as malnutrition adversely affects the developing brain so does sensory deprivation."[30]

The effect of sensory undernourishment in childhood is sensory craving in the adult. Prescott calls this a neurophysiological addiction to sensory stimulation. In seeking unmet sensory needs, the deprived adult turns to drugs, crime, and violence.

However, all sensory stimulation is not equal. Sight, hearing, and smell are of considerably less importance to the healthy development of the cerebellum than two others: vestigial stimulation (movement) and touch. It is the touch studies that we will now explore.

The monkey literature points squarely at a relationship between lack of childhood stimulation and bizarre, dysfunctional adult behavior.

The best known of the studies were those conducted by Harry Harlow, whose comparison of cloth and wire surrogate monkey mothers has had so much exposure as to need no retelling here. To give the briefest of summaries, Harlow demonstrated that:

   (a) Cuddlyness is a more important maternal quality to an infant rhesus monkey than feeding; and

   (b) Even those monkeys raised on a cuddly mother surrogate were, as adults, unable to function as mates or mothers.[31]

Charles Kaufman's studies of pigtail and bonnet monkeys showed the importance of physical contact, both in uninterrupted maternal-infant relationships and in re-establishing relationships after separation. One of his valuable contributions was to point out differences in the behavior of the two species. Bonnets touch each other more in almost every social situation than do pigtails.[32] This is a useful, cautionary reminder of the limits of generalization from animal studies, and it also reminds us of what we know from other sources about human touch; that humans, both individually and in groups, differ in their needs for and expression of touch.

Gary Mitchell is the primate-research scientist who probably had the greatest influence on Prescott. His review of social isolation studies showed that animals raised in structures that allow them to see, smell, and hear each other, but not touch, suck, or cuddle, grow up with immense problems in living. Their symptoms include self-mutilation, inability to mate or mother, excessive fear and violence, and failure to integrate into the dominance order. They also groom themselves and others less frequently than those who were not sensorially deprived, and they tend to make repeated bizarre movements, including pacing, rocking, and self-clasping. They masturbate a great deal but copulate only with difficulty.

From the point of view of Prescott's theory, the most interesting of Mitchell's observations concerns the pattern of fear and violence:

> Our long-term studies found that the behavior of monkeys reared in isolation gradually changes from cringing fearfulness into prominent displays of hostility in adulthood. This change occurs gradually but becomes salient around puberty, especially in the males. The longer and more severe an animal's early social isolation, the later in life will this change from fear to hostility occur.[33]

With this animal evidence in place, Prescott began to assemble the human pieces. Using Textor's Cross-Cultural Summary as a guide, he studied child-rearing and adult violence in 49 cultures, from the Ainu to the Zuñi. He found what he described as, "a strong significant statistical relationship between the degree of deprivation of infant physical affection and adult physical violence."[34] Prescott was satisfied that he was able to accurately predict adult violence patterns in 73 percent of the cultures he studied. Dividing the other 27 percent according to their attitudes toward premarital sexuality, he found that those that were repressive and punitive were also marked by violence. By feeding this information into his classification system he was able to achieve near-perfect predictability.

There is something about near-perfect predictability that makes me nervous. I think Jim Prescott's work is important for the line of research it opens up, but I confess I don't believe that a simple, one-to-one relationship exists between infant handling and adult peacefulness. For one thing, I'm not entirely satisfied with the data.

Prescott has himself reclassified one group, the Samoans, whom he originally classified as Low Infant Physical Affection/Low Adult Physical Violence. He now recognizes that they are more aptly classed as Low Infant Physical Affection/High Adult Physical Violence, thus fitting better into his theory. But he has also wrongly classified the Maori, whom he describes as high in infant physical affection and low in adult physical violence. Prescott's infant description is correct, at least until the birth of the next child, for it's the baby who gets the lion's share of affection in the traditional Maori family. But categorizing adults as low in violence would make most Maoris laugh, since they have always regarded themselves as the warriors of the Pacific. In pre-European days, human flesh contributed significantly to the protein content of the Maori diet. They took slaves, made human sacrifices, and were highly skilled in the tactics and strategies of warfare. Maoris practiced facial and body tattooing with stone chisels, an extremely painful form of self-adornment or mutilation. They had a highly refined code of *utu*, or revenge. Today, Maoris in New Zealand are well represented in contact sports, the army, and the prison system. I suggest those 49 cultures need rechecking.

There is another problem as well—one that applies more to books like this than to any individual piece of research. It is the problem of oversimplification, usually rooted in the fertile soil of enthusiasm. If violence, dwarfism, dyslexia, acne, and baldness were caused only by insufficient touch, it is likely that such a relationship would have been discovered long before the first graduate school of psychology was built. If touch offered an easy cure to these curses of humanity, medical schools could have stopped teaching biochemistry years ago. Touch is not offered in this book as the Prevention and Cure of All Diseases, but as an understudied, undertaught, and underpracticed healing tool. It cannot and should not be offered as the one key that will open the door to human understanding. As John Money pointedly reminded me:

> It would be stretching an hypothesis beyond credibility to attribute all these biochemical anomalies to touch deprivation alone. Beware of the marketer's folly of putting all the eggs in one hypothesis. Nature is usually incredibly complex, once the etiology of what at first looks like a single-unit problem is unraveled. It then becomes multivariate, and hierarchically reducible.[35]

### The Child Touched in a Disturbed Way Will Suffer

It is tempting to conclude that if lack of touch is always bad for the developing organism, an abundance of touch is always good for it.

Wrong.

There are ways of touching which can be damaging, devastating, sometimes even life threatening. In extreme cases they bring about death. We will look at two forms of negative touch in this section, the second of which is a killer. The first is the incestuous touch.

There has been so much written on incest from so many viewpoints —anthropological, psychological, religious, genetic, legal, etc.—that it is futile to attempt even the scantiest of summaries here. I will therefore limit myself to two recent developments, one a finding from research and the other a trend among researchers.

The sexually provocative parental touch has, until recently, been condemned by nearly every psychiatrist since Freud as destructive to the child's development. There has been general agreement that such a touch is both confusing and overwhelming to the child and that it raises oedipal conflict to vertiginous heights. In extreme forms the sexually provocative touch becomes the literally incestuous touch, and incest is a practice condemned by societies old and new, from Tahiti to Transylvania. Any event so universally tabooed is more than likely to have disastrous consequences for those who risk the wrath of the gods by indulgence. Indeed, I have yet to see a psychological study that shows that children benefit from sexualized parental touch.

In fact, there is new evidence that incestuous relationship with parents may have specific deleterious effects for the child. In two articles, written separately but simultaneously, clinical researchers have recorded hysterical seizures as an aftermath of incest. Six of the cases were from New Mexico,[36] and four, involving incestuous rape, were from Ohio.[37] All involved teenage girls. The New Mexico team found some interesting historical precedents for this type of reaction:

> Galen, the second-century Greek physician, believed that seizures were the result of premature intercourse in childhood. This is not too distant from Freud's perception that the hysterical seizure repeats a traumatic event. The Navajo Indians have recognized for centuries a syndrome that includes incest, seizures, and witchcraft. When a Navajo has a seizure, it is often assumed that she has experienced incest and may be a witch.[38]

Just as interesting as recent research finding is a trend among recent researchers. Of all the sexual taboos, incest is the one that has received the greatest support, both from ancient custom and modern psychiatry. But now even this most sacred of cows is being eyed by the butcher. A number of sexologists have begun to question whether the incest taboo might just be obsolete.

One can take this in two ways. It can be seen as a legitimate inquiry into a previously sanctified area of social conduct, or it can be perceived as a pernicious plot by a group of publicity-craving academics. *Time* magazine has chosen the latter course. Describing the inquiries as an "attack" and "a propaganda campaign," calling the researchers "lobbyists" and "pushy ham-handed amateurs," *Time* concludes that this may be "the most reprehensible" trend in the (presumably, already reprehensible) field of sex research.[39]

I am one who believes that all human behavior, the incest taboo included, should be subject to investigation, and I do not share the view that those who do the investigating are reprehensible propagandists and/or ham-handed amateurs. In fact, most sexologists are neither of the above. Yet I believe that constraints against intrafamilial sex, particularly between parent and child, are important to maintain in order to protect children from parental exploitation. I also believe that some of the statements made by those who reject the taboo are just plain wrong. When, for example, James Ramey describes "the withdrawal of all touching contact" as "a peculiarly American problem,"[40] he is merely demonstrating ignorance about the rest of the world. Americans touch considerably more than English, Scots, Irish, and Australians. They probably touch more than Germans and Austrians as well. When Ramey concludes that with more touching in the family, America might reduce "the present rash of feverish adolescent sexual activity outside the home,"[41] he is merely expressing a pious wish that supports another present-day taboo. Not all things are best when done with the family.

However serious the psychological damage caused by the incestuous touch, another wrongful touch more than matches it and results in terrible physical damage as well. Sometimes it ends in death. This is child battering.

The history of child-beating is long and grim. Children have been whipped by their teachers for at least 5,000 years. The practice is alive today in New Zealand (where it never died), in a few English towns (where it is back by popular demand), and showing stirrings of life-after-death in the United States (where the Supreme Court has resurrected it). This punitive touch is usually reserved for boys, who receive the hand or the cane "for their own good" or for religious reasons. Roman lads were taken by their parents to be flogged before the altars of Diana, and Christian children were dealt an annual bruising—ironically, on Innocents Day.

Christian dogma was frequently the source of brutal advice for parents. For example, the *Domostroi*, a sixteenth-century household guide compiled by Russian Churchmen, cautioned fathers against playing with their sons. Patrick Dunn quotes its advice on punishment:

> Punish your son in his early years and he will comfort you in your old age and be the ornament of your soul. Do not spare your child any beating, for the stick will not kill him but will do him good; when you strike the body, you save the soul from death. . . . If you love your son, punish him often so that he may later gladden your spirit. Punish your son in his youth, and when he is a man he will be your comfort and you will be praised among the wicked, and your enemies will envy you. Raise your child in fear and you will find peace and blessing in him.[42]

Islamic children fared no better under the rigors of Mosaic law. There is nothing wishy-washy about Mosaic law; it calls for unruly children to be put to death. It was adopted as law by the Commonwealth of Massachusetts in 1646. Connecticut followed three years later but usually substituted public whippings for death. (They have always been sort of wishy-washy in Connecticut.) Not so its northern neighbor. While you can't chop your mother up in Massachusetts, you can—or could—murder your apprentice. In 1630 a master was acquitted of this crime by a jury of his Salem peers on the grounds that the boy was "ill disposed."

Samuel Radbill's excellent historical survey of child abuse traces reform movements as far back as A.D. 100, when Plutarch urged his fellow Romans to stop whipping their children with the *scutia*, a leather-thonged whip. Sir Thomas More had a nice way of making the same point to his fellow Englishmen; he beat his daughters, but substituted peacock feathers for a whip. American reformer Samuel Halliday described the beatings small children received at the hands of their parents in *The Little Street Sweeper; Or, Life Among the Poor*, published in 1861. A decade later the Society for the Prevention of Cruelty to Children was founded in New York.[43]

The founding of the Society was undoubtedly influenced by Halliday, but the immediate impetus was the plight of a poor New York girl named Mary Ellen. She was starved and beaten by her adoptive parents. Alarmed church workers alerted local authorities and the police, but neither showed any interest in her situation. Parents had a sacred right to do whatsoever they wished to their children in nineteenth-century America, much as the father in ancient Rome enjoyed "the privilege to sell, abandon, offer in sacrifice, devour, kill, or otherwise dispose of his offspring."[44]

Finally the church workers found an interested organization; it was the SPCA, the Society for the Prevention of Cruelty to Animals. Arguing that Mary Ellen was a member of the animal kingdom and thus subject to the laws against animal cruelty, the SPCA had her legally removed from her parents.

Doctors have from time to time alerted their colleagues and fellow citizens to the existence of parental abuse. In the tenth century Rhazes made mention of injuries to children caused by intentional striking. In the late seventeenth century both Paul Zacchius and Theophilus Bonet recorded postmortem findings of battered and injured children. In 1860 Ambroise Tardieu described the symptoms of abuse, and a century later Henry Kempe rediscovered these same symptoms.[45] Kempe drew international attention to what he called the battered child syndrome, and it is he, more than any other person alive today, who has created a new awareness of the problem and new ideas for its prevention and solution. Kempe, a pediatrician at Colorado Medical Center, persuaded two psychiatrists there, Carl Pollock and the late Brandt Steele, to join him in studying the phenomenon of child battering.

Steele's work is still classic in the field. He estimated that each year in the United States at least 40,000 children are seriously injured by their parents. It was a gross underestimation. In 1978 the National Center on Child Abuse and Neglect estimated one million cases of child abuse, and a 1979 government survey suggested that three million was a more realistic figure.[46] Alcohol abuse, absence of support networks (usually friends and relatives), poverty, overcrowded housing, unemployment, and broken families all constitute stress factors that may result in battering, but it can occur without their presence and at all levels of society. The most constant factor in child abuse is the psychological set of the parent. The best predictor of this set is the type of parenting the parent received as a child. So often, the battering parent was the battered child.

Child abuse is not limited to a too-hard spanking; the things par-

ents do to their children are numerous and horrifying. Steele lists
some of them:

> Some parents frequently slap and spank during all routine care-
> taking acts: they whack, poke, or severely pinch the infant each
> time they pass the crib, and they may burn the infant with a
> cigarette or hit him with handy household objects. . . . Other
> infants have periods of relatively good care interspersed with
> isolated attacks of yanking and hitting of great severity, causing
> fractures, massive bruising, lacerations, or visceral injury. . . .
> Frequently seen are welts and bruises produced by belts and
> electric cords, burns from hot electric appliances or dipping in
> hot water, bruises and fractures caused by choking, shaking, or
> throwing the baby against the wall or side of the crib.[47]

The observations that parents do unto their children as they were
done unto is not limited to the human species. When the female
monkeys raised by Harry Harlow on wire and cloth mother-
surrogates grew up, they were no more suited to motherhood than
their inanimate "parent." They withdrew from contact with their
infants and failed to protect them from threats of harm. Some of the
monkeys went further; they struck their infants, beat them, and even
ground their faces into the floor. And as the law now does in cases of
human battering, so did the experimenters: they finally removed the
young to protect their life.

It is a sad business, this child battering, and the consequences
reach much further than the welts on a youngster's back. A list of
well-known adults who were maltreated as children would have to
include the following names: John Wilkes Booth, Arthur Bremmer,
Lee Harvey Oswald, James Earle Ray, and Sirhan Sirhan.

# The Restoring Touch

**5**

If children can be harmed by lack of touch and by the wrong kind of touch, it is reasonable to assume that application of the right kind of touch may help undo that harm.

This chapter looks at that assumption and how to apply it. One might also reasonably assume that the proposition *Bad or insufficient touch can lead to harmful consequences; therefore, good and sufficient touch can help reverse those consequences* is so obvious that the helping literature will have already enumerated the applications of touch to the touch-damaged child and her family. That would make this chapter unnecessary. Sadly, the assumption, however reasonable, is not supported by the facts. The mainstream literature on child abuse and neglect rarely mentions touch as a potential healing agent.

Take the basic text of readings on child abuse, Helfer and Kempe's *The Battered Child.*[1] This book outlines the appropriate roles of those involved with abusing families. Somewhere, one of the authors should know something about the restorative use of touch. Yet Ray Helfer makes no mention of it in his chapter on the role of the physician.[2] Elizabeth Davoren never discusses it in "The Role of the Social Worker," although her otherwise faultless article explores virtually every other interpersonal therapeutic possibility.[3] It is not surprising that Jack Collins speaks of laws, not touches, in "The Role of the Law Enforcement Agency,"[4] but it is a tribute to the strength of the touch taboo that psychiatrists Brandt Steele and C. B. Pollack ignore human touch in their famous chapter, "A Psychiatric Study of Parents Who Abuse Infants and Small Children."[5]

The absence is especially notable in this chapter for two reasons. First, the paper is lengthy, well thought out, and inclusive of almost every other strategem in the diagnosis and treatment of the battered child syndrome. Second, the chapter contains a vignette which demonstrates the power of touch to reach, to restore trust, to *heal* the unloved child who is now a battering parent, *and the authors miss it.*

The parent's name was Sally. She was an uncared-for child who grew up to become a rigid, controlling, physically abusing parent. She was admitted to hospital for observation and while there began slowly to build a relationship with a social worker on the staff.

> At a crucial time in one interview, during which Sally was crying and the worker put a sympathetic hand on her shoulder, they were interrupted by the ward personnel demanding Sally come out and join in the routine group therapy scheduled at that time. She later described the situation as follows: "When Mrs. D. put her hand on my shoulder, I felt a sense of hope for the first time in my life, and then they ruined the whole thing."[6]

Here we have a direct statement from a patient about the healing power of human touch—"When Mrs. D. put her hand on my shoulder, I felt a sense of hope for the first time in my life . . ." and the authors completely miss its significance. They make a brief interpretation of the patient's "intense need for mothering," but, like so many others who have not been trained to tune-in to touch, they miss the therapeutic significance of this simple gesture, a sympathetic hand on the shoulder of a woman who has never experienced a sympathetic touch. They never mention it again.

Although Helfer and Kempe published this edition in 1974, most of the articles were written earlier, and it could be argued that the times were not yet ready for touch as a therapeutic tool. But in 1976 the United States Department of Health, Education, and Welfare published a series of well-researched booklets entitled *Child Abuse and Neglect,* with articles by the leading figures in the field, and somehow therapeutic touch gets no mention then either.[7]

Nor is the omission limited to American researchers. In 1979, the International Year of the Child, a national symposium of child abuse was held in New Zealand. Contributors included pediatricians, psychiatrists, psychologists, social workers, judges, and politicians. The report of the proceedings, a fairly inclusive summary edited by pediatrician D. C. Geddis, makes no mention of the use of touch in working with parents or children.[8] Its pervasive absence is a blind spot, a black hole in the therapeutic literature.

One thing that is mentioned again and again in articles on abusing parents is that in whatever other respects they may differ these parents hold one trait in common: they are hard people to reach. As individuals and as a group, they distrust motives, break appointments, disconnect their phones, change doctors, and do whatever else they can think of to keep the would-be helper at a safe—and helpless—distance. They make poor clients for the easily discouraged.

Workers have often commented that abusing parents are put off by talk, which they interpret as criticism, and by silence, which they interpret as silent criticism. Well. If you are a health worker, and you cannot talk, and you cannot not-talk, you are in something of a dilemma, especially if all you have been trained to do is talk and listen. And if in the course of your training, you have gotten the message that you never touch a client whose head is higher than your knee cap, then your only remaining alternative is to leave the room.

But as Sally's comment—"When Mrs. D. put her hand on my shoulder, I felt a sense of hope for the first time in my life"—showed, human touch can sometimes make contact when all else fails. People who work with the unparented, the brutalized, and the unloved need both permission to touch, and training in the skills required for therapeutic skin-to-skin contact.

The first such skill required is knowing when not to touch. And the first law of non-touching is this: Touch only when you feel like touching. (Older's second law, which we'll come back to later, is: Don't always touch when you feel like touching.)

The first law is not to ensure that the therapist has a good time. It is to maximize the chances that the touch will convey what is intended. Touch is a sensitive medium, and it is not hard for most people to detect an insincere touch. This is especially true of people who distrust signals from those around them, and such a group includes many battering, neglecting, and abusing parents. They will quickly pick up the contrived touch for what it is, and the result will be greater distrust, not a stronger bond.

Therapeutic touch need not—*should* not—be the sole preserve of the therapist. Parents can be encouraged to give pleasurable touches to each other. One good way of doing this is to teach them massage. Self-help groups have become a major source of support to abusing parents, and they can incorporate physical contact into their operations. It can be as simple as arranging chairs so that people make knee contact with one another, as light as games involving touch, or as intimate as massage, hugging, or a group press.

The children of these parents also require touch retraining. They must learn that physical contact with an adult need not take the form of a slap or a swat across the room. The child who flinches from a hand on the shoulder needs to experience benign touch.

But this is not to say it will be easy. If the therapist's touch is premature or precipitous, it will be rejected. If it is brusque or perfunctory, it will be disliked. In short, the helper must attune not only to her own feelings and to her own touch but to the immediate situation and long-term needs of the client as well.

I myself am involved in an experiment involving restorative touch with a group of mothers, some of whom have battered or neglected their children and others who have aroused concern that they are potential child abusers. The setting of the experiment is a weekly meeting to which they have been invited. Several men were also asked to come along but, except for me, none did. Between 30 and 70 women show up ever Friday at the children's outpatient clinic within the hospital grounds for tea, conversation, a lecture on some child-related topic, and touch.

Soon after the group was formed, occupational therapist Franceska Banga and I organized a lecture on the subject of touch. After arranging the chairs in a circle so that knees at least occasionally brushed against one another, I gave a short talk on touch, emphasizing Harry Harlow's monkey experiments and the observation that people who were not touched as children often have trouble touching their own children. I then broke the group into pairs and asked the partners to tell each other about childhood memories of being touched. This took about 15 minutes. Each person was then invited to tell the whole group one item from the discussion. The items were of considerable interest. Two women had no recollection whatsoever of childhood touch, and another felt "too confused to say anything coherent." Still another remembered being slapped and prodded as her introduction to touch in the family. A nurse recalled having fairly distant parents but a "lovely, sloppy old grandfather who used to massage my legs." I kept the focus on their own childhood memories as touch recipients, resisting an attempt by one of the helpers present to talk about how important it is to touch your children lovingly. I thought their own needs were too great for that. At the end of the discussion Franceska asked one member of each pair to stand behind her seated partner; she then led the whole group in a gentle touch exercise. One woman was not at all sure she wanted to join in, but her partner cajoled her into trying it, and from then on she and everyone else participated fully.

The exercise has six steps. In the first, the standing person taps her fingertips rapidly and very lightly on the shoulders of her partner. This we call *snowflakes*. Following snowflakes comes *raindrops*, in which her fingers tap simultaneously and with greater intensity. Then she *glides* across her partner's back using the heels of her hands in parallel strokes. Next, with hollow palms she claps her hands across the back and shoulders, creating the sound of *horsehooves*. The fifth stage is *whirlpools*, a penetrating massage of circling thumbs. Finally the recipient of the exercise is asked which touch she preferred and is given an extra dose of that. Each stage lasts two or three minutes. When they are all done, the partners switch places, and the sequence begins again.

I was exceedingly nervous before this exercise began, for I knew we were going in at a point where theories conflict. My assumption was that people with severe parenting problems involving touch were themselves badly or insufficiently touched as children; I further assumed the intervention of therapeutic touch, even this much later in life, could have a restoring effect. But I was also aware of a convincing body of literature that shows that in human and monkey, untouched infants grow up to be touch-aversive adults. If this held true for the women in the room, they would quickly—perhaps even violently—reject our offer of touch.

The answer came shortly after we began. A slowly growing feeling of relaxation infused the room. Smiles appeared. The woman who had been "too confused to say anything coherent" began to beam. (This was particularly significant. Not only was it the first time she had smiled in several weeks of these meetings, but when earlier in this meeting the staff had presented her with a birthday cake for her one-year-old son, she had not reacted at all.) But the real test came at the end of the exercise. I asked the mothers to decide whether we should do some more of this touching at the beginning of next week's session or whether we should let the idea go. The vote to have it continue was unanimous.

The next week virtually everyone returned, and Franceska and I opened the session with a repeat of the touch exercise. As we began, I suggested as a last minute thought that anyone who was holding a baby might, if she wished, do to the child what was being done to her. Since I was one of the ones holding a baby, I modeled this behavior. At the end of the exercise there was again unanimous support for its continuing the next week.

The massage program has now been an integral part of the weekly meetings for nearly a year. Those few times it was skipped, the mothers have asked where it (and where I) was. They have taught their friends how to do massage, and some of those with husbands or mates have managed to get touched in this positive way at home. One women told me that she once rubbed her child's back rather than hit him.

I do not want to make unsupportable claims for the efficacy of the procedure. All that can be said is that mothers who are potential or actual child abusers find it relaxing and enjoyable and ask for more. To discover its effects on child abuse will require a carefully controlled research project.

In considering the limitations of the massage program, I pointed out to Franceska that it was, after all, only a few minutes of physical contact a week. Her answer put that remark in context. She said, "For the person who never gets touched, ten minutes a week is an enormous dose."

Occasionally, one has the privilege of seeing a healer gifted in the use of touch at work. I have seen a few people who have that gift—a nurse in Western Australia, a professor of surgery in New Zealand, a child-care worker in Baltimore. Even more occasionally, a writer manages to capture the skills of this rare breed in print. One who has done so is Mary MacCracken, author of *A Circle of Children.* Here is her description of the restorative touch used by a teacher of severely disturbed children:

> Most of her touching was light and firm and quick. She used it to communicate affection, support, pride in the child; usually she touched the back, shoulders, arm, or head; she used it alone or

with a few simple words. She also used another kind of touching. It was really more holding. It said in effect, "I am here. We will survive." She reacted this way during violence, when a child tried to kick her or bite himself—holding him, restraining him from the destructive act and at the same time comforting him with the solidness of her body.[9]

The one emotion she never expressed with touch was anger. "Striking a child may cause him to become fearful of your touch, and this is too valuable a tool to lose, too high a price to pay for giving in to momentary frustration."[10]

Touch messages travel in both directions in therapeutic relationships, something McCracken came to realize as her own skillfulness as a teacher grew: "There are other ways for other people, but I could almost hear the children through my fingertips, and I think I almost spoke to them." She also observed that disturbed children have their own ways of communicating through direct physical contact. Stuart, who always had to prove his awfulness to the adult he was with, employed it with great subtlety:

> He used touch in an odd way. If he had a difficult morning, immediately after lunch he would begin to fiddle with the light switch, then he would revert to his old trick of kissing Dan's hand—finally he evolved one for me. He would deliberately wet his forefinger and then as I bent to sip my coffee, he would move quietly behind me and slip the wet finger into my ear.[11]

When I was a child-care worker, I had a few experiences like this myself. My most memorable was with cute little Davey. "Pick me up, Mistah Oldah," he said in that irresistibly adorable tone of his.

I picked Davey up.

Davey socked me in the jaw.

"I twick you, Mistah Oldah," said the dirty little sneak.

Despite the danger of an occasional clout in the snoot, most health workers find it easier to touch children than adults. Even the most orthodox Freudian analyst will waive the no-touch dictum in child therapy. One of the few clinical researchers who has advocated sensory contact with inadequately parented adults is James Prescott. Working backward from his theory that the untouched child is more likely to become the violent adult, he strongly recommends human touch as an integral part of the rehabilitation of the violent offender. He writes:

> The tactile sensory system must be retrained and re-educated to experience pleasure and not pain. . . . We must deal with the sensory modality that has been rendered dysfunctional by sensory deprivation. This will not be easy since one consequence of tactile deprivation is an avoidance and aversion to touching. Therefore barriers to touching for pleasure must *gradually* be broken down.[12]

Prescott goes on to suggest ways that this gradual barrier breaking can take place:

> This can be accomplished by enjoying a long hot bath or shower; whirlpool baths; swimming in the nude; and massage. The home shower can be effectively used in this sensory re-education process by alternating between hot and cold water which will awaken the skin receptors to be responsive to a broader range of stimuli. This effect is analogous to a sauna which is followed by rolling in the snow or jumping in a pool of cool water (also highly recommended).[13]

For me, these suggestions seem a bit too simple; like the Prescott theory, I think their ultimate usefulness lies in pointing a direction for further work rather than in their inherent truth or healing power. Most are also solitary pursuits. I believe human contact is the essential ingredient in therapeutic touch.

We have seen how tender loving care in a hospital can promote a sudden growth spurt in a psychosocial dwarf and how the love of a family can kindle an intellectual flame in an institution-imbecile. The restoring touch is a spectacular sight when used in these extreme cases. Yet there is another kind of case which is in some ways even more extreme. And touch has a role to play here, too.

From time to time throughout history a child has been captured in the wilderness who is a complete stranger to civilization. Wherever they have been found, these wild children have become instant objects of fascination. They do not speak or write or wear clothing; they are reputed to run on hands and feet; they are suspected of having been raised by a wolf mother.

When these feral children do make contact with village or city life, the civilizing efforts of teachers and appointed guardians are always difficult and sometimes fatal. One of the most interesting and historically important of such cases is the wild boy of Aveyron, the young teenager later named Victor, who emerged from the forest in central France on January 8, 1800. The largely unsuccessful, but terribly intensive, efforts to reach and teach him left their mark not only on Victor (who survived only a few years of his new life), but on the course of education from that time forward. As a result of the labors of his guardian, a 26-year-old physician named Jean-Marc Itard, ideas emerged that still affect the teaching of the deaf, the handicapped, and the very young. We have also gained some worthwhile information about the role of touch in these processes and its role in establishing contact with the child who is otherwise beyond reach.

These observations have been preserved through the efforts of Harlan Lane, author of *The Wild Boy of Aveyron*.[14] In researching the book, Lane dug out a massive number of official French documents, newspaper accounts, and journal entries concerning Victor's capture and his progress through early nineteenth-century France. Touch plays a prominent role throughout, as the following quotes indicate.

• From the district commissioner whose home first held the newly captured wild boy:

> When I noticed that he gave no response to the various questions that I put to him, both loudly and softly, I concluded erroneously that he was deaf. I took him affectionately by the hand to lead him to my home; he resisted vigorously, but repeated caresses and particularly two kisses I gave him with a friendly smile decided him on the spot, and he trusted me a good deal from that time on.[15]

• From a newspaper report of his arrival in Paris eight months later; note the metaphor of touch in the descriptive language:

> He occasionally seems touched by the care he is tendered, and he offers his hand of his own accord to those who express any interest in him.[16]

• From a scientist's observations of his behavior in captivity:

The young Aveyronnais is naturally distrustful and on his guard
... if he is afraid of something, he throws himself in the arms of
his caretaker and pushes him urgently toward his room.[17]

- From Dr. Itard's notes:

  ... when I go to his room in the evening just after he has gone to
  bed, his first movement is to sit up for me to embrace him, then
  to draw me to him by seizing my arm and making me sit upon his
  bed. Usually he then takes my hand, draws it over his eyes, his
  forehead, the back of his head, and holds it with his upon these
  parts for a very long time.[18]

Whether Victor was abandoned by unloving parents or made his
own way into the forest, and whether he was retarded at birth or
simply failed to develop intellectually in his woodland environment,
were hotly debated issues in France and remain unresolved today.
Not all children who are different are damaged, and not all children
who are damaged were harmed by their parents. Many conditions
are of genetic origin; many more must still be declared "origin
unknown."

Autism is one of the unknowns. Sometimes called childhood schizophrenia, the condition was originally—and erroneously—thought
to have been caused by distant, intellectual, unexpressive parents.
The symptoms of autism include an unwillingness or inability to
relate to people, a fascination with objects and patterns, repetitious
behaviors, and sometimes mutism. The condition is extremely difficult to treat, *and* nearly every technique has a high rate of failure. (A
controversial exception will be discussed in the Body Therapies
chapter.) Within this somewhat discouraging context, physical contact is proving a useful tool in the habilitation of autistic children.
Even behaviorists, who are not commonly thought of as touchers,
have found that an enthusiastic rub on the head is a better reinforcer
than the traditional reward of a piece of candy popped in the mouth.
  One of the problems in working with autistic children is that they
often have an aversion to any human contact, including touch. When
they do make contact, it is sometimes done by turning the person into
an object. I well remember the amazement on a child psychiatrist's
face as he recounted his experience of this. "The child obviously

wanted to leave the room, probably to get away from me," he said, "but the doorknob was out of his reach. After studying the situation a while, he took my hand and led me to the door. But though he held me by the wrist, he never once looked at me. In this same way he guided my hand to the knob and pushed my arm like a ratchet handle to open it. It was absolutely clear that I was nothing to him but a mechanical tool."

Most workers with the autistic see the main task, and the often insurmountable problem, as establishing human relationships. Physical contact has often been used toward this end, both by established institutions like Bruno Bettelheim's Sonia Shankman Orthogenic School in Chicago and by individual families searching for ways to break into the self-contained world of their strange child. Barry Kaufman, the father of one such child, has published his family's efforts in *New York* magazine and in a book, *Son Rise.*[19] Reading the article, I was filled with admiration for the Kaufmans' courage, and with sadness when I thought of the odds against a miraculous cure. I was also struck with the role physical contact played in almost every activity they constructed to break into the world of their autistic son. When other avenues are cut off, touch is the only road.

But the problem remains that autistic children usually have an aversion to ordinary touch. The most ingenious solution to this problem I have encountered does not, so far as I know, appear in the literature. It was conceived in Vermont by child-care worker, Meredith Leavitt-Teare. One year she found herself with two groups of children in her class. One group was autistic, the other had Down's syndrome. The latter is a form of retardation that results from chromosomal abnormality; it used to be known as mongolism. Despite their limited intelligence and rather odd facial features, Down's syndrome children tend to be cheerful, loving, and cuddly. These traits are appreciated by their families but by few others; there is not much market for a happy, affectionate, not-too-bright, funny-looking kid.

But it was just what Meredith needed. She taught her Down's syndrome students to hug her autistic students and to reinforce their responding behavior. The autistic children, who would not tolerate the touch of an adult, apparently felt less threatened by these same-size huggers, and they quickly grew quite tolerant of their touch. This should be viewed as an experiment worthy of replication. It offers contact to the hard-to-reach and useful work for the hard-to-market. And that is a hard combination to beat.

Touch has also had a part to play in the education of the retarded. Behaviorists today rub retarded children on the head as a reward for learning just as they rub autistic children as a reward for relating. But behaviorists did not discover touch as a teaching aid; its use goes back to the first school for idiot-level retarded children, which was founded in 1839 by Edouard Seguin, a physician and student of Itard. Orthodox medicine at that time held that idiots were unteachable and constitutionally unable to learn. Seguin disproved that. Visitors from Europe and the United States were astonished by the progress the students were able to make under his training program. The program was one of sensory education, and the sense of touch was the rock on which all others were built.

> The first sense to operate is touch . . . the second is sight . . . the third is hearing . . . it is not until much later that taste and smell distinguish flavors and odors. I did not arrange this order that I assign to the awakening of the sense to please myself; I have observed it in young subjects, whether normal or idiotic.[20]

Children at Seguin's school were systematically trained in the development of the senses, beginning with the sense of touch. Blindfolded, they learned to distinguish first hot from cold, then warm from cool, by plunging their hands into tanks of water maintained at different temperatures. Using similar methods, they were taught the meaning of heavy and light, rough and smooth, long and short, and so on. When touch was mastered, they went on to explore the other senses.

The legacy of Itard and Seguin is with us today. Both normal and retarded children routinely receive sensory training, some from kindergarten, most from Sesame Street. ("This is hot, Grover, and *this* is *cold!*") The international network of Montessori schools bases its teaching theory and practice directly on the sensory training program of Itard and Seguin. Tactile learning helps children with reading problems learn the alphabet in the United States and the Soviet Union.

Finally, human touch can mean the difference between learning and not learning in certain situations. Teaching juvenile delinquents is tricky business because the potential for an explosion is often just a word away. The teenager who is a walking jar of gelignite can either be set off or defused with a touch. The tricky part comes in knowing whether your touch is going to be a defuser or a detonator. If you guess wrong, the feedback is instantaneous. Among young delinquents, almost all fuses are short ones.

Here is an example of a wrong choice from Esther Rothman, principal of a New York City school for delinquent girls. It occurred shortly after she took up her job at the school. At an assembly, one of the girls created a deliberate disturbance.

> "Stop it," I told her in front of everybody. Loudly, too.
>
> "Make me," she said. She turned and faced me, and suddenly all eyes were turned toward us . . .
>
> I then did the one thing I should not have done. It was not the time to touch, and, completely ignoring the warning signals that were flashing in my head, I put my hand on her arm and told her to come with me to the office. As soon as I made it, I realized it was the worst move I could possibly make.
>
> "Take your fuckin' hands off," she threatened menacingly.

Frightened of the student and afraid of losing face, Rothman tightened her grip. The student slapped her, and the room exploded.

> Chairs went flying—girls began to scream gleefully. It was directed at me, and then it turned. One girl hit another, and the fuse was lit. Old feuds, new feuds, undreamed-of, later-to-be-developed feuds erupted. Girls clawed at each other and tore at each other's hair. Clothing was torn, faces and hands were scratched to the point of blood.[21]

But Esther Rothman is a quick learner. Many months after the melee, another student came screaming into her office, threatening to kick a male teacher's "cold-blooded ass in," and then raced out to start kicking. The principal took off after her.

> I had to run faster than she. I waylaid her on the stairway. I was puffing audibly, and tentatively, gently, I touched her on the arm. She did not shake me off, so I let my hand stay there, and we stood silent for a few moments.
>
> "What do you want?" she asked angrily.

"Good God, I can't even breathe," I told her, "and you want me
to answer? Let me get my breath first." I needed time to study
her mood, to know in what direction she would go.

"Look," I finally said, "it's cold here on the stairway and I want
a cup of coffee. Come on down to the office where we can talk and
have coffee."[22]

This is the kind of touch-sensitivity that is lovely to behold. It is
extremely effective and more efficient by far than words, drugs,
restraint, or calling the police. A few come to it naturally, and all but
a few can learn it. It works.

One more observation from Esther Rothman—one with implications not just for delinquents but for all who need a restorative touch.

The psychologists and psychiatrists call it a lack of a prime sense
of identity. And many of the girls show it not only by their
confusion and their anger, but by the way they cling physically
to adults. Iona, for instance, would frantically wrap herself
around a teacher's body. She practically crawled in. She clung
and touched and intermingled with the teacher's physical presence. Other girls fight this tendency. They are fearful of admit-
ting their need to be part of another individual's life. Hands off.
They don't touch and are fearful of being touched. But oh, how
they want it and need it! Progress indeed when Elaine, aloof,
guarded, straight and distant, bent over me and tenderly tightened my earring. She was truant for five days afterward. The
closeness frightened her. She couldn't yet admit she wanted it or
even needed it.[23]

When I returned to the United States after six years of living
abroad, within the first few minutes I received two powerful messages about touching. Taken together, they tell a lot about this fascinating, infuriating land of my birth. They may also be omens of
things to come.

I got the first message in Los Angeles International Airport.
Weighted down with too much luggage, numbed from too many
hours in the air, children in tow, lost, and all of that, I was suddenly
accosted by a cheery young man who pushed a small, plastic flower
onto my shirtfront, flashed me a toothy Los Angeles smile, and held
out his hand for me to shake. I put down my suitcase and shook. He

locked my hand into his and began reciting a prepared spiel about a religious convention he and his friends were holding, and how they needed some money to—

I pried free my right hand, wearily picked up my bag, and continued across the lounge to where Effin and the kids were watching from behind a pillar. "Did you see that?" I asked.

"I sure did," she answered, "And you sure looked uncomfortable. He ran the whole show."

That should have been the end of it. But I suddenly recalled that my next-door neighbor, a beekeeper, had told me that the same thing had happened to him in L.A. Airport, and that this had been his first encounter with an American in the United States. He had been so unnerved by the experience that he gave the guy the five dollars he demanded and fled to his hotel room until he could get a flight out to Canada. That sort of bodily intrusion, that unwanted touch, would simply never be thrust upon a stranger in New Zealand.

Effin saw the glint in my eye and tried to say something, but it was too late. I put down my bag and started back. I called over my shoulder, "See who looks uncomfortable this time."

When I reached the middle of the room a smiling clone of the first supplicant stuck a plastic flower on my chest, bared his fangs and stuck out his paw. I pulled the flower from my shirt and pushed it, with perhaps a mite more force than actually required, firmly onto *his* chest. He was already into his patter by this time, and his words came to a rather surprised halt. I stared at his outstretched but still unshaken hand. I could hear him changing cassettes, and he started on his back-up routine, "I don't know what's the matter with people these days why they won't even shake hands with you isn't it an unfriendly world and wouldn't it be nicer if—"

I cut him off. "It's not nice," I said evenly, "to use a handshake to shake down a stranger."

"Get out of my way," he hissed, no longer sounding all holy and lovey. We were now eyeball to eyeball.

With my usual maturity and reserve, I replied, "No, *you* get out of *mine!*" Now our foreheads were touching, and in a moment more, we played the mountain rams in mating season. Lacking horns, we pushed head to head, each unwilling to break off the glaring contact. For long moments we maintained the struggle, but in the end my anger was too much for his holiness, and he gave way. Then, like my neighbor, I too fled Los Angeles.

The second message was very, very different. I first saw it shortly after we touched down on American soil, and later I was to see it again many times in many states. The message was in the form of a question which, if answered in the affirmative, would obviate the need for most restorative touch. The question, which first appeared to me on the back bumper of a 1972 Volkswagen, addressed itself to the most basic form of preventive touch, the kind that protects kids and nurtures them, the kind that will build healtheir adults and may build a more peaceful world. The question was this:

Have you hugged your kid today?

# Massage

6

The physicians do the work of Apollo, versed in the knowledge of remedies, but the result does not always correspond to their efforts. From a little pain a great ill grows which does not yield to soothing remedies but at other times, laying on of hands re-establishes promptly the health of a man sunk in dangerous and painful disease.

—Solon

As a form of healing, massage has moved in and out of favor many times. In 1883, British physician Julius Althaus noted that what had been for a long time "the Cinderella of therapeutics has recently seen a considerable change in its fortunes, and become . . . thoroughly fashionable . . ." He viewed this trend with some alarm, ". . . lest a procedure which does good in a limited class of cases should suffer by the excessive praises of injudicious partisans, and eventually be thrown aside altogether."[1]

When there were but few medical procedures available to the physician, massage loomed large. Indeed, Chinese physicians some 5,000 years ago were massaging patients suffering from paralysis, chills, and fever,[2] and by the T'ang dynasty (619–907 A.D.) massage was elevated to one of the four officially recognized medical techniques. (The others were acupuncture, internal medicine, and exorcism.)[3]

But lack of healing alternatives cannot account for the latter-day re-emergence of massage. In an era of nuclear medicine, ultrasonic diagnosis, and laser surgery, massage has once again arisen from the ashes of the hearth to dance the night away on the prince's back. Massage centers are opening in the provinces as well as in the flesh-pots of New York and California. Professionals from all across the United States are leaving secure jobs in social work and computer analysis to open body shops above vegetarian restaurants and coffee houses. The field is aswarm with people who gave up jobs they worked from the neck up for one they do from the elbows down. Folks who were pushing buttons on calculators now find themselves strok-ing, striking, kneading, rubbing, and vibrating other people's bodies to soothe and heal them.

I think this may be accounted for by a general cultural mood that affects healing practices no less than it affects music, politics, and religion. This mood is a conglomerate of many factors, including feelings about the body, increased or diminished need for distance, formality vs. informality, high or low conflict about pleasure, and so on. Today there are two additional factors. One is a longing for roots, whether they be racial, national, or medical. And massage is healing roots. The second, much discussed and analyzed, is disenchantment with modern medicine. Massage is part of a widespread alternative, the holistic approach to health, which will get a longer look in the next chapter. Whatever the reasons, massage is back in strength today in forms little changed from those practiced when its use was first recorded. And the history of massage is as old as human attempts to treat sickness; its practitioners as far-flung as human habitation.

The earliest known medical text from India is the *Ayur-Veda*. Compiled around 1800 B.C., it lists massage along with diet and exercise as the leading health-restoring practices of the time. The English word "shampoo" is derived from *champna*, an ancient Indian word meaning "to press."[4]

From Egypt comes the *Papyrus Ebers*, a major medical document from the sixteenth century B.C. It too prescribed massage, notably for female disorders caused by a wandering uterus, or hysteria. Accord-ing to Ilza Veith's classic of medical history, *Hysteria*, Egyptian physicians of the day employed "ointments compounded from a va-riety of unpleasant ingredients, that were used to rub the affected parts of the body in order to drive down the uterus."[5] Hysteria continued to intrigue and perplex medical men over the centuries, and massage continued to play a part in its treatment. The great Galen pioneered a rather specialized form—he applied "digital manipulation" to hysterical women in order to bring on sexual release.

For men, the use of massage as an invigorator and restorer goes back at least as far as ancient Greece. There, athletes were rubbed down to strengthen their bodies before events and to soothe and revitalize them after. Ordinary citizens were massaged to hasten convalescence after disease. Ulysses and other war heroes had their weary bodies refreshed at the hands of beautiful Greek women. The leading Greek physicians and philosophers were advocates of massage; among them were Hippocrates, Praxagoras, and Aristotle.

Greeks brought the healing use of massage to Rome, most notably in the temples of Asclepiades. The mystic healing rituals there were mixed with earthier practices including bathing, diet, drugs, wine, and massage. Massage was specifically prescribed for dropsy, leucophlegmasia, and certain forms of mental illness; it was recommended for torpor, spasm, and stomach pain. Aretaeus, one of Asclepiades' leading disciples, inaugurated the use of massage after heart disease in order "to preserve the remaining spark of life."[6] Today this same spark of life is preserved through heart massage.

Aretaeus also used massage to treat headache and vertigo though, strangely enough, he rubbed the legs to treat both. Galen, who was physician to Marcus Aurelius as well as a great medical innovator, described and classified nine types of massage and the diseases for which each was indicated. Today massage is generally divided into only six types. In order of increasing pressure applied, they are:

1. Effleurage, or stroking. Its best known use is in natural childbirth. The woman in labor strokes her abdominal area with light, fingertip massage as an aid to managing labor pain.
2. Friction. Movement of the hands over the body with more force than effleurage.
3. Pressure. No movement involved.
4. Petrissage, or kneading. The hand is stationary, but the fingers move, working their way into sore muscles.
5. Vibration. The only form of massage better adapted to a machine than the human touch.
6. Percussion. Slapping, pounding, tapping.

Since ancient times massage has been an adjunct to labor and delivery. It has been employed to ease labor pain, to hasten delivery, and to stop postpartum bleeding. In the sixth century, Aetius of Amida urged midwives confronted with "strangulation of the uterus, to rub the part gently and for a long time, so that the thick and irritated humor which clings to the uterus may come out."[7] He also prescribed massage as a cure for infertility. In the mid-nineteenth century massage was prescribed for relief of postpartum atony and dysmenorrhea.

Sometimes, advice from earlier ages was more graphic and less clinical than that given today. Dr. Fleetwood Churchill, writing in 1872, advised midwives:

> If, however, the breasts become hard and knotty and painful, in spite of the efforts of the child, you may afford great relief, and facilitate the flow of milk, by rubbing them gently with a little warm oil—rubbing them *gently*, I say, not as if you were polishing a mahogany table.[8]

We have already seen the ways midwives use massage today, something I was able to observe firsthand last year. A young Vermont couple whom I had never met was told by their midwife that someone interested in touching and birthing would be visiting the hospital and would probably arrive before the baby. How would they feel about a stranger's presence at the birth? The woman, who had already been in labor for several hours, said she would like to meet him first. I did beat the baby to the hospital, and after a brief meeting with the prospective parents I was warmly invited to the event. This was their first child, and the labor was a long and difficult one. They worked and groaned and sweated together through the night. Sometime between two and three in the morning I found myself kneading the husband's shoulder muscles as he bent over his laboring wife, stroking her tired thighs. An hour or so later, a fat, healthy baby joined us, and we all celebrated with champagne (except the baby, who preferred colostrum). I thanked the parents, then drove across the state to give a somewhat dazed, all-day workshop on touching and healing.

A month later I met the midwife at another workshop. I asked her how the family was doing. "Just fine," she said. "And when I saw them for a post-partum check-up, the woman told me something I think you'll find interesting. She was saying how delighted they were with the baby and the birth, and went on to say, 'By midnight I was tired, and as time rolled on and I was still in labor, I got more tired and a bit spacey. In fact I was in kind of a daze and was getting a bit discouraged and worn-out. But at one point I looked up and saw that touch-guy massaging Dave's back, and I snapped out of it completely. I just felt great that someone was taking care of him too.'"

The touch-guy was touched.

In the Middle Ages friction was prescribed for hydropsy and colic; flagellation, for mania. A nice distinction. In the Renaissance surgical patients were massaged to speed healing and to improve their general condition; today, specialized forms of massage are used as an adjunct to plastic surgery. Discomforts and disorders of the joints were rubbed then, as they are today.

Other uses of massage have not survived the test of time. From the seventeenth century come two that have disappeared along the way. The first is from Francis Glisson's 1671 tome on rickets in which he recommended massage as part of the management program; the addition of vitamin D to milk ended the need for such management, at least in the industrialized world. The second proposed use was suggested toward the end of the century. Massage was then prescribed as a cure for syphilis. I can see how massage as an alternative to sex might serve a prophylactic function, but as a morning-after measure it seems of limited efficacy.

By mid-eighteenth century, abdominal massage was being prescribed for chronic constipation and later for skin lesions. Massage's usefulness in the treatment of sprains was also recognized.

At the beginning of the nineteenth century, Barclay's anatomy text described a case of severe muscle contracture as follows: "After resisting all treatment, it was finally cured by simply percussing the affected sterno-cleido-mastoid."[9] In that period there was some controversy about the efficacy of massage in the treatment of gout, but for many other conditions it was standard procedure. The great English physician John Grosvenor employed women "rubbers" to treat contractions of the joints; to restore movement in strained, fractured, or wounded limbs; for paralysis and chorea. Another Englishman, John Shaw, preferred massage to the then-orthodox management of scoliosis, which consisted of months of enforced rest on an inclined plane.

Meanwhile, in France, Martin reported on 100 cases of lumbago

that were cured by massage, and Bonnet, one of the first rheumatol-
ogists, massaged patients suffering from pain associated with rheumatic diseases. French masseurs were also advised to work on older
people. In 1875 Reveille-Parise wrote, "Dry frictions, more or less
often repeated, are an excellent method of giving back vitality to a
part. The aged will always derive great advantage from this hygienic measure."[10]

In the history of the healing massage there is a special place for
disorders of the eye. Aetius of Amida treated glaucoma with full
body massage and paralysis of the eyelids with massage of the lower
extremities. I can think of no reason to suppose that these practices
were of any more use than that of massage to cure syphilis. The
seventeenth-century Italian anatomist Valsalva claimed to have restored eyesight in a woman blinded through trauma by manually
compressing her optic nerve. A century later Sabatier reported
similar results using the same method. A century after that, in 1872,
Donders wrote of the usefulness of eye massage in treating keratitis
and corneal opacity.[11]

Application of massage to promote health and treat disorders in
the very young is a widespread practice. Indian mothers routinely
stroke and knead every part of their infants' bodies, a practice
Leboyer recommends to the rest of the world. In New Zealand,
pre-European Maori mothers massaged their children's noses to
improve the shape and their legs to lengthen and straighten them. Te
Rangi Hiroa, better known outside of New Zealand as Sir Peter
Buck, recalls his own mother looking approvingly at his legs and
saying, "My hands made your legs what they are."[12]

Nose and leg massage for healthy babies may be seen as a legitimized way of maximizing physical contact between mother and child,
but it cannot account for the Maori treatment of clubfoot. The disorder has a higher incidence among Polynesians than among any
other racial group, and the Maori are not excluded. In his genetic
study of clubfoot, Beals observed:

> The European era witnessed a tradition of treatment of clubfoot
> in infancy by continuous massage by the older women of the
> family, a tradition passed down through the generations. This
> "Maori grandmother" method of management often produced
> surprisingly good results and examples are still occasionally

seen. This practice has virtually disappeared and the child with clubfoot is now treated by conventional European methods.[13]

This method of treatment was not confined to New Zealand; it was practiced in much the same way in New England. An old-time Vermont midwife described it like this:

> Once in a while you would get a baby with a clubfoot, and of course Mama would cry and carry on a good deal, but that is the time it could be fixed. You would say, "Now the bones are soft. Here, feel the baby's foot! See how nice it is. Well, I'll massage it back and we'll work on it, and if it isn't going to come back very good, we'll wad up a little piece of cloth and tie it on the other end and fold it a little bit. And I'll take it off now and then, and we'll massage it and work on it, and that little foot is going to be just as good as the other."[14]

According to the midwife, the treatment usually worked if the deformity was not too severe; if it was, the doctor would be called in when the baby was about a month old. Whether it changed the shape of the foot or not, the practice was of major importance in the mother-child relationship and in the child's image of himself as he grew from infant to adult. It acted in several ways. First, the midwife's words gave hope at a time of despair ("that little foot is going to be just as good as the other"). Second, she made herself a model of acceptance, a model she encouraged the mother to emulate ("Here, feel the baby's foot! See how nice it is"). Third, she engaged the mother in long-term healing work that involved regular touching of the ill-formed appendage ("I'll massage it and work on it"). The result was likely to be immediate reduction in guilt for having produced an imperfect baby combined with instructions which should lead to acceptance—the mother will have many opportunities to see for herself "how nice it is" as she cares for her child. Finally, the memory of a mother's loving touch will help the growing child to accept himself as he is, whether or not the foot grows normally. In short, the midwife's routine is a masterpiece of physical and psychological rehabilitation.

Massage has been part of traditional medicine in many parts of the world and continues in that function to this day. In North America the Navajo use massage as part of their elaborate healing rituals.[15] In Cuba massage is used by the *curandero* and the *santera*—the faith healer and the witch—whose roots go back to Africa. For *el mal de madre* a garlic and oil massage is prepared and applied to the stomach. "The hand must slide smoothly and always in the direction of the navel. Meanwhile, put two garlic cloves in each nostril . . ."[16] A common Cuban disorder is *el empacho*, a meal that lodges in the stomach where it causes pain and fever. The treatment is massage, with salt now added to the oil. Both stomach and spine are rubbed, the latter in a descending motion from the neck to the waist. The sound of a snap in a vertebra signals that the *empacho* has been cured. Not so incidentally, this is the same snap that Americans listen for when they undergo treatment from *their* traditional healer, the chiropractor.

On another island on the other side of the world from Cuban *curanderos* and American chiropractors, the healing touch is also widely used. In Samoa, traditional healers employ massage and annointment for almost every disorder from migraine to diarrhea. The treatment involves filtrations made from certain tree leaves, roots, herbs, and Samoan oil—a mixture of coconut milk, fragrant flowers from the *mosooi* tree, flowers from the *aloalo manogi* plant, and roots of grasses. The concoction is massaged into the skin for conditions as far-ranging as burns, headaches, backaches, stomach troubles, and broken bones.

> In the case of a broken limb, the *taulasea* [the traditional Samoan doctor] is helped by two members of the family in setting the bone right. This is done especially for an open fracture. When the bone is set, the *taulasea* then massages the lesion. Four straight pieces of wood from the coconut leaf frond are tied around the affected limb. Each day the patient comes to the *taulasea*. The sticks are removed and the limb is massaged. The outcome is usually good.[17]

From Africa to Indonesia the picture is the same, as can be seen in this observation by E. Fuller Torrey, a man who has studied healing in both places:

> In regard to body contact in the therapist-patient relationship, therapists in other cultures almost invariably use it more than

Western therapists do. For instance the Nigerian *babalawo* rubs the patient's body extensively, and carefully holds his head as he makes shallow cuts for the medicine. During my brief observations of a Balinese *balian* I noted that approximately one-half of the healing session included some kind of body contact, usually the rubbing of medicated oils into the body.[18]

If the *babalawo* is the traditional healer of the Nigerian and the *balian* of the Balinese, is there an equivalent tradition for the educated, wealthy, white European? Of course not, you say, falling neatly into my trap. There is indeed, and considerably more than one-half of their healing sessions include body contact.

The traditional healing temple of Europe is the spa. While usually associated with the mountains of Switzerland, they may be found across the Continent and even in darkest England. Do spas use massage? Do sparrows fly? The spa is a veritable orgy of massage, performed by every means yet conceived by the human mind. Here are a few entries plucked from the journal of a British journalist who spent a few days at the Henlow Grange Beauty Farm in Bedfordshire.

> Each morning Ursula gave us one of her superb, vigorous Swedish massages which really get the circulation going, pummelling at the fat and, funnily enough, making you feel on top of the world. Just in case we were still feeling sluggish, Dawn gave each of us in turn a brisk going over with the very effective G.5 electric vibratory massage machine. . . . The first morning also included a high-frequency scalp treatment—it felt like pins and needles, but wasn't at all unpleasant. . . . This is followed by a steaming, conditioning scalp massage and, finally, a shampoo and set.
>
> I began with the hydro underwater massage—a splendid idea that gives incredible results. Hydro massage means a huge, very deep bath filled with warm water in which you lie, first on your back and then on your front, while an experienced girl goes up and down the areas you want to lose with a hose of high pressure water. The pressure is so strong that you can see the skin indenting and rippling as she moves. . . . Another fat breaking up process is achieved with the Traxator, applied only where you need it. This takes the form of a plastic vacuum suction cup

which scoops up excess fat, breaking down the tissues under the surface.

Still on the spot-reducing theme, I tried out the Parafango—a brown, hot volcanic mud specially flown in from Italy, which is wrapped around, in my case, hips and thighs.... On Wednesday I tried the French massage.... I tried the wax bath ... the superb Finnish sauna ... the Panthemol machine ... dry facial ... hot compresses . . . Italian skin peel . . . a baby facial Traxator machine, which helps to contour the face by lifting the muscles with a cupping (kissing) action ... fresh fruit mask—a glorious combination of cucumber, oranges and carrots ... the ultrasonic machine ... a drying magnesium mask ... they threw me in the seaweed bath. It looked terrible and smelled awful. "But it's good for you," insisted Ursula, so in I climbed![19]

And if I ever hear you talk about primitive natives again, so help me I'll throw you right in that seaweed bath.

While the late-twentieth-century revival of healing massage has been largely a non-medical, and sometimes even an anti-medical phenomenon, there have been exceptions. The innovative Family Medicine Program at the University of Miami keeps a masseur on call for patients. Khalil Wakim of the Mayo Clinic has long been an advocate of the medical use of massage; in 1960 he described its applications as follows:

Systematized massage, consisting of stroking, kneading, wring-ing, pulling, percussing and vibrating, brings about the follow-ing important effects: (1) improvement of circulation and movement of blood and nutritive elements, (2) increase of warmth to the skin and improvement in its condition, (3) more rapid elimination of waste, (4) dissolution of soft adhesions, (5) reduction of swelling and induration of tissues, (6) soothing of the central nervous system and the peripheral nerves.[20]

He added that massaging the muscles of the abdomen both strength-ens the abdominal wall and aids in exciting peristaltic activity, which eases constipation. The Chinese had discovered this many centuries before and had devised wooden rollers for constipation-massage.

One of the most unusual forms of massage is in the treatment of prostatitis, the enlargement of the prostate gland, which is so common in men over 50. What makes prostate massage different from most others is that it involves direct contact with internal organs. A finger is inserted in the patient's anus, and the prostate gland is at first gently, and later vigorously, palpated. While not every doctor agrees about the efficacy of this treatment (which is more in favor in America than in the Commonwealth), one leading urologist, Gordon Dilmer, has described it as the "most satisfactory" treatment of the condition. In many cases it may be a more effective (and certainly more conservative) approach than surgery or drugs.

But there is considerable resistance among urologists to getting into the prostate massage business, and it is not hard to imagine why. If sex and general touch are suspected of holding hands, imagine the connection that will be made between sex and a touch that is applied only through the male anal sphincter. In the case of prostate massage the taboo has been so strong that when Dr. Abraham Wolbarst described an apparatus for improving the efficacy of this unusual form of therapeutic touch in the 1931 *Journal of Urology*, he not only disguised the face of the patient but that of the doctor as well.

Massage has other relief functions as well. It is commonly used both for preventing and treating pressure sores in bed-ridden patients. It has been suggested for the relief of static edema and varicose ulcers. And gum massage has been recommended by Naboru Muramoto for the treatment of pyorrhea.

Through the ages practitioners of massage have chosen sides around the issue of pressure. The hard-liners maintain that for massage to do any good it must go deep, a position equivalent to the theory that for cough medicine to work it has to taste bad. The other side puts more emphasis on feelings of warmth and pleasure and on the personal contact offered by soothing hands. The issue is alive today, with the softies practicing Swedish and Esalen strokes that gracefully sweep down the muscles of the back or the length of an arm. The toughies practice Rolfing.

Rolfing is a series of deep and often painful massage techniques conceived by the late Ida Rolf. The founder of Gestalt psychology, Fritz Perls, says that Rolf's treatment saved his life after a heart attack. A midwestern social worker said that after one session he looked down and found that his body was a different shape than it had been an hour before. A very sane and somewhat conventional young psychologist astonished me by calmly stating that he paid his Rolfer $25 an hour to do things like massage the inside of his throat. He described it as exquisitely painful.

I am not one who finds pain cute, much less exquisite. In fact, I would have to be pretty near death before I would even dream of letting someone massage the inside of *my* throat. Yet Rolfing is one of the great and continuing successes of the human potential movement. I have yet to meet a dissatisfied customer.

The precursor of Rolfing, another deep technique also created by a woman, has enjoyed a large medical following in Europe for much of this century. The method is called connective tissue massage; it was developed by Elisabeth Dicke, a German physical therapist, in 1929. The method is painful; a pull with a hooked index finger is one of its mainstays. Advocates of connective tissue massage prescribe it for neurologic and metabolic diseases in children as well as for orthopedic and rheumatic conditions, diseases of the circulatory system, functional disorders of the viscera, polio, gangrene, frostbite, and a long list of other ailments.[21]

I confess that lists like this make me almost as nervous as the thought of someone massaging the inside of my throat. Massage is a great calming agent, a wonderful adjunct to other treatments, a marvelous means of making contact. But it is not the universal panacea. Throughout the ages, proponents of massage (like those of so many other forms of treatment, from tonsillectomy to psychosurgery) have claimed for it results that are beyond its power to achieve. Then an inevitable reaction against the procedure sets in, and it falls into general disfavor. Years pass, and the lost procedure is "rediscovered" until once again someone pushes it past its natural limitations.

The problem is still with us. James Cyriax, a contemporary expert on medical massage, recommends it for edema, traumatic periostatis, insomnia, neurosis, bronchiectasis and pulmonary abscess, asthma, chronic sepsis, painful neuromata and postherapeutic neuralgia, cardiac arrest, injury and nerve palsy, varicose ulcer, rosacea, gingivitis, and obesity.[22] Massage may be of use in these conditions, but the danger of overenthusiasm may well overwhelm whatever benefits derive.

Overstatement of the benefits of massage has not been limited to proponents of skin-to-skin contact. Vibration too has been hailed as a panacea, particularly so earlier in this century when electricity became widely available for home use. Thus, when the Hamilton-Beach Company brought out a home vibrator, they gave away with every purchase a book edited by Charles Bryson entitled *Health and How to Get It.* Along with intelligent uses of vibration (for instance, for aching feet), the book offered a host of dubious ones, such as treatment of adenoids and anemia. According to Bryson, the way to get health is to get the Hamilton-Beach Vibrator. And why not? The machine not only cures falling hair but also falling wombs. It is good for fractured bones and fading beauty. It helps one gain immunity from disease, it aids indigestion, and it offers help for impotence.[23] What more do you want?

Historically, there have been a number of cautionary voices raised against overprescribing massage. Hippocrates was among the first. In *On Articulations,* he pointed out that the effects of massage can be harmful as well as helpful: ". . . rubbing can bind and loosen, can make flesh and cause parts to waste . . ."[24] Asclepiades did not permit the abdominal area to be rubbed at the beginning of a disorder, and the Roman medical encyclopedist Celsus cautioned that ". . . prolonged frictions are contraindicated in acute disease . . . except as a soporific for a madman." He added a word of caution about dosage: "It is difficult to determine the exact number of frictions to apply to a person since this will depend upon the strength of the individual. . . . Thus, we must be more careful in applying them to women than to men and to children and older people more than to young adults."[25]

In nineteenth-century London, Cleobury warned his colleagues that massage could be dangerous in certain conditions. He stated: "1. In all cases of inflammation it is highly improper, as it will not fail to accelerate symptoms, 2. In scrofula, 3. In cases of inflammatory gout or rheumatism it will do mischief, 4. In cases of ankylosis it can be of no service."[26]

In this century there have been further cautions. François Françon, honorary president of the French National Society of Physical Medicine, is a leading advocate of massage as a basic and powerful therapeutic agent. But Françon advises that certain maneuvers are to be avoided, the most important of which is massage given with such force as to be painful. There are specific areas of the body to be avoided as well; they are "the large vascular and nervous plexuses of the axilla, the neck, the triangle of Scarpa and the popliteal fossa."[27] In discussions with neurologists about massage, they always single out the neck as a potential danger area and one to be avoided by the nonmedical masseur.

James Cyriax, whose long list of disorders that benefit from massage has already been presented, has an almost as long list of contraindications. Among his "don't massage" disorders are arthritis, inflammation caused by bacterial infection, bursitis, pressure on a nerve, phlebitis, and cellulitis.[28]

In summary, massage is an ancient and honorable healing technique that has suffered both on the swings of overenthusiasm and on the roundabout of lost interest. Let us then close this section where it began, with Althaus' century-old concern "... lest a procedure which does good in a limited class of cases should suffer by the excessive praises of injudicious partisans, and eventually be thrown aside altogether."

"To do massage is to physically help someone, to take care of them," says George Downing, author of *The Massage Book*. He continues:

> The core of massage lies in its unique way of communicating without words. In itself this is not unusual; by touching and hugging, for example, we often let those around us know that we like them, or that we sympathize with them, or that we believe in their worth. Massage, however, can transpose this kind of message into a new and different key. When receiving a good massage a person usually falls into a mental-physical state difficult to describe. It is like entering a special room until now locked and hidden away, a room the very existence of which is likely to be familiar only to those who practice some form of daily meditation.[29]

Downing's description of massage as the key to an inner room was echoed by another massage practitioner who recounted to me what it was like for her to receive a massage. Her terms and Downing's are strikingly similar though she begins on a very different note:

> I do not always feel warm, open, or invigorated after a massage. Not uncommonly I feel incredibly tired, sad, or solitary. But always relaxed. I figure that I can get so busy, overextended, and mentally preoccupied for weeks at a stretch that until I relax (as

with a massage), I don't realize how much of myself I'd closed off to keep my steam up. Massage, for me, is a way of quieting my myriad mental voices that can be the walls and ceilings of a very separate reality. If I haven't been caring well for the rest of myself, leaving those private rooms may not be a pleasurable experience although it's certainly a wonderful opportunity to know myself better.

Earthbound creature that I am, I have found no separate realities while undergoing massage, nor even any secret rooms. What I have found is a deep relaxation, a fabulously sensual experience, and a most soothing form of contact with another person. I have received welcome relief for stiff and spasming muscles. And I have welcomed the gift of human comfort as my wife's fingers lift the veil of a dark mood from my eyes.

On the giving end, I have been able to use massage effectively to relieve cramps of the uterus and of the stomach, to loosen knotted muscles, and to relax a tense body.

Massage can also serve as a diagnostic tool. It has been used in this way by a range of practitioners that runs from Georg Groddeck, physician and psychoanalyst, to psychics who examine the "aura" surrounding their patient with their hands. What physician and psychic have in common is the development of their hands as a trained, clinical instrument. There are several nice descriptions of this training process in the literature of massage. The medical team of Bischoff and Elmiger put it this way:

> The physical therapist must be taught to use his fingers skillfully, accurately and perceptively to achieve the desired effects. . . . The therapist must also be taught to develop his visual and tactile powers of observation . . .[30]

Emphasizing the learn-it-yourself approach of the nonmedical masseur, George Downing spelled out the same message in considerably more detail:

> After you have looked for signs of tension with your eyes, the next step is to "look" with your hands. This, of course, is most easily done during the massage itself. In the long run you will find that by touching another person you can tell even more

about the patterns of muscular tension in his body than you can by looking at him.

What do your hands "look" for? . . . In a particularly tight area—especially in the upper back just above and beside the shoulder blades—your fingers are likely to find tiny lumps, anywhere from the size of a pea up, buried under the flesh; normally these are either deposits of waste matter or knottings of the connective tissue. In general, however, where somebody's body is tense the flesh simply feels tight, feels stiff and resistant to your handling of it. Being able to sense this with any precision is a skill you will develop only by doing a lot of massage on a number of different people with different body types.[31]

The message from the medics and the masseur is identical to that of midwife Reva Rubin quoted earlier. In order to use touch in a skillful way, touch skills must be developed. We train the eye of the radiologist to perceive patterns in an X-ray film that would be invisible to the rest of us. We train the ear of the cardiologist to pick up sounds through a stethoscope that the neophyte would never notice. The time has come to increase the tactile sensitivity of our diagnosticians and healers so that they may have one more means at their disposal in preserving and restoring their patients' health.

As with psychotherapy, there are many schools of massage, each more or less convinced that its specialized technique or underlying rationale is more efficacious than the others. Their names tell much about their origins: Swedish, Esalen, Shiatsu, Acupressure, Polarity, Applied Kinesiology, Rolfing. Some stroke, others press, still others prod and jab. But whatever the differences in origin, theory or technique, I believe that it is only the territory they share that is of real importance. As with psychotherapy, the belief system of the masseur is of little consequence compared to what actually goes on in the room with the client. In the realm of psychotherapy, this point has been made by a number of researchers, Truax and Carkhuff,[32] Morris Parloff,[33] and Jerome Frank[34] among them. I predict that massage studies will show the same. I base this prediction on personal experience.

I have found that a person with beliefs about the meaning of massage as different from mine as Mars is from marzipan can still give me a most wonderful going-over while one whose beliefs I share entirely can dish out some pretty indifferent stuff. It's not what is in their heads that matters so much as what goes on where skin meets skin.

What does go on in healing massage? I think there are several components. The most important is legitimized skin-to-skin contact in a safe situation. Massage offers the best of a limited number of opportunities for this sort of encounter. Consider that the average visit with the family doctor lasts seven minutes and is declining, that the fifty-minute psychotherapy hour in many places now lasts forty-five minutes and is declining, and that neither priests nor social workers are taught to touch their clients. Massage, for many, is the only alternative.

A second component is the masseuse's acceptance of the client's problems and pain combined with a readiness to treat them actively. This combination is often lacking in other forms of treatment. Some patients are rejected as having conditions unsuitable for medicine/surgery/therapy, etc., and many others can be given nothing more tangible and satisfying than a prescription. By offering something as physical and inherently comforting as active skin-to-skin contact, massage can give more.

Another factor is direct, caring attention to hurt parts of the body, parts that often have direct links to hurt feelings. Attending to a sore shoulder can release feelings about aging; massaging a disabled leg can bring out feelings about deformity. Thus can massage connect mind and body, or, perhaps more correctly, close the imagined gap between them.

The legitimization of a relaxed, passive, let-me-take-care-of-you attitude makes massage particularly beneficial to groups whose credo is take-charge, get-going, take-care-of. This includes doctors, psychotherapists, teachers, nurses, and executives whose lives are organized around doing; massage lets them be done to.

Finally there is the expectation of positive results, an aid to almost any form of healing, and in massage, a natural result of the combination of other components.

These elements transcend beliefs about polarity, *ch'i* energy, acupressure, chiropractic, or osteopathy. If they are present, the client is likely to arise from the table feeling warm, open, relaxed, and invigorated. If they are not, forget it.

The healing massage is not the only form that is in fashion today. In the business of sex, the massage parlor has done to the whorehouse what Frigidaire did to the iceman. The ads promise beautiful girls, hotel-room service, nude masseuses, "relief massage" (what a felicitous phrase!), and a—nudge-nudge, wink-wink—*good time.* In terms of clientele, the relationship between the massage parlor and the holistic healing massage center is about the same as that between Country and Western music and authentic Olde Englishe Ballades. They are both on records, but you will listen long and hard before you hear Cynthia Gooding trilling Barb'rie Allen over WWVA. You've got the same chances of finding a Center for Wellness Through Massage in Times Square.

The lurid reputation of the massage parlor presents something of an image problem for the healing masseuse, and the problem is anything but new. In 1894 the image issue in England was so vexing that four women called a meeting "to discuss the possibility of putting massage, which had fallen into great disrepute in this country, into its proper place, and making the profession a safe, clean and honourable one for British women."[35] As a result of the meeting, the Chartered Society of Physiotherapy was founded.

The situation is similar today. Healing masseuses flee from the stigma of the parlor as the Romans from the Huns. "They're not our sort, dear." Of course they're not . . . yet, in a way, they are. Their clients, too, are touched and caressed; if they are well treated, they too arise feeling relaxed and content, their yin and yang balance restored. Then why the stigma, why the need for distance? The simple answer is that in this case, as in so many others, the sex taboo threatens to overwhelm the healing use of touch. Aware of this threat, the touching healers know that one way to survive is to draw as clear a distinction as possible between themselves and the hand hustlers. My understanding of this strategy swelled rapidly when I left New Zealand for a year of research in the United States. After a few months I started to hear transoceanic rumors, via letter and phone, that I was engaged in all sorts of wild sexiness and that my "research" was in truth nothing more nor less than open slather. When I told this tale to the healing masseuses I was interviewing, they nodded in resignation—they had been there before. One told me about a recent experience she had had. Her answering service is run by sweet little old ladies. Early one Sunday morning her phone rang. On the line was the sweetest and oldest of the operators.

"Sorry to disturb you, Bea," she said, "but there's a man calling who wants to know if you'll come up and give him a blow job."

"What!"

"There's a man calling who—"

"Right. Tell the man that we don't offer that service."

"Just thought you'd like to know, dear."

In their efforts to distance themselves from the ladies of the parlor, many healing masseuses deny that there is anything sexual about their treatment. But there is. When two people meet in a warm and comfortable room, and one lies down with no clothes on while the other rubs his or her body with skilled hands and soothing oils, there is a reasonable chance that s-e-x-ual feelings are going to be aroused. The real question is what is done about them. If they are denied, suppressed, and disapproved, then the therapeutic effect is reduced. One cannot disclaim that essential an element of human experience and still claim to be treating the whole person. If the feelings *are* catered to, to the exclusion of all else, then it is not massage but masturbation.

There is a third alternative. If sexual feelings are accepted and appreciated but not allowed to overwhelm other feelings that may arise—such as sadness, nurturance, anxiety, and reassurance—then massage may take its rightful place among the healing arts.

There is, in fact, one place where the massage healer and the massage parlor come together, where God and Mammon are reconciled, where art and commerce join hands, where Jean Ritchie lies down with Johnny Cash. This Demilitarized Zone of the massage world is to be found in the sexual dysfunction clinic. We will have a look at that in a later chapter.

As the end of this chapter draws nigh, let us examine two life situations in which massage can perform healing miracles, or, in more conservative terms, can accomplish more than other therapeutic techniques, both physical and psychological. One is old age; the other, treatment of people with missing or damaged parts.

It is a safe generalization that the old are touched less than the young. Everyone wants to hold the baby. Parents kiss the child's hurt away. Teenagers pet, adults cuddle, men jostle each other in pubs, women have their hair set, and the double bed is still the creature-comfort center of the home. But what happens when the occupant of half the bed dies? What happens when skin is no longer smooth and inviting; when flesh no more is firm and exciting? From what source springs touch then?

In many cases the spring simply dries up. There are people whose dry, wrinkled skin seems to be more the result of lack of physical contact than the product of sun and age. Others displace their affection, satisfying what educational psychologist Sidney Simon calls their "skin hunger" by lavishing attention on pets and plants.[36] Massage may offer a more satisfying alternative.

> . . . as people relaxed and enjoyed their massage, they became lovelier, pinker, and wrinkles vanished. Lines of tension eased away. They began to look really vital and beautiful. They would get up after a massage and look at themselves in the mirror with sparkling eyes, pleased.[37]

These are the words of Gay Luce, founder of SAGE, a group established in 1974 and dedicated to exploring the possibilities and excitements of old age. Massage is one of the cornerstones of the SAGE experience and the subject of more than one chapter in her lively and useful book, *Your Second Life*. Working in groups, elders involved with SAGE learn to massage first themselves, then each other. Discussion of feelings always precedes the hands-on exercise. And because the feelings aroused by the idea of 80-year-olds taking off their clothes and rubbing each other run pretty high, these discussions are as vital to the outcome as the massage itself. In fact, all SAGE exercises are designed to maximize choice as to how deeply the participant wants to plunge, to minimize competition as to who can do it best, and to proceed slowly enough to reduce uptightness to a speck on the horizon. This cautionary approach could well be adopted to groups of any age:

> Contact is very personal, and some people are afraid of it. Be sensitive to that. You might begin by saying aloud, "I'm going to place my hand on your hand. Is that all right?" Then do it. Ask yourself what you would like.[38]

People with experience in massaging the elderly regularly report two observations. The first is how much their touch is appreciated, how great the skin hunger in their clients. The second is the lack of stored tension in old bodies. Deep massage techniques that are often used as tension reducers simply are not necessary when working on people in their seventies.

There are special benefits as well. As one masseuse told me:

> Old people need to be reaffirmed that they're valuable enough to touch. That they're here. In many cultures they aren't considered very useful, and their wellness relates to their feeling functional. If they are attended to enough to merit touching, it's reaffirming that they're OK, that they're worth caring for, that they're there.

Those are the words of Julie McLane, a Vermont therapist, teacher, and masseuse. She has developed a special touch technique for aiding elders who have lost mobility in a limb through accident or arthritis. While it does not involve massage, I include it here as a variation that others may find a useful adjunct to massage.

There are three stages to the approach. First, the elders are told to concentrate on deepening their breathing. (Deepened breathing is a key part of the SAGE program as well.) Next, they practice the exercise, which is usually one which has been prescribed by their doctor. As they exercise, Julie places her hand under the limb being moved. "Just by touching them and having them breathe really fully, they're getting emotional support, tactile support (although I'm not physically supporting the limb), and they find themselves surprised by how well they can do the exercise." The third stage is to have them visualize using the limb with full mobility while Julie holds a similar picture in her mind. The combination of exercise, breathing, tactile support, and visualization enables them to stretch the limb—and themselves—further than they have been able to do previously.

Perhaps the biggest problem about massaging older people is the feeling many of them have that they do not like to be touched. Talking to elders about touch and sex, one quickly comes to realize just how far the young in our culture (and that includes American, Canadian, English, Scottish, Australian, and New Zealand cultures that I know of firsthand, and undoubtedly many more that I do not) have opened themselves in these areas. Their grandparents are two generations and an eon behind. Add to this a shared cultural feeling that you can't teach an old dog new tricks, and you have both a real and an expected resistance to massage among the elderly.

But once these initial barriers are worked through by discussion and slow, hands-on experimentation, people who previously thought that they were not touchers—who for 60 or 70 years had not been touchers—suddenly discover what they have been missing. One 83-year-old spinster was *sure* she did not like being touched until the day she got her first, limited massage in a SAGE group. When it was over she said, "You know, John was stroking my arm, and I thought, 'I feel like purring.' I really liked that. My whole body felt as if I were being stroked. I felt so good I decided I liked being touched after all.'[39]

This discussion of massaging our elders should end with a quote from Gay Luce, the person who has probably done more than any other to bring touching to the aged.

> Touching is nourishment. To touch is far more than to soothe and massage the body physically. It is the kind of nourishment that mothers give their infants, that lovers give each other, and that most adults give to cats and dogs—but not to each other. If it were possible to give a massage or be massaged each day, it would revitalize a sense of human connection that is all but abandoned after maturity. A massage a day would keep isolation away.[40]

What massage has to offer those with missing or damaged parts is in some ways similar to what it gives to the aging. In both cases it improves circulation, muscle, and skin tone, and induces a feeling of general well-being. But even more important is its capacity—an almost unique capacity—to imbue people with a sense of their lovability, touchability, and worth. The difference is that in cases of damaged or incomplete bodies, the area of need is specifically related to one part. By openly looking at, touching, and caring for the sensitive region, the masseuse or masseur is able to give one of the most basic forms of reassurance a person can receive. The analogy to psychotherapy is inescapable—if this one person can accept me, imperfect and damaged as I am, perhaps I can dare the risk of exposing myself to others.

What follows are the thoughts of therapist-masseuse Julie McLane on this subject. Her conclusions are useful and sound; the way she reaches them (via Kirlian photography) leaves me searching for my roadmap. For me, this disparity provides a good example of a phenomenon I have encountered time and again in this research—that is, the irrelevance of the healer's belief system to day-by-day practice. I feel wholeheartedly positive about Julie's practice; Kirlian photography leaves me just as negative. I can't get it in focus.

Here are Julie McLane's thoughts on massage for those with damaged bodies:

> My sense about body parts that are missing is that the consciousness is still in that part of the body. This is based on my having seen Kirlian photography of leaves that have been damaged. Take a photograph of the leaf before it was torn in half, and the aura of the leaf is total; then tear the leaf in half and rephotograph it, and the Kirlian photo will show the whole energy pattern of that leaf similar to what it was before it was cut in half. Although there are some changes, the whole form is there. I sense that the body does the same thing. If one is missing an arm there are still sensations and still the awareness of the whole arm space, the whole arm form there. I can't massage an arm that's not there, but I certainly can attend to the area where it was connected.
>
> For women who have had mastectomies I am particularly attentive to the chest area because I feel a woman has a lot of consciousness there. And it wants attending to. This is very much a woman-part regardless of how deformed it is, so I attend to it especially carefully. In terms of healing a damaged area, the person gets support from this attention, and it brings more energy to the region, so the trauma which occurred there can be healed. The healing takes place at a physiological level and an emotional level. To bring energy to that part is to bring caring to it. And caring—focusing energy on something—creates more rapid healing.

I watched Julie work with a client and was struck by the free flow of touch and dialogue between them. Talk, massage, more talk, specific area massage, rest, more talk, then an embracing good-bye until the next, as yet unscheduled session. The client was Louise Sunfeather, herself a healer, specializing in work with the so-called terminally ill. Louise insists on the "so-called" because she believes that determination to live is the most important factor in healing.

She came to this position after intensive work with her first patient—
herself. Louise had breast cancer that resulted in two mastectomies.
She described her work with Julie as follows:

> Massage with Julie has certainly contributed to my sense of
> wholeness. There's something about being touched deeply which
> is affirming of being alive. That's really what the decision's
> about. The work I did after the cancer was to claim being alive.
> Being touched is an acknowledgement that you're here. At the
> very basic level there's that, and at a more sophisticated level
> there's "I'm here, and I'm beautiful." Because part of the work
> was not only to accept the cancer and the life and the death, but
> even the beauty of my scars. The lovingness of her touch and the
> ability to just lie there while she "does" me is affirming from
> both sides—from inside me and outside me.

Both Julie McLane and Louise Sunfeather approach healing from
a holistic perspective. We will have a look at that in the next chapter.
But before we go, let us share a last word about massage:

> Tranquilizers have been called a biochemical backrub.
> Massage is a non-chemical tranquilizer
> With no side effects
> Other than
> Pleasure.

# Holistic
# Healing

**7**

People ought to practice love every day. If you go to bed hating half
the people you met that day, you'll have a drain of energy, energy you
need for healing and health.

—Nicola Tauraso

If you haven't seen an American newspaper for a couple of years, if
you've avoided talk shows and stayed away from bookshops, you
might just have managed to avoid coming across the phrase "holistic
healing." But even those measures will not be enough for long; the
words will be ubiquitous before we are very far into the 1980s. What
began as an "alternative" movement ("alternative" being the ubiquitous phrase of the late 1970s) will no doubt be absorbed by American
commerce just as one-time alternative phrases like "natural" and
"organic" have come to describe every product on the supermarket
shelf from room deodorizers to refined sugar. I predict with great
confidence that the time will not be long in coming before a
wholesome-looking lass seated in a wooded glen looks you in the eye
from your television set and with ingenuous sincerity urges you to try
Ex-Lax—the Holistic Solution. I can't wait.

There is a wide range in the way holistic healers define themselves,
and most of their self-definitions tend to be inclusive rather than
exclusive. The result, at least for now, is a general overlap rather

than strict division into distinct camps or schools. A good example of
these definitions may be found in the introduction to the *Vermont
Holistic Health Director*, edited by Hobertha Wreagh. It begins:

> The Holistic approach recognizes men and women as whole
> beings having purpose and meaning in a meaningful universe,
> with the capacity to direct their own growth to ever higher levels
> of integration, organization and harmony. Within this context,
> psychological or physical dis-eases are considered to hold mes-
> sages, pointing us to the removal of blocks on the way to full
> self-actualization and utilization of our qualities and abilities.
>
> Holism de-emphasizes the elimination of symptoms in favor of
> discovering root causes, thus allowing the system to balance
> itself and unnecessary manifestations or symptoms to fade
> away.[1]

A journalist-observer of the movement nicely summarized the
holistic approach after participating in a week-long healing festival,
high in the Rocky Mountains. He wrote:

> —that we are irreducible beings, our minds and bodies working
> as one—that good health is mainly an attitude and that, likewise,
> an infected toe reflects a more general malfunction. They focus
> not on the symptoms of illness but on the principles of wellness.
> Instead of regarding disease as an alien invader to be combated
> with drugs, they believe the cure lies within. In these days of
> inflated doctor and hospital bills, their message is: Patient, heal
> thyself.[2]

*Many Hands*, which describes itself as "more than just a yellow
pages" of holistic health centers in the greater Connecticut River
Valley, carries ads for everything from Adlerian counseling, Aikido,
and Alpha Awareness through chiropractic, clairvoyant readings,
and clinical psychology to dream exploration, healing music. Rites of
Passage, stress reduction, Universal Astrology, and Womancraft. A
not-quite-random quote gives the flavor of at least one facet of the
holistic spectrum; it is from an ad whose headline reads, "Bach
Flower Remedies and Consultations."

Bach Flowers, discovered by Dr. Edward Bach, are a healing

system of 38 remedies made from wild flowers, trees and a healing spring. The remedies develop the "opposing virtue" of an emotional or mental disharmony in the personality thus relieving tensions and imbalances in our psyches and bodies. . . . Here are some samples of remedies; *Larch*—for those who do not consider themselves as good or capable as others. *Gentian*—for people who are easily discouraged. *Pine*—for those who blame themselves. Even when successful they think they could have done better. *Gorse*—balances those who have feelings of great hopelessness.[3]

It was probably the gorse that caught my eye, as it would anyone who has spent more than a few days in New Zealand. In that country, gorse *causes* feelings of great hopelessness, particularly among farmers who can't keep the bloody gorse from taking over their fields and pastures.

Holistic healing is more a concept than a category, more an alliance than a school. Those who identify with it share a number of general beliefs and antipathies, the most significant of which are:

- that we are a union of mind, body, and spirit, none of which can be ignored in the process of maintaining or restoring health;
- that energy, or energies, flow within each person as well as within the universe;
- that freeing/unblocking/releasing this energy, or balancing/harmonizing/restoring equilibrium to these energies, is the work of the healer;
- that wisdom flows from ancient, Eastern, and mystic sources;
- that raw is better than cooked, fasting healthier than feasting, vegetables nicer than meat, diet preferable to drugs, and *anything* beats modern medicine;
- and that touching is a legitimate and effective treatment modality.

Of these tenets, it is the first that gets the most emphasis. Chiropractors (who are recent and enthusiastic converts to holism), palmists, iridologists—all preface discussion of their speciality by a ritual affirmation that they are Treating the Whole Person. While my own trinity tends to be mind/body/emotion rather than mind/

body/spirit, like almost everyone else I think healers have to be aware that there is a person attached to the gall bladder in Room 201. But these days even the most benighted surgeon pays homage to Treating the Whole Person in his lecture to medical students, even if in his practice he makes it a point of honor to do nothing of the kind. The fact is, I would not mind a moratorium on the phrase, or at least a partial ban, limiting its use in conversation to those who are prepared to spell out what they mean by Treating the Whole Person and how they apply it in practice.

My basic problem with the holistic movement has to do with evidence as a basis for belief. The problem of evidence is not limited to holistic healers; it plagues medicine and psychology as well. But in those fields, tremendous effort is expended trying to sort sense from nonsense while holism tends to accept *everything* that is not late-twentieth-century American medicine. Tarot readings, *t'ai-chi*, megavitamins, Laetrile, macrobiotics, acupuncture, psychic surgery, Bioenergetics, and Ginseng root—they are all acceptable because orthodox medics don't like them. Twentieth-century *Chinese* medicine is O.K.; *eighteenth*-century American medicine is O.K.; everything goes as long as it's not currently taught at medical school. It's just a matter of time before *New Age* starts running ads for leeches.

There are many holistic healers to whom this generalization does not apply; they do not reject all modern medicine—some are doctors, themselves—and they do not accept all forms of alternative practice. In fact holistic attitudes toward organized medicine are complex, as scientist Donal Gould observed at a British meeting organized by Health for the New Age, Ltd. He wrote:

> This love-hate relationship with the orthodox medical profession, involving a wish to be recognised and valued by proper doctors, and to become a part of the formal system of medical care, was not, apparently, shared by all the members of the audience, for, more than once, reference to conventional physicians and their attitudes produced derisive groans and laughter . . .[4]

But, despite the exceptions and ambivalence, the state of the movement now is one of accepting all things from one direction and almost none from the other. A philosophy so all-embracing risks ridiculousness; one so all-rejecting flirts with madness.

The reception given Wilhelm Reich by the holistic movement illustrates the madness. There is no question that Reich's emphasis on the somatic component of neurosis was a major contribution to psychological thought; he recognized that bound-up emotions could find expression in bound-up muscles and that the condition could be attacked through the musculature as well as the mind. But there is also no question that toward the end of his life, Reich was as mad as a snake. He thought he had the power to divert hurricanes (a feat, by the way, that Transcendental Meditators are just as convinced they can perform today), that hostile spaceships were watching the earth, and that "deadly orgone" was the cause of nuclear pollution and disease. Yet after acknowledging that some of Reich's ideas "seemed incredible even to his sympathizers,"[5] holistic writer Mary Coddington goes on to defend them. Her supporting evidence derives from a book, written a year after Reich's death, that states that there is now "full proof" that alien invaders are indeed keeping an eye on us. The source of this corroborating evidence is called *Flying Saucers, Top Secret*.

More worrisome still is the tendency of the movement to accept unsubstantiated treatment methods for no other reason than that they are written by nonmedical chiropractors or others who give the nod to Treating the Whole Person. For example, in *Touch for Health*, a book highly praised by holistic healers, and whose cover describes it as "a practical guide to natural health using acupuncture, touch and massage to improve postural balance and reduce physical and mental pain and tension," author John Thie offers the following advice:

> When the abdominal muscles are weak, this is often due to the parietal bones being jammed together at the top of the head. Pulling apart the scalp along a middle part, using hard pressure, is very effective in strengthening the abdominals.[6]

I have been unable to find a neurologist who can discover even a very small grain of truth in this assertion. Nor have I been able to evoke any perceptible abdominal reaction in those whose scalps I have parted. Yet like so much else that calls itself holistic, it is offered as simple fact.

*Touch for Health* also helps provide an example of what happens when a group adopts too all-embracing a philosophy. An illustration neatly shows the points at which the wrists are connected to the heart, liver, and kidneys (left) and the lungs, spleen and "circulation-sex" (right). Fine. These points derive from Chinese beliefs that have been around for at least 5,000 years. But Shiatsu, a form of Japanese massage that has also found holistic favor, links these same organs to the fingers and thumbs. And Reflexology (also of Chinese origin) ties the organs of the trunk to small areas on the soles of the feet. Iridology, which is also practiced as a form of holistic healing, insists that both the organs and their diseases show up in the iris of the eye. And even the otherwise sensible *The Massage Book* can suggest:

> Stop when you find tightness or when your friend says "Ouch!" Check the accompanying charts, determine what body part corresponds to the right (*sic*) or sore part of the foot, and let your friend know that he either has a health problem or a strong potential for one in that particular part. . . . Or, if you already know of some health condition that has been bothering your friend, you can go right to the corresponding area of the foot and begin working there.[7]

It is possible that there are links between your kidneys and your wrists, your pancreas and the sole of your foot, your spleen and a particular slice of your iris, your liver and the ridge of your ears (which are used as symptom revealers in another diagnostic-healing system), but I doubt it. That all these systems work equally well is unlikely; for me it is both too all-embracing and too unsubstantiated. In the end this lack of critical thought saps the strengths of the holistic movement.

And strengths there are. In my contacts with them, I have found many qualities about holistic healers that I like and admire. And this includes some of their major beliefs. By emphasizing the importance of good food, clean air, pure water, harmonious relationships, and harmonious lives, they are attending to the principal determinants of health. It was known long before Illich wrote *Medical Nemesis*[8] that economics and environment have more effect on health and longevity than medicine and surgery. Enough food, a safe water supply, and a decent sewage disposal system increase the chances of a healthy life to a much greater extent than do cobalt treatment, C.A.T. scanners, and convulsive therapy. Not smoking today works a lot better than chemotherapy tomorrow. And there is ever-increasing evidence that familial and community relationships exert a major effect on the physical health of our species. This last point has been effectively argued and convincingly supported by James Lynch in *The Broken Heart*.[9] (Lynch's clinic at the University of Maryland Medical School is also a model of what other clinics—holistic or otherwise—could be like. It is one of the few places I have seen that really does try to treat the whole person.)

Another aspect of the movement worthy of praise and emulation is its determination—at times naïve—to place responsibility for health in the hands of the individual. Unfortunately this is often treated as though it were the obvious solution to a simple problem, when in fact neither problem nor solution is simple. Self-knowledge is not the same as self-treatment. Both causes and cures are complex phenomena. Governments have a major role to play in the protection of health as do doctors and other healers. But this said, the holistic approach is a welcome relief from the guild mentality that so often pervades medical practice. To their credit—for they face fire from two fronts—the doctors who affiliate with holism are frequently among the strongest proponents of health in the hands of the people.

Still another admirable aspect of the holistic movement is its attempts—also, at times naïve—to heal philosophically the mind-body split, that crevasse that both underlies and undermines the structure of our language, medicine, psychology, and even our universities. The movement speaks of mindbody, of wholeness, and of all-pervasive Energy: each an attempt to free language and thought from the separatist ideology of dualism. The dualistic concept is so deeply ingrained that we do not recognize it as a way of looking at the world but think instead that we are seeing things as they really are.

These holistic attempts at unification carry over to clinical practice as well. Holistic healers talk to the physically diseased and massage the emotionally disturbed. They think cancer can be caused by negative thoughts and cured by positive ones. Schizophrenia may be the result of vitamin deficiency, low blood sugar, or allergic reaction. In *The Massage Book*, George Downing cautions his readers, "... don't fall into the trap of trying to separate 'physical sensations' from 'emotional qualities.' To tune in to the energy which is your body is to feel neither just the one nor just the other, but the common root of both."[10]

This way of looking at the world is full of interesting possibilities, but in the end, what I like best about holistic healers is much simpler than ideas about dualism or notions of personal responsibility for health. What I like best is their willingness to say nice things to people. The practice, it is true, fits into their theoretical position on the importance of holding positive ideas, but it comes across in a way that is more personal than theoretical. They speak well of people—*to* people—and they do so openly, directly, and frequently. I feel good when I'm around them. Their friends feel good. Their patients feel good. And that is as good a place as any to begin healing.

# Miracle of Miracles

8

Two friends clasped her hands while a third held her head and took each earlobe between thumb and forefinger, wiggling them and chanting, "Come home, come home, Brave Orchid, who has fought the ghosts and won."

—Maxine Hong Kingston

In the course of researching the subject of miraculous healings involving touch, I have, myself, been healed several times. It is an experience that gives one a richer perspective on the subject of healing. Something that surprised me was the variety of miracles available. For a flavor of this, allow me to describe two healings—my first and my worst.

My first and still favorite took place after a lecture on miraculous healing in the South Island of New Zealand. The audience was told that if any of us had a problem we wished dealt with, the speaker, a stern and fiftyish woman, would see us privately after the question period. It says something about the difference in national character between New Zealanders and Americans that I, a Yank, was the only one who stayed.

"What's the trouble?" she asked, no less stern in person than during the lecture.

"I've been having lower back pain," I answered truthfully.

"Sit here," she instructed, directing me to a piano stool. I sat, and she observed me from behind. After a long minute she placed one hand lightly on my spine and moved it in an impersonal way over several vertebrae. Silently she continued to observe me, her fingers resting lightly on the small of my back. Then she prodded me sharply and abruptly with the heel of her hand, saying, "No wonder you have back trouble. Just look at that posture! Sit up straight!"

And that concluded a highly successful healing. I consciously sat and stood straighter for the next few weeks or months and during that time had no more back trouble. A miracle indeed.

My worst healing also involved back pain, this time brought on by competitive waterskiing with younger relatives in northern New England. In the next town lived a spiritual healer whom I had been intending to interview for some time. Now, with a real ailment, I called him and arranged a night visit. Effin drove me to his isolated farmhouse, and we both got our first glimpse of the man whom several of our farmer neighbors had assured me was The Real Thing. The Real Thing stood in the porch light, unshaven, beer-bellied, a cigarette drooping from his lip. Through the open windows we could hear a Montreal station broadcasting the Pittsburgh Pirates game in French. Effin wanted to drive on, but I insisted that we stop.

With a diffident handshake and a mumbled greeting he ushered us into his office, a room decorated entirely with lighted pictures of the Virgin Mary, plaster casts of Jesus, ornate scrolls bearing greetings from the Pope, and a framed set of faded snapshots of a faded rose in a crystal ball, which he told us had miraculously changed colors as patients suffering from different diseases entered his chambers. Unfortunately and alas, his ex-wife had smashed the miraculous object in a fit of pique.

Aside from the religious objects and faded photographs, the healing room contained only a few chairs (Effin was waved into one of them), a plastic-covered examination table (to which I was directed), and the radio, still blaring the game at full volume in French.

The healer motioned for me to lie face-down on the table and roll up my pants legs; the roll-up, however, was not to aid the diagnosis, but to protect the practitioner. He was, he explained, "allergic" to cordu- roy, plush, and velvet, and to touch any one of them even lightly was enough to throw him into an instant faint. I tried to digest this information as the smell of foot powder drifted from the table to my nose. The healer stood at my feet and surveyed the soles of my shoes. "It's bothering you on the left side, eh?" he half-asked, half-asserted.

"Actually, it's the right."

"Hmmm." Gently, he lifted my right leg and moved it in a small circle, telling me to relax. Just as I started to, he suddenly and powerfully yanked my leg straight toward him. Equal measures of fear, anger, and pain projected my yell over miles of surrounding countryside. But before I could protest further, he grabbed me again and yanked my leg several more times in rapid succession. "Get up," he commanded.

Get up? I wasn't even sure I still had a leg to stand on. But ever the obedient patient, I slowly and painfully swung my feet toward the floor and stood, supporting myself as well as I could on the table's edge. I could see the look of horror etched on Effin's face while on the face of the healer sat a triumphant grin. "Now you are cured," he said. "Bend over and touch 'zee toes."

Touch 'zee toes? I could barely stand! Still gasping from the leg pulls, I shook my head. He scowled and motioned me to a chair. Placing a towel between his hand and the deadly corduroy, he reached into my pants and placed his right hand on my buttock. Soon, he said, I would start to feel intense heat. I did not. We remained in that position, linked by his increasingly clammy hand, for about five minutes. During that time he smoked, drank tea, and listened to the game. Then he removed his hand and told me that if I were still in pain next week to come back and see him. He said that serious cases like blindness, heart disease, cancer and epilepsy—all of which he had successfully treated—sometimes took several visits to heal. I left a five-dollar bill on the table which he snatched up before I had time to turn around. My back felt worse than before the healing, and I spent the next several days in bed writing these memoirs.

When I first began researching the subject of miraculous healings involving touch, I was happily convinced that those miracle healers who were not outright charlatans were suffering from delusions. Today, after reading incredible stories ("Jesus filled seven of his tooth (*sic*) that had cavities. He filled them with silver"),[1] after listening to extraordinary tales ("I heal through crystals, pyramids, feathers, and spirit guides. My cat is a healer too"), after undergoing several misdiagnoses ("You have ulcers, don't you?" "No."), and after talking personally to many healers, I am no longer happily convinced that they are suffering from delusions.

Now I am sadly convinced.

Sadly, because other than the Pirates fan described above, I have encountered no charlatans, but, rather, an exceptionally nice, open, giving, helpful group of people who believe things that I cannot see, feel, experience, and ultimately accept, as anything other than delusional. The delusion is usually benign, sometimes beneficial, and occasionally—as when a patient avoids medical care that works in favor of a miracle that does not—dangerous.

Delusions, however, are not so simple as simple-minded psychology would have it. Delusions are false beliefs held despite invalidating evidence, and we are all subject to them. If you believe sugar is bad for you, running is good for you, and cholesterol gives you heart attacks, the odds are that at least one of these popularly (and medically) held beliefs of our time will prove delusional a little further on down the road. And around another bend someone will discover that we ancients were right all along, and the new belief will be relegated to the status of a quaint, once-popular delusion. And so on. In fact some definitions of delusion try to accommodate this uncomfortable reality (or delusion) by excluding culturally held myths. Your sanity will not be called into question if you profess belief in the virgin birth of Jesus, but I wouldn't suggest going around talking about the virgin birth of Jules.

Both Frank in *Persuasion and Healing*[2] and Torrey in *The Mind Game*[3] have convincingly argued that a major factor in healing is a shared belief system between healer and patient. I once wrote, "Cultural attitudes toward health, disease and medicine can profoundly influence the patient's reactions to medical intervention. Understanding these attitudes can sometimes mean the difference between success or failure of treatment."[4]

But understanding and accepting is not the same as believing, and after considerable investigation, meditation, and consideration, I still cannot believe that the six-foot Tibetan spirit guide whom the miraculous healer can see peering over my right shoulder is really there. Sorry.

On the other hand, I do not think that this is the only kind of delusion currently afloat in healing waters. It might be worthwhile to compare briefly the miracle movement with the two most influential movements in orthodox psychology—psychoanalysis and behaviorism. I think that anyone who truly believes in the extremes of either one is also delusional. Claims have been made for both that neither can begin to fulfill. Freudians used to think that they could account for every aspect of human behavior from the Washington Monument to the successful businesswoman by invoking the precepts of phallic symbolism and penis envy. As for behaviorism, I have heard a leading Skinnerian state positively that behavior modification could effectively dispatch all symptoms of schizophrenia. His statement was made in a ward full of schizophrenics in the middle of a hospital full of schizophrenics. Remember, delusions are unaffected by invalidating evidence.

Yet neither psychoanalysis nor behaviorism seems nearly as mad as the beliefs of the miracle healers. Perhaps it is just that both are widely accepted in the circles in which I travel, and I accept them much as a Botswana tribesman would accept spirit possession. I prefer to think, however, that there is simply a much larger grain of truth in the ideas of Freud and Skinner than in the ideas of those who see auras, dowse the human body for illness, make blind diagnoses by mail, or perform surgery with their bare hands. Regardless of one's feelings about castration anxiety, Freud's insistence on the importance of the irrational and on the influence of the early years must be seen as an enormous contribution to human awareness. Skinner's methods have not cured all ills, but his observations of the behavior patterns of pigeons have given us a new way of looking at animal behavior, including the complex and difficult human animal. The combined contributions of thousands of visionary guides, ghosts, and spirits have had considerably less impact.

False beliefs need not be bad beliefs. If I believe that running the roads before breakfast is going to make me live longer, no harm at all is done even if I die right on my actuarial schedule. If a miracle worker has given me hope or strengthened my will to live when ordinary doctors have done all they could, then my belief in what she tells me may be doing me good. Only if a false notion has kept me away from real healing has harm been done. Unfortunately, this does occur, particularly when belief in the healer is mixed with fear of the doctor's diagnosis. Some miraculous healers have taken advantage of this combination, provoking surgeon William Nolen to write, "When healers treat serious organic diseases they are responsible for untold anguish and unhappiness; this happens because they keep patients away from possibly effective and life-saving help. The healers become killers."[5]

To be perfectly precise, neither in reading the literature nor through personal observation have I encountered a really miraculous healing, with the possible exception of Jesus filling teeth, as quoted above. After all, a miracle is an event that is unexplainable by the laws of nature, and what passes for miracles, even by the stringent standards of a place like Lourdes, falls far short of that. There are unusual cures at Lourdes and inspiring ones, but none that defy natural law. A broken arm may be healed, but no one has ever grown a new arm there. Or a third arm. Cancer may go into remission (as it occasionally does in London or Los Angeles), but a seventy-year-old never comes out looking like fifteen. Or like an artichoke.

Still, an unexpected cure feels miraculous to anyone who has been ill. An improvement that the doctor did not expect seems like a miracle. And any change that follows prayer or laying on of hands is experienced as truly miraculous.

Touch has always been an enhancer of these sorts of healing miracles, and they have been around as long as people have prayed for relief from suffering. Many religions are based on miraculous tales, but of the world's major religions Christianity has been singularly effective in the promotion of miraculous healing. The practice is as old as the church and as widely dispersed.

In the Gospels, Jesus is seen healing the sick no less than 39 times, and the Acts of the Apostles records another 18. Since many of the healings involved multitudes, it is clear that large numbers of people experienced Christian healing in the early days of the Church. The disorders cured included blindness, deafness, dumbness, stammering, dropsy, hemorrhage, devil possession, paralysis, leprosy, withered limbs, and apparent death. The range of healing techniques was equally impressive. The apostles made use of shadow healing (". . . they brought forth the sick into the streets and laid them on beds and couches, that at least the shadow of Peter passing by might overshadow some of them.")[6] handkerchief healing ("So that from his [Paul's] body were brought unto the sick handkerchiefs, or aprons, and the diseases departed from them, and the evil spirits went out of them,")[7] conversion healing ("And immediately there fell from his eyes as it had been scales: and he received sight forthwith, and arose, and was baptized,")[8] healing by command, by exorcism, and by the laying on of hands ("And it came to pass, that the father of Publius lay sick of a fever, and of a bloody-flux: to whom Paul entered in, and prayed, and layed his hands on him, and healed him.")[9]

Jesus himself employed a number of healing techniques. He touched, was touched, suggested, commanded, granted absolution, and spit.

Spit. It is astonishing the number of active, Bible-reading Christians who manage to miss the saliva cure, no matter how well they know the rest of the Good Book. But it's there, all right. In Decapolis a deaf stammerer was brought to Jesus, who "put his fingers into his ears, and he spit, and touched his tongue . . ."[10] Confronted with a blind beggar, "he spat on the ground, and made clay of the spittle, and he anointed the eyes of the blind man with the clay . . ."[11] And at Bethsaida he healed a blind man by touching him and spitting in his eyes.[12] Note that all these cures involved touch as well as spit, just as anointing with oil involves the hands as much as the oil. Nonetheless, the healing power of saliva long predates the birth of Jesus. According to Weatherhead, saliva had long been associated with curing disorders of the eye. The Roman Emperor Vespasian used the same method as Jesus to restore sight, Galen and Pliny both recommended it to practitioners, and the ancient Egyptians thought that spittle could cause and cure blindness.

Anointing, whether with saliva, oil, or water, involves physical contact. The Christian healing touch involves physical contact, though not always skin-to-skin. A woman "diseased with an issue of blood twelve years"[13] was made whole by touching Jesus' garment; when Mary Baker Eddy, founder of Christian Science, led a parade through the streets of Chicago, several believers stepped out from the crowd, touched her dress, and claimed healings.

Laying on of hands is pure physical contact. Since the triumvirate of healing methods in the post-apostolic church was laying on of hands, anointing with oil, and prayer, it is clear that two out of three involved touch. In fact, all three do. The traditional Christian prayer position calls for self-touch, as the hands stretch heavenward palm to palm, fingers to fingers.

The laying on of hands has been part of Christian miracles from the time of Jesus and the apostles until today. The practice was referred to a dozen times in Matthew, Mark, and Acts, and it has long been practiced in fundamentalist Protestant churches, particularly in southern, rural, and black America. Today it is enjoying a revival in more staid, mainline churches as well. And the revival has reached Catholics and Episcopalians, groups that have traditionally stood apart from too much pressing of the flesh.

The Reverend Gary Eley is a well-educated, articulate, turned-collar, Episcopal priest. He is also a layer on of hands. After Sunday services in his northern, suburban church, those who have taken communion are invited to remain kneeling at the altar rail for spiritual healing. Many choose to do so. Father Eley removes himself for a few moments of contemplation/relaxation, then moves to the line of communicants. He stands before each in turn, holding his or her head in his hands. He asks God to remove pain and sickness and thanks Him for His presence. The procedure takes a minute or less per person.

I asked Reverend Eley if he would try healing me to relieve a daily nosebleed that developed after moving from moist New Zealand to woodstove-dry Vermont. "Sure," he said. "Let's try it after lunch."

When we left the restaurant and went upstairs to the Massage Center, we found an empty room where I knelt on the carpet with my eyes closed. Following instructions I had read in *New Age*, I visualized the inside of my nostrils and pictured them healing. Reverend Eley asked God to be present and to heal me. (I expected him to say, "Lord, heal the nose of this Jewish kid from Baltimore," but he didn't.) While he was praying he placed the palms of his hands on the top of my head.

I have asked several ministers how they know where to put their hands since I have been unable to find specific instructions in the Bible. I have had three answers: 1. "It's the part that's nearest heaven." 2. "It's the part that's easiest to reach." 3. "I never thought of that—I guess it's traditional." Whatever the reason, the hands on head position that Reverend Eley uses is the same as used in black fundamentalist churches and by a young, Jewish, Viennese doctor by the name of Sigmund Freud. All lay hands on head to promote healing, but the results they get are determined by the style of their constituents.

Freud's Victorian, female patients uncovered repressed memories after the laying on. Eley's white suburbanites make no visible sign but sometimes tell him later that the experience brought them relief. In black "roller" churches, the results are considerably more spectacular. At the end of the service, the congregation is invited to receive the holy spirit. Those who wish to, line up, and in their turn stand beneath the outstretched arms of the minister, who is usually on a stage or platform at the front of the church. He presses his hands to each parishioner's head and invokes the spirit to enter. The response is immediate.

The supplicant reels under the minister's touch as if shot through with a bolt of lightning. The reaction looks very much like unmodified electroconvulsive therapy or grand mal epilepsy. As the body convulses, stiffens, and writhes, the supplicant sometimes collapses into the waiting arms of two deacons who support her while she regains the strength to walk. Then she shudders and heaves herself back to her seat, never hurting herself or anyone else in the process.

As for my own healing, I would call it a qualified success. For the rest of that day and that week as well, I had no nosebleeds. This was the first blood-free period longer than 24 hours in at least two months. On the eighth day I had another bleed, but the problem was permanently (and miraculously) cured by a trip to the healing sun of Florida the next month. Amazing grace.

It is clear that miraculous healing has worked better in some periods of history than others. The founding of the Church was the peak time. Then there was a gradual decline coinciding with official acceptance of Christianity, followed by periodic revivals in the years since. The rise and fall of Christian healing is nicely illustrated in the history of one healing practice which involves both faith and touch, the anointing ritual.

It has its roots in Mark 6:13, "And they cast out many devils, and anointed with oil many that were sick, and healed them," and in the Epistle of James, 5:14, "Is any sick among you? Let him call for the elders of the church; and let them pray over him, anointing him with oil in the name of the Lord."

James went on to speak of forgiveness of sins, but biblical scholars are in general agreement that this was secondary to physical healing. Yet, over the years the position of the Catholic Church on the anointment ritual changed from physical healing to preparation for death. What began as a rite of healing became the Last Rites.

This was not true of the Greek Church, which steadfastly maintained that anointing with oil can bring about physical healing. Then why the change in the Roman Church? According to MacNutt, "The first stage took place when healing began to drop out of the ordinary experience of the church in the third and fourth centuries."[14] St. Jerome's 400 A.D. official Vulgate translation of the

Bible obscured the meaning of James, changing the focus from real to symbolic healing for the next 1,500 years. There were other changes as well, one of which limited those who were allowed to anoint. While oil itself had to be blessed by a bishop, it originally could be applied by friends, family, or any concerned lay person. But in the Carolingian reform of liturgy in 815, lay anointing was suppressed, and the ritual was delayed until after the rite of deathbed penance. Schlemon, Lin, and Lin cite a number of reasons behind the changes. One was that after Constantine made Christianity the official religion of the Roman Empire around the year 300, the loss of martyrs willing to die for Christ led to a willingness to suffer for Christ, bringing a redemptive quality to pain and illness and making the hair shirt and the flagellant's whip prized religious articles. Another was that in the fifth century extreme penances were regularly imposed after confession of sins. Rather than spend years fasting or in the exile of a monastery, "most people put off confession and anointing by a priest until they had dug their graves."[15] Finally, there were abuses. There was big money in selling sacred oil and relics of martyrs' shrines, and the church tried to reduce the profitable combination of greed and superstition by restricting the use of the oil to priests.

A simpler explanation for the change has been put forth by Weatherhead, who maintains that the gradual loss of interest in physical healing came about because the healings no longer worked. What had been a powerful tool of the early Church gradually lost its power over the ages. Perhaps in religion, as in medicine, the dictum should be, *Try it while it still works.*

I think there is still another possibility. It may be that the giving up of physical contact played a role in the decline of the healing powers of church rituals. As the numbers of Christians grew, the laying on of hands and anointing with oil were gradually replaced with a symbolic gesture. Confronted with ever-increasing multitudes, the bishop now extended his hands *over* the supplicants. Physical contact was replaced by symbolic touch. Since touching is such an integral part of healing, it may well be that this loss of touch contributed to the diminution of the church's power to heal.

The policy of de-emphasizing religious healing continued over the years. By 1549 the Council of Trent had watered down the doctrine of healing to a declaration that unction is good for the soul "and, sometimes when it is expedient for the soul's salvation, recovers bodily health." In 1718 there was an attempt to resurrect the healing use of unction, but as time passed this function was once again lost.

And thus the situation remained until the Second Vatican Council. Then the "danger of death" requirement was removed from anointing, and it was renamed the Anointing of the Sick. A new rite was written that went into effect on January 1, 1974. After that date, both priest and laity could once again anoint, and the purpose of the ritual returned to healing, as originally prescribed by James. And laying on hands again accompanied the anointing.

Another Christian ritual involving physical contact is exorcism. First Jesus and later his followers cast out many a devil and unclean spirit until spirits became passé in the twentieth century and the devil went out of fashion. But there are signs that along with holistic healing, speaking in tongues, and old-timey religion, Old Harry too is making a comeback, and with him a renewed interest among the clergy in casting him out. (The Anglican Church had the great foresight to maintain the rite of exorcism all along.) I have personally known two Christian medical students to practice exorcism: one to cleanse his house of a troublesome spirit; the other, as part of his abundant fear of the devil.

Origen, who lived two hundred years after Jesus, was one whose use of touch in the rite of exorcism has not been lost to time. He made the sign of the cross on the head of the possessed parishioner, then had him kneel while he sprinkled holy water on his brow. After asking the devil his name (as Jesus himself had done) and imploring him to leave the sufferer alone, Origen layed his hands on the patient's head and intoned, "I exorcise thee, unclean spirit, in the name of Jesus Christ; tremble, O Satan, thou enemy of the faith, thou foe of mankind who hast brought death into the world, who hast deprived men of life and hast rebelled against justice, thou seducer of mankind, thou root of all evil, thou source of avarice, discord and envy!"[16]

This procedure was not very different from one described in the Vulgate version of the *Arthurian Romances*, collected by Sommer. Volume IV of this tale told in Old French contains an exorcism involving a laying on of hands. It is the tale of the rich woman from Tuscany, recounted from *Lives of the Fathers*. When the woman learns of the hour of her death, "the devil entered into her as quickly as the fear in her flesh made her forget the salvation of her soul." Her spiritual advisor, a holy man, prays for her as he holds her in his arms. God hears his prayers and grants him the power of the healing touch. "As soon as the holy man put his hand on her to make the true sign of the cross, the devil came out of her body crying and howling and braying so vehemently that the whole earth trembled therefrom. And as soon as the lady had come to her senses, she agreed that this had all happened to her through failure to believe."[17]

There is nothing like the *Arthurian Romances* to banish feelings of despair for our own age. Reading these tomes makes Camelot sound a lot less fun than Fort Wayne, Indiana, on a bad night. Chivalry too loses much of its charm when the realization sinks in that it amounted to little more than lopping off any head at which a fair damsel pointed her pretty little finger. The *Romances* contain almost nothing save head lopping, magic, an occasional swoon-filled sexual encounter, and more head lopping. *Monty Python and the Holy Grail* was a bloomin' documentary!

But amidst the carnage and the gore were some interesting examples of miraculous cures involving touch. One that occurs near the end of Volume III is a cure for madness.

Lancelot, imprisoned by the king's enemies, refuses food or drink and becomes violently and totally demented. He is finally released and taken to the apartment of his swooning lover, the Queen. But he remains as mad as ever until his fairy godmother, the Damsel of the Lake, arrives. The Damsel is able to calm him by seizing him by the wrist (a variation on a technique I have used in work with madness and which will be described in the psychotherapy chapter) and pronouncing the name she used to call him at the Lake. Then she cures him by anointing him with precious salve: "She places her hands on him and anoints his eyes and arms and both temples and his forehead and his fontanel."[18]

Lancelot sleeps and the Damsel departs. Before she goes she instructs the Queen to give him a bath when he awakes, after which he will be healed. He does eventually awake, "cured but very feeble," and after the bath gradually regains his strength.

Volume V finds Lancelot sharing the cold, filthy water at the bottom of a well with vermin and serpents. Just as his legs are beginning to swell from the attacks of his well-mates, a damsel with a long rope happens along and rescues him. She takes him to her daddy's castle. Although still far from recovered, Lancelot does manage to dispatch 20 knights who are watching a chess game, throw their bodies out the window, ride off on a horse, watch a knight lop off a damsel's head, chase the villain all day, beat him up when he finally catches him, ride off again, rescue another damsel from burning, catch the mob that was trying to roast her, "Mow them down like mute beasts," and, at day's end, rest for a while at the home of a widow.

It had been a pretty ordinary sort of day except for the serpents, but they had taken their toll. The widow notices Lancelot's swollen limbs and immediately sends for her sister, the herbalist. The sister arrives and anoints his legs with a potion. In four days Lancelot is well, and he rides off to seek more adventures. He finds them.

Lancelot and Arthur were not the only royal personages associated with miraculous healings. For centuries in both France and England the king was thought to be endowed by God with the power to heal a specific disease with a touch of the royal hand. The disease was scrofula, or tuberculosis of the cervical lymph nodes, a condition marked by ugly swellings, abscesses, and scars on the body and face. Scrofula was widespread in England and Europe where it produced both great discomfort and repulsion but almost never proved fatal. Thanks to the meticulous research and gifted writing of historian Marc Bloch, a thorough history of the disease and its miraculous treatment is available in a book appropriately named *The Royal Touch*.[19]

In France the royal touch goes back at least as far as the mid-eleventh-century ruler Philip I, and the power to heal scrofula was passed down through his Capetian descendants. The story was much the same in England where the Plantagenets beginning with Henry II (who died in 1189) possessed the healing gift. Shakespeare mentions in *Macbeth* that Edward the Confessor had the power:

> strangely visited people,
> All sworn and ulcerous, pitiful to the eye,
> The mere despair of surgery, he cures,
> Hanging a golden stamp about their necks,
> Put on with holy prayers; and 'tis spoken,
> To the succeeding royalty he leaves
> The healing benediction.[20]

This royal power to heal with a touch (the golden stamp Shakespeare mentions was a later variation that followed the touch) has some roots in Christian beliefs about the healing power of saints and still deeper roots long predating the birth of Jesus. Bloch writes:

> Like the pious healers whose stories were familiar to them, they used to touch the sufferers with their hand, most often it would seem on the affected parts themselves. They were thus unconsciously repeating a very ancient custom, going right back to the oldest beliefs of the human race. The contact of two bodies, made in one way or another and more particularly through the agency of the hand, had always seemed the most effective method of transmitting invisible forces from one individual to another.[21]

In time other rituals were added to direct touch. The water in which the king washed his hands after a day of touching scrofulous tumors acquired its own healing properties; it was collected and drunk by sufferers. Gold coins were handed to other supplicants, and this relic was also endowed with magic healing powers.

Use of the royal touch was widespread. Because the English kept particularly good records, we know, for example, that Edward I touched 938 of his scrofulous subjects in the 28th year of his reign and 1,219 four years later. Edward II performed only 79 healings in his 14th year. Physicians and surgeons of the period fully accepted this unusual form of treatment in both France and England, and the power of the royal touch lasted nearly eight centuries. Then it failed.

Bloch attributes the demise of the miracle to the Reformation (miracles attributed to saints and kings filled Protestant hearts with detestation) and to loss of respect for the powers and privileges of royalty. But while the demise may be easily explained, what can account for nearly 800 years of success for this well-documented, popularly and medically accepted healing miracle?

Bloch explores several theories, ancient and modern, including a very likely one; to wit:

> ... the sick people were stirred in spirit by the solemn occasion and the pomp of the royal ceremonial, and above all by the hope of recovery, and thus underwent a kind of nervous shock capable in itself of bringing about a cure. In short, the royal touch was a sort of psychotherapy, and the kings were unconscious Charcots.[22]

The combination of desperate hope, religious ceremony, and expectation of results undoubtedly accounts for most miraculous healings, today as well as then. But there are other explanations as well. For one thing, among the king's subjects there was no expectation that the cure would be immediate. While some felt better immediately after the touch, there were others whose symptoms gradually abated over weeks or months. For another, there were few follow-up studies in those days. One that was carried out in France showed that of 125 people touched, only eight were cured, and three of these were of dubious certainty. On top of that, we now know that scrofula is a disease that frequently goes into periods of apparent remission in which external symptoms disappear—for a time. The illusion of cure (a subject we shall return to shortly) is well-suited to such a disorder.

After weighing the evidence, Bloch reaches an ironic conclusion:

> Thus it is difficult to see faith in the royal miracle as anything but the result of a collective error—a more harmless one, incidentally, than most of those which bestrew the human past . . . whatever opinion might be held about the efficacy of the royal touch, it possessed at least one advantage: it was not in any way harmful. And in that it was greatly superior to a good many of the remedies for scrofula contained in the pharmacopoeia of older times. . . . From this purely negative point of view we are no doubt quite right in imagining that more than one poor sufferer may have owed a debt to his prince for the relief of his ills.[23]

Before we turn to the subject of cures and illusions, there are two other miraculous healers whose lives may throw light on the topic. The better known of the two was Anton Mesmer; the other was Valentine Greatrakes, a/k/a Greatrakes the Stroaker.

Greatrakes was the best-known healer of his time. That in itself was no small achievement, for his time, the seventeenth century, was one of the golden ages of healing miracles. The Prince of Orange cured his soldiers' scurvy in 1625 with a concoction of camomile, wormwood, and camphor. Kircher the Jesuit treated a hernia by having his patient swallow a magnet. Wounds inflicted by sharp weapons were dosed with a mixture that included "moss from the head of a thief who has been hanged and left in the air."[24]

Into this world came Greatrakes, a man whose only healing instrument was his hands, but with them he outshone the others as the sun does the moon.

Greatrakes' discovery of his healing powers has been described with loving cynicism by one of the great disbelievers of the nineteenth century, Charles Mackay. In his *Memoirs of Extraordinary Delusions and the Madness of Crowds*, published in London in 1852, Mackay writes:

> He was the son of an Irish gentleman, of good education and property, in the county of Cork. He fell, at an early age, into a sort of melancholy derangement. After some time he had an impulse, or strange persuasion in his mind, which continued to present itself, whether he were sleeping or waking, that God had given him the power of curing the king's evil (scrofula). He mentioned this persuasion to his wife, who very candidly told him that he was a fool. He was not quite sure of this, notwithstanding the high authority from which it came, and determined to make a trial of the power that was in him. A few days afterwards, he went to see one William Maher, of Saltersbridge, in the parish of Lismore, who was grievously afflicted with the king's evil in his eyes, cheek, and throat. Upon this man, who was of abundant faith, he laid his hands, stroked him, and prayed fervently. He had the satisfaction to see him heal considerably in the course of a few days; and finally, with the aid of other remedies, to be quite cured. This success encouraged him in the belief that he had a divine mission. Day after day he had further impulses from on high that he was called upon to cure the ague also. In the course of time he extended his powers to the curing of epilepsy, ulcers, aches, and lameness. All the county of Cork was in a commotion to see this extraordinary physician, who certainly operated some very great benefit in cases where the disease was heightened by hypochondria and depression of spirits.[25]

Mackay's description differed only in tone from Greatrakes' own account of his awakening: "I had an impulse, or a strange perswasion in my own mind (of which I am not able to give any rational accounty to another) which did very frequently suggest to me that there was bestowed on me the gift of curing the King's Evil . . . whether I were in private or publick, sleeping or waking, still I had the same Impulse."[26]

When Jesus practiced healing he ran into trouble with church authorities and drew vast crowds of supplicants around him. The same problems afflicted Greatrakes. So great was his success that wherever he went, multitudes of infirm souls followed. They were so numerous that county magistrates expressed concern lest they infect local residents with their illnesses. From dawn to dusk Greatrakes laid hands on all who sought his help, and many claimed to be cured by his touch. Nevertheless, despite his successes and his description of himself as a mere instrument of God, the Church did not look upon him with favor. Finally, the Dean's Court forbade him to continue his laying on hands. But responsible only to a Higher Authority, Greatrakes stayed at his work.

His life presents a number of paradoxes. He almost never took a fee yet lived very well. Attacked by the church, this religious healer was defended by several prominent physicians. Though he cured by touch, in time his spittle and urine acquired healing powers. His glove was once successfully used to end a hysterical fit.

As to Greatrakes' technique, some detailed information has been preserved. One of his critics wrote that his cures required repeated touching sessions, that relapses were frequent, and that his strokes were useless once decay had set in. Still, he was credited with healing the blind, the deaf, and the cancerous. His techniques varied with the problems that confronted him. According to Laver:

> For pain, he used only his dry hand on the spot. For ulcers or running sores, he would first spit on his hand or finger. For scrofula, he stroked and then ordered poultices of boiled turnips applied until it came to a head; then he would lance and empty the swelling. He was able to draw out pain, to anesthetize limbs and to stop bleeding.[27]

Whatever Greatrakes' successes, the ever-doubting Mackay remained unconvinced: "Whether his pretensions were more or less absurd than some of his successors, who have lately made their appearance among us, would be hard to say."[28]

One of his successors gained a reputation as a healer that has lasted to this day; whenever someone says, "He mesmerized me," unconscious tribute is paid to the influence of Anton Mesmer. Mesmer was an eighteenth-century Viennese physician and promoter of the theory of animal magnetism. Just as twentieth-century physician Wilhelm Reich maintained that all nature was pervaded by orgone energy, Mesmer decreed that the universe was suffused with magnetic fluid. (And just to show that if you wait long enough all ideas will come around the wheel again, Milton Trager, yet *another* physician, holds that there is a universal electromagnetic force field that infuses all matter. Trager is alive and well and living in Hawaii.)[29]

Mesmer tried to proselytize his theories in Vienna and then Switzerland but encountered either resistance or, at best, sheer lack of interest. In 1778 he moved to Paris. This was a felicitous move, for within a short time he was all the rage there. Rich and poor, men and women—but especially women—flocked to his sumptuous home, fitted with stained-glass windows and mirrored walls, filled with the smell of incense and the sound of harps. It was here that the supplicants gathered, and here that they went into trances, convulsions, sobbing, laughter, and other altered states under Mesmer's hypnotic influence. Like most miraculous theories, his notion of a ubiquitous magnetic fluid was undoubtedly wrong, but his results were awesome. And touch was very much involved in the process.

Mesmer's healing sessions were group affairs. In the middle of the room was a *baquet*, a four-foot oval vessel that contained wine bottles filled with "magnetized" water. Water was poured into the vessel until the bottles were just covered, and iron filings were added from time to time to enhance the magnetism. The whole affair was then covered with an iron lid drilled through with holes. A rod, also of iron, was placed in each hole, and the patients applied these rods to the diseased or disordered parts of their bodies. They sat holding hands with one another and pressing knees tightly to facilitate the flow of magnetic fluid amongst them. From this point, Mackay's description cannot be improved upon:

> Then came in the assistant magnetisers, generally strong, handsome young men, to pour into the patient from their finger-tips fresh streams of the wondrous fluid. They embraced the patient between the knees, rubbed them gently down the spine and the course of the nerves, using gentle pressure upon the breasts of the ladies, and staring them out of countenance to magnetise them by the eye! All this time the most rigorous silence was maintained, with the exception of a few wild notes on the harmonica or the pianoforte, or the melodious voice of a hidden opera-singer swelling softly at long intervals. Gradually the cheeks of the ladies began to glow, their imaginations to become inflamed; and off they went, one after the other, in convulsive

fits. Some of them sobbed and tore their hair, others shrieked and screamed and yelled till they became insensible altogether.[30]

When the frenzy reached its peak, Mesmer himself made a dramatic entry. Dressed in a lilac-colored silk robe and holding a white "magnetic" rod, he cut a grand figure indeed. With his hands he stroked his patients' eyebrows and down their spine. With his wand he stroked their breasts and abdomen. In his presence the room grew quiet, the patients calm. Many reported experiencing streams of cold or burning vapor pass through them.

The fate of Mesmer and animal magnetism is worth pondering. At the height of his popularity, when all Paris buzzed with tales of his wondrous healing powers and intellectuals argued whether he was a quack, a benevolent genius, or the agent of the devil, Mesmer boldly challenged the Faculty of Medicine to examine his work. But he stipulated that the terms of reference should not include how the cures were produced, only whether they took place.

The Faculty refused to so limit the inquiry, and that, for a while, was that.

Mesmer then wrote to Marie-Antoinette, suggesting that as a token of appreciation of his work the French government should grant him lands and build him a chateau. The monarch's response was to offer Mesmer both great honors and a sizable pension if he would but communicate his discoveries to physicians nominated by the king. This he refused to do and instead rather suddenly left Paris "for his health."

It was beginning to look as though Mesmer had lost whatever faith he once had in his theory, a theory he was still espousing and indeed was teaching to French followers at considerable profit to himself. But if the master was becoming a skeptic, his most devoted follower, a physician named d'Eslon, was growing ever more true in his beliefs. He demanded an examination and got two; the first by the Faculty of Medicine and the second, by the *Académie des Sciences*. The former was composed of physicians, while on the latter sat the most eminent men in the country, including Anton Lavoisier and Ben Franklin. Mesmer always found reason not to present himself to the commission though d'Eslon both attended and demonstrated magnetic effects on the body.

After months of observation and experiment, the commission from

the *Académie* published its report. It was regarded as both impartial
and intelligent. The commissioners concluded that the only evidence
supporting the existence of animal magnetism was the effects it had
on patients, and that these same effects could be produced without
magnetism. Furthermore, the wand waving produced no effect if it
was done without the patient's knowledge. Therefore, the commission concluded, they were dealing with a mental not a magnetic
phenomenon.

With the publication of the report, Mesmer's reputation in Paris
plummeted, and he took the large sum of money he had managed to
save and left the country.

Reputations of individual healers may rise and fall, but belief in
miracles carries on. Why? Because they usually work. Most people
who look for miracles find them in one way or another. If you are not
physically healed, you find new peace. If you can't extend your life,
you come to terms with death. If you don't find a permanent cure,
well, at least you experienced one glorious moment of ecstatic tran-
scendence. Most miracles work, whether or not they are based on
delusion.

The question with which healers (and observers of healers) must
come to terms is whether the cure or the delusion is more important.
Does the recovery justify the lie that led to it? Should we abide by the
old Spanish proverb *Hagase el milagro y hagalo Mahoma*—"Let the
miracle be done, though Mahomet do it?" Let us debate the issue.

You take the affirmative—it's the results that count, not the way
they are achieved. But then what if the cure is only in the eye of the
beholder? What if the condition remains the same, and the patient
only thinks, i.e., suffers the delusion, he is cured? It happens all the
time.

In fact, we need not start our debate there; still more extreme
examples exist. Let us begin with a case in which the patient, her
family, and outside observers all agree that there has been no cure,
but the healer remains unshaken in his belief that there has. This is
not fiction—the healer was Anton Mesmer, the time was the late
1770s, the place was Vienna, and the patient was Maria Therasia
Paradis. Mesmer was at the time ambitiously trying to build his
reputation in a city where, on an earlier visit, he had been scorned by
his medical colleagues. He found a patient on whom he could demonstrate his powers and set to work. Here is Mackay's account of what
happened:

He undertook to cure a Mademoiselle Paradis, who was quite blind, and subject to convulsions. He magnetized her several times, and then declared that she was cured; at least, if she was not, it was her fault and not his. An eminent oculist of that day, named Barth, went to visit her, and declared that she was as blind as ever; while her family said that she was as much subject to convulsions as before. Mesmer persisted that she was cured. Like the French philosopher, he would not allow facts to interfere with his theory. He declared that there was a conspiracy against him; and that Mademoiselle Paradis, at the instigation of her family, feigned blindness in order to injure his reputation![31]

Since Mesmer's reputation as a charismatic charlatan has always rivaled his reputation as a charismatic healer, it may be worth recalling that Sigmund Freud once accused a patient of dreaming the wrong sort of dream in order to disprove *his* theory. ("The dream showed that I was wrong. *Thus it was her wish that I might be wrong, and her dream showed that wish fulfilled.*")[32]

In the case of Mesmer we can probably agree that the word of the patient, her family, and the oculist should be taken and that of the healer dismissed. But what of those times in which both patient and healer agree that there has been a cure while family and expert are just as certain that there has not? This is common after religious conversion, particularly when a cult is involved that yanks its new members away from their family roots. When the family has also joined the cult, it gets even trickier. Patient, family, and all their new friends may agree that a miraculous healing has taken place, leaving the poor doctor to mutter that his patient is just as blind as before.

This is just the situation that prevailed in Greatrakes' day. Its effects on nonbelievers and the quandary in which it placed them were described in the *Miscellanies of St.-Evremond*, published in 1665:

So great was the confidence in him, that the blind fancied they saw the light which they did not see—the deaf imagined that they heard—the lame that they walked straight, and the paralytic that they had recovered the use of their limbs. An idea of health made the sick forget for a while their maladies; and imagination, which was not less active in those merely drawn by curiosity than in the sick, gave a false view to the one class, from the desire of seeing, as it operated a false cure on the other from the strong desire of being healed. Such was the power of the Irishman over the mind, and such was the influence of the mind upon the body. Nothing was spoken of in London but his prodigies; and these prodigies were supported by such great authorities, that the bewildered multitude believed them almost without examination, while more enlightened people did not dare to reject them from their own knowledge. The public opinion, timid and enslaved, respected this imperious and, apparently, well-authenticated error. Those who saw through the delusion kept their opinion to themselves, knowing how useless it was to declare their disbelief to a people filled with prejudice and admiration.[33]

You were saying that results alone are important, but it appears that results can be spurious. Maybe you got the wrong side in the debate. Try the other position, that a cure based on delusion is likely to be a false cure. And now I must ask you who is better qualified than the sufferer to determine whether a cure has taken place. The oculist? Medical arrogance! The family? They have experienced neither the suffering nor the relief. No, surely it must be the person herself who knows best.

On the other hand, if a blind patient swears she has been healed but still can't read the eye chart and stumbles over your desk on her way out, has a cure really taken place?

These are questions that must be raised and considered, but not necessarily answered. For whatever conclusion one comes to, the opposite can be argued just as persuasively. It is the consideration of the issue that is important, for it is that which offers protection against delusion and deception. To understand how, let us ponder for a moment the nature of truth.

Mesmer: "The nature of truth? What does truth have to do with healing those who suffer? When you are dealing with people's pain, young man, truth is irrelevant. The only matter of importance is discovering and using what works. Animal magnetism, dream analysis, Laetrile, touch, Tarot cards or the moss from a hanged thief's head—the remedy is truth to the afflicted."

Seeker after truth: "When cures are based on delusion, crimes, too, can be so based. Along with religious healing has come religious torture and murder. The number of women who were slowly burned to death for drying up the neighbor's cow or souring the milk probably exceeds the number healed through magnetism or the royal touch. A searcher for truth would not be so easily deluded nor act with such depravity."

Mesmer: "Searcher for truth, is it? Have you not yet learned that the search for truth is a snipe hunt, an illusion? What was taught as modern medicine 100 years ago is today seen as quaint at best, and deadly more often. Do you really think today's 'truths' will be regarded any differently 100 years from now?"

Seeker: "No, not at all. But last century's truth was the best they had to offer then; ours today is the same. I do not believe that it is within our power to grab hold of the truth and keep it true forever, but we do have the power to search for it actively."

Mesmer: "Still searching, eh? This truth for which you so earnestly—so touchingly—scour the earth would be, if you ever chanced to stumble over it, disastrous. The surgeon, the internist, the psychologist, the *healer* who limits himself to what he knows to be true will have little to say, less to do, and in a very short time, not a patient left on whom to practice it."

Seeker: "You're talking about facts, not truth. And what you say about them is true. We cannot limit ourselves to known facts, but we can strive to minimize our delusions about them. And, Dr. Mesmer, we can certainly avoid lying about them, either to ourselves or to our patients."

Mesmer: "Avoid lying—how noble. How charming. How stupid. Seeker, have you not heard of the placebo? How many studies, double-blind trials, and experiments will it take to convince you that half the power of the healers of your own age comes from placebo? Have you read nothing in the last decade? Let me recommend *The Silent Pulse* by G. B. Leonard[34] or *Mind as Healer, Mind as Slayer* by Kenneth Pelletier[35] as catch-up reading."

Seeker: "How do you define placebo?"

Mesmer: "The patient's delusion swallowing the doctor's lie. In tablets."

Seeker: "The study of the placebo is part of the search for truth. From what combination of attitudes and needs does the placebo gain its strength? Does a white coat enhance it as much as a lavender robe? Does touching the patient add to its power? If so, what kind of touch, where, and at what point in the interview?"

Mesmer: "You are searching for something that does not exist. Give it up!"

Seeker: "No. We search for truth not because we are suddenly going to find it because the act of searching helps steer us away from the extremes of madness and badness. The Inquisition was the search given up."

Mesmer: "Your age hasn't been exactly free of such purges."

Seeker: "We're talking about staying honest with ourselves, not about ages. Yes, we've had our share of inquisitions all right, from the master race to the red menace."

Mesmer: "And have you false cures today as well?"

Seeker: "Oh yes. Just look at the psychic surgeons of the Philippines. Thousands have made the pilgrimage to Manila to have chicken entrails pulled out of a crease in their abdomen. After a week or so of such tricks, they come back healed."

Mesmer: "Ah. Healed."

Seeker: "They *feel* healed. That is important. And the fervent desire for health, the expensive journey, the mystery of it all may indeed relieve pain or lift depression or calm an agitated soul. But when the claim is made that through spiritual power one can open the body with a hand instead of a scalpel, when the healer swears it is diseased organs, not chicken parts, he's removing, when the cure depends on sleight of hand—then not only is the truth lost, but with it the search for truth, and the door has been opened to exploitation, madness, and evil."

Mesmer: "Madness—like truth—is in the eye of the beholder. You are from what is supposed to be an enlightened age (though I have yet to see an age which does not consider itself so). But perhaps you've slept through it. Have you not heard of the idea of cultural relativity? It applies to healing as much as anything else. Read *The Mind Game* by E. Fuller Torrey. You'll discover that psychiatrists and witch doctors perform the same function and use almost the same techniques. The one is not more scientific, nor the other more magic-ridden. The psychiatrist comes from a culture that believes disorders come from wicked parents; witch doctors, from one that believes they stem from wicked spirits. Neither theory has an edge on the truth, and they both work. Sufferers visit a psychiatrist who tells them they harbor bad feelings about their parents, whereupon they feel better. Sufferers visit a witch doctor who tells them they are haunted by the spirit of an ancestor, whereupon they feel better. Which is truth, oh Seeker, and which is delusion?"

Seeker: "Listen, Mesmer. If you're still talking about "truth" over *here* and "illusion" over *there*, you're missing the point. They're both affected by time and place. Introjected parents are closer to the truth in New York, and unappeased spirits are closer to the truth in Nairobi. But neither is the ultimate, eternal truth in either place. Psychiatrists *and* witch doctors sometimes get stuck in their own orthodoxies, but neither of them has to. Both can—and often do—continue the search for a better truth."

Mesmer: "How 'better'?"

Seeker: "A better truth? One that accounts for more facts; one that heals more people or just more effectively; one that welcomes new information and adapts to new findings. There's an ancient prayer which goes:

> From the cowardice that shrinks from new truth,
> From the laziness that is content with half-truths,
> From the arrogance that thinks it knows all truth,
> O God of Truth, deliver us."

Mesmer: "How sweet to end your discourse on truth on a religious note. Is the Bible, too, your source of truth?"

Seeker: "Look everywhere, Mate. The Bible, *The Interpretation of Dreams, New Age,* even animal magnetism. There's some truth and a lot of illusion in all of it. But since you're so scornful of biblical truths, let me rest my case with a quote from a children's book. It's from *The Chestry Oak,* by Kate Seredy.

> For yesterday and for all tomorrows,
> we dance the best we know."[36]

# The Age of
# Miracles
# Hasn't Passed

9

Just because the troops are marching in step doesn't mean they're going in the right direction.

> —Jim Moody

Yes, Virginia, miraculous healings still exist, and touch still plays a major role in their occurrence. In fact, miracles today are very little changed from those that astonished onlookers in Mesmer's Paris apartment, in Greatrakes' stately home, or beside the dusty roads trod by the apostles. Features common to healing miracles, ancient and modern, include the following:

The supplicant feels a great need for change;
The healer has a reputation for extraordinary powers;
An event that defies the laws of nature precedes the healing;
The healing technique is a mysterious one.

These are the features that prepare the way for change. Need and reputation join forces to create both the expectation that change is possible and the hope that it can be brought about by the healer. The miraculous event "proves" that a healing miracle can be performed; it heralds the main event. And the mystifying form of the healing technique carries its own power in the world of the miraculous.

There are also adjuncts to the healing process that are nearly the same today as in times gone by. They are frequently, but not always, part of the event, and they serve to enhance the inherent power of the situation. Included among them are:

A group, to increase pressure and add encouragement,
A relic, to give tangible form to the miracle,
A shared, irrational belief system, usually of a religious nature, and
Highly charged emotions in the supplicant and in the onlookers as well.

In addition, physical touch plays a role in miraculous healing as much in our day as it did in Mesmer's. It often serves as the immediate stimulus to the actual event; the signal, perhaps, that a miracle is about to begin. A current example will demonstrate how very few have been the changes over the centuries.

Father Ralph DiOrio is pastor of St. John's Catholic Church in Worcester, Massachusetts. Some years ago he felt the call to charismatic healing and answered it; today he draws ever-increasing crowds to his Thursday and Sunday healing services as his reputation spreads throughout the Eastern seaboard. This reputation is built on his prowess not only as a healer but also as a "slayer in the Lord." With a look or a touch, Father DiOrio is able to induce swooning in his own congregants and among those who have made the pilgrimage to Worcester.

The healing services last for hours, during which an air of hopeful expectation slowly grows into barely contained excitement. After a long preliminary period, the priest turns his back to the parishioners and the congregation begins to pray. Suddenly DiOrio's voice interrupts the prayer—"I see a woman in a white beaded blouse . . . I think there's a gold chain . . . there's a respiratory problem . . . I see her chest area . . . there's perhaps a spot of cancer . . ."

A woman's wail breaks out from one of the pews. To the fascinated onlookers, the priest announces, "There's been a healing. Thank you, Jesus."[1]

A skeptic will note that:

(a) Father DiOrio spent the long preliminary period among the congregants and may have actually seen the beaded blouse before he had a vision of it, and

(b) When there was no response to "respiratory problem" (which is a nice broad category to start with, particularly if the woman has been coughing and wheezing), he changed his preliminary diagnosis to cancer, of which,

(c) "There's perhaps a spot," a diagnosis tentative and ambiguous enough to tap the fears of many, many people, and finally,

(d) Apart from one anonymous wail, there is no evidence of either accurate diagnosis, proper identification of the sufferer or, indeed, a healing of any kind.

But there's much more to it than that. The people there *felt* that they had witnessed a healing, just as in the days of the apostles. There was an emotional wail, just as in Mesmer's practice. And someone may have *felt* healed, just as did Greatrakes' patients, whether or not there actually was a spot of cancer and whether or not it actually went away.

Yes, but if she didn't actually have cancer, wasn't it a false healing? Oh. We're back to that.

If the woman who shrieked thought she had cancer but did not, and after the healing thought she no longer did, was that a false healing or a true one? If she really did have cancer before and still had it after, but before the service was incapacitated with worry, fear, and self-absorption, whereas afterward she felt relieved enough to return to the pleasures of an active life, was *that* a true healing? If she had cancer before but did not have it after, like the 15 percent of the population who spontaneously recover from this particular type of cancer, was that a true healing? If she had cancer before, showed no sign of it after, but the symptoms returned after ten years, was *that* a true healing? How about after ten days?

The "true" answer to any of these questions will not be found in a yes or a no. A better way to sort out the complexities of healing is to look upon it as a multi-level phenomenon rather than as a yea or nay proposition. I divide healing into six levels: one for healing the well plus five for healing the sick.

*Level One* (Healing the well)
Imagined recovery from an imagined disorder.

Father DiOrio provides an unwitting example of this when he describes his first experience as a miraculous healer. A woman rushes into his service and shrieks that her husband is "bleeding inside his stomach." She demands that DiOrio pray over him. When he does, the man falls to the floor and says, "I feel great. My ulcer doesn't seem to be bleeding any more. Hallelujah!"[2]

The literature of faith healing is filled with such tales. No evidence is offered of either a real disorder or a real cure. No outside opinion is sought, and no follow-up undertaken. Yet this form of "healing" maintains its popular appeal year after year, generation after generation. It is in vogue these days to attribute the appeal of faith healers, spiritualists, and quacks to the failure of an ever-more impersonal medical profession to provide tender loving care to its patients. I have always shared this view, but, after examining the depth and breadth of the phenomenon, I now think that doctors' failures only account for part of it. Another part of the appeal is that large numbers of people are strongly attracted to the irrational. For them, absence of verifying evidence, of logic, of demonstrable results, of plain common sense is not a liability—it is a powerful asset.

### Level Two

A real disorder remains, but the feelings and attitudes that surround it change.

A woman whose vision is deteriorating has lost 90 percent of her sight, and she considers herself blind. At a revival meeting she has hands laid on her and experiences an overwhelming sensation of healing. The experience has a profound influence on her attitude toward her condition. Now she thanks God every morning for the 10 percent of sight she has left instead of cursing him for the 90 percent that is gone. Although there has been no physical improvement whatsoever, her life has dramatically changed. She is active in her church, does volunteer work at the hospital, attends plays, and re-enters life in more positive ways than before her condition developed.

### Level Three

Real but temporary improvement in the disorder.

This is also common in revival meeting healings. The desire (perhaps "need" better describes it) to regain health, the charisma of the healer, and the excitement of the crowd give the sufferer the strength to throw away his crutches. But by the next day or the next month, that strength ebbs as the memory fades. Surgeon William Nolen followed up a number of such cases in *Healing: A Doctor in Search of a Miracle.* Invariably, a night of joyous release was followed by return to the wheelchair, the ecstasy replaced by resignation and gloom. Nolen's reaction may be seen in his description of the girl with the withered leg who limped onto the stage holding her brace after healer Kathryn Kuhlman had called for someone with a brace to, "Take it off, come to the stage and claim your cure." Nolen writes:

> The scene was, to my mind, utterly revolting. This young girl had a withered leg, the result of polio. It was just as withered now as it had been ten minutes earlier, before Kathryn Kuhlman called for someone to remove her brace. Now she stood in front of ten thousand people giving praise to the Lord—and indirectly to Kathryn Kuhlman—for a cure that hadn't occurred and wasn't going to occur. I could imagine how she'd feel the next morning, or even an hour later, when the hysteria of the moment had left her and she'd have to again put on the brace . . .[3]

Weatherhead has recorded how the temporarily healed feel the next morning. A British Ph.D. suffering from chronic encephalitis attended a nighttime healing service in Liverpool. After the sermon the pastor went into the audience and began laying on hands. Here is how the recipient of the healing described the experience:

> After enquiring about the nature of the complaint, he laid his hand on my right temple and prayed fervently. I then felt what can only be described as a current of healing power pass from him to me. As a result, I could walk a few steps without limping and the tremor ceased. He then asked was I cured, and, on receiving my reply in the affirmative, asked me to repeat, "Thank you, Jesus." This, I am ashamed to say, I did. He then proclaimed my cure to the meeting. The effect, however, soon wore off. I estimated a period of about five minutes before the limp returned. The tremor, however, was absent, and I remained free of it even at breakfast next morning. I repeat I was quite detached and had no emotional feelings whatever beyond curiosity. I cannot explain the temporary cure, but I have heard

of similar cases, in one of which a patient suffering from diabetes was cured temporarily.[4]

Another case reported by Weatherhead involved a young woman parishioner who suffered from lameness. During an emotion-filled healing ceremony she walked on crutches to the stage where the preacher layed hands on her and told her to believe she was healed and could walk unaided. Enormously excited, she did what is done in these situations and threw away her crutches. She made it back to her seat without them and continued to walk unaided for three weeks. Then she began to limp and finally collapsed, returning both to her crutches and to her former condition.[5]

*Level Four*
Curing: physical healing by physical means.

Surgery for appendicitis, massage for cramp, aspirin for headache: at first glance this appears to be a level without controversy. But when you begin to look at life stress as a causal agent, positive attitude as a healing agent, and placebo effects as a confounding agent, the apparent simplicity of it all quickly disappears.

*Level Five*
Emotional strengthening/social improvement.

These are the psychological therapies. They include psychotherapy, family therapy, social-skills training, relaxation and meditation.

*Level Six* (Extraordinary healing)
Dramatic improvement or reversal of a disorder that defies explanation in ordinary terms.

Though it is usually called miraculous healing, I am reluctant to attribute the improvement to divine intervention. There is also a difference between defying explanation and defying nature—as I have said, you may have a broken arm healed at Lourdes but no one there has ever grown a new one. And while the healing process may defy explanation, the conditions that lead up to it are, as already described, often highly stereotyped, little different today from earlier ages. In the following observations of Father DiOrio by the American journalist Donald Gropman, note the build-up of emotion, the religious atmosphere, the anticipation of "miraculous" events— even the latter-day relic.

> It was a curious mixture of emotion and technology, spontaneity and choreography, God and show-business. . . . Some of the trappings—the small pieces of polyester knit that his attendants handed out as "prayer cloths," the prolonged testing of the sound system, the anticipated faintings of the members of his ministry as he blessed them—were jarring notes. But the air of hope, the emotional release that seemed to be found by the people DiOrio touched, made the experience moving and worthwhile to us.[6]

Mesmer would have been proud.

Reading about polyester prayer cloths and mass swoonings, one might be drawn to two conclusions. The first is that only the simple, the gullible and the naïve would fall for such far-fetched claims and show-biz techniques. The second is that these miracles are the last dying vestige of another age. Both these conclusions are logical, and both are wrong.

Let me correct the first, first. During the course of preparing this book I have encountered people smarter, wiser, and more experienced than I who firmly believe absolutely outrageous healing tales. I have met others who for me epitomize the wisdom of age who, if they do not fully believe, accept them as "probably" true. Believers I have met include scientists and ministers, the hip and the naïve, psychiatrists and surgeons. For an example of a surgeon-believer, read either *A Doctor's Thoughts on Healing*[7] or *Surgery of the Soul*,[8] both by William Standish Reed. "No Cures Without Jesus," is his overriding principle of medical practice. I have met a general practitioner who thought that he and other Transcendental Meditators were responsible for diverting a hurricane from the capital of New Zealand. I have listened to an Australian psychiatrist explain that his wife can influence the laws of chance with her thoughts. I have lunched with an American minister-psychologist who *knows* that his broken neck was healed in Iowa by a prayer said for him in Philadelphia.

As for the second conclusion, that modern miracles are a last vestige of the past, I think not. We are now in the midst of our own golden age of miracles. And new believers turn up in the most unexpected places. I was deeply saddened to read that my own personal candidate for a Nobel prize, Dr. Elizabeth Kübler-Ross, has joined the miracle rush-hour crowd. She is a Swiss-born psychiatrist and the author of *On Death and Dying*,[9] one of the most valuable, perception-changing, influential books written in our time. Through it, Kübler-Ross helped my wife and me nurse my grandmother at home through her last days of life. I feel intellectually enriched, emotionally expanded, and personally indebted to her. But now she is talking to ghosts under the guidance of a self-ordained minister and miraculous healer who is either having it off with the women of his flock or has found a way to bring "entities" back to earth for both social *and* sexual intercourse. This Zombie's Jamboree takes place at a luxurious ranch which Kübler-Ross has helped finance. Jackovitch quotes the ghost-coital question raised by one who was there: "How is it that an entity, a pure spirit, has cigarette breath?"[10] Elizabeth Kübler-Ross replies to critics by first acknowledging that some think she has lost her marbles, "But I'm convinced that what I am sharing is verifiable. I would not risk my reputation if I were not 100 percent sure."

Wake up, Lizzie! Listen to your own words! There is little in this world, less in psychiatry, and less still in the world of fornicating ghosts about which you can be 100 percent sure. Back off, take a vacation, go to the mountains. We need you too much down on the ground to lose you to astral travel and sexy spirits. Come back home.

Kübler-Ross's performing ghosts are an example of the kind of magical event that so often precede a miraculous healing. A Philippine healer performs his sleight of hand and then pronounces the cure. A Mexican medium makes his magic and *then* gives down-to-earth advice. A California general practitioner writes a prescription for sugar pills or Valium before telling his patient to stop working so hard. It is the magic that gives power to the common sense that follows. It is his ability to perform that magic that gives the healer's words a power all out of keeping with their actual meaning. They may be the same words the patient's brother-in-law has always told him but, coming from one endowed with the status of healer, their effect is transformed. For a demonstration of this effect, listen to any radio preacher or catch the Oral Roberts show on T.V.

Oral Roberts also provides a rare example of bringing the healing touch to the electronic age. After a career as one of America's most successful faith healers on the revival-tent circuit, Roberts took his talents to television. On his widely viewed weekly program, he asks sufferers to make contact with him by touching their television screen.

People—electronic age people—raise themselves from their E-Z-Loungers, shuffle their slippers over to the Sony, and place their fingers on the TV screen.

While we were working together stacking a truckload of hay, one of my Vermont neighbors told me that his mother swears that her piles were cured in just this way. He stopped between bales and looked thoughtful, in the manner of Vermont story-tellers. Then he continued. "The only thing I kin figger is that [another thoughtful pause] is that she musta accidentally sat on the antenna."

Yes, Virginia, the healing touch (miraculous variety) is alive and well in the age of technology.

Which brings us to Dolores Krieger, Ph.D., R.N. Dr. Krieger is a physiologist, a professor, and a nurse, but she is best known as a hands-on (well, almost on) healer. She is the author of *Therapeutic Touch: How to Use Your Hands to Help or Heal*,[12] and she has trained more than 5,000 health workers in the use of her method. The method consists of the practitioner moving her hands along the patient's body looking for parts that are out of kilter. The hands never actually touch the body but are held about four inches above the skin. Once the area of disturbance is found, the practitioner places her hands on it, or, more often, just above it. But, Dr. Krieger cautions, "Therapeutic touch is not just putting your hands over a painful area nor is it a massage to loosen muscles. You have to be taught to concentrate and direct your healthy energy to get proper results."[13]

Therapeutic Touch consists of five stages. To begin with, the healer centers herself, achieving a state of relaxed concentration. Then she makes an assessment of the healee's (Krieger's term) "field," the invisible aura that, according to Krieger, both surrounds us and reveals our state of well-being. Next, the healer "unruffles" the field at its rough spots by waving motions of her hands in the air. The fourth step is either rearranging the healee's energy or directing the healer's own energy into him. The final stage is knowing when to stop.

Krieger frequently and explicitly states that her method is not miraculous. But it most certainly is. In fact, Therapeutic Touch is a modern-day classic of a miracle. It includes an inexplicable event in the form of the mysterious diagnosis and treatment of the invisible field. It works in mysterious ways, with the healer's hand not quite touching the healee's body but relying instead on some form of energy transfer. The traditional relic even puts in an appearance in the form of a bit of "magnetized" cotton that assumes the healing powers of the one who magnetized it. And as if that were not enough miracles, Krieger has moved on from Therapeutic Touch to telepathy, body dowsing, and psychokinesis.

Dr. Krieger is by no means the only healer operating today who uses a non-touching touch. Those who practice Mahikari, or True Light, use their hands in almost identical fashion to Therapeutic Touchers despite the vastly different origins of the two movements. Mahikari began at five o'clock on a February morning in 1959 when Mr. Yoshikazu Okada, a Tokyo businessman, had a revelation that if he were to hold up his hand he could purify the world. He did so, and—like Greatrakes and DiOrio—at once began healing all manner of disorders and diseases. From Japanese miracles to international ones, Mahikari grew, and the movement now has offices in North and South America, Europe, New Zealand, and all over Australia.

Mahikari promises to cure everything from hepatitis to bad grades, to make plants grow and keep dogs from biting, to purify food and improve sex. And it is all done by a three-day course, a "divine pendant," and some by now familiar hand work. The healer simply holds his hand about a foot behind the supplicant's head and various parts of the body. He maintains that position for about ten minutes, and several such sessions are usually required for healing to occur. What sounds like a Japanese chant of exorcism marks the end of each session.

I had the Mahikari miracle worked on me by one of the international leaders of the movement but, alas, I never saw the Light. Neither did I feel any different at the end of the session from the way I felt at the beginning, and I found the healer's reasoning disappointing, his case histories unconvincing, and the members far from enlightened. But just in case you are picturing this healer as some slavering buffoon, let me hasten to report that he is in fact a highly regarded, widely published neurophysiologist who got caught up in miracles while a visiting professor in Japan. Like Dr. Krieger, he is far from an intellectual slouch.

I think I have made it clear that I do not regard polyester prayer cloths, divine pendants, and magnetized cotton as dancing the best we know. But I also want it clear that I think Dolores Krieger has made some important contributions to the practice of helping and healing. She has brought touch consciousness into a university nurses' training program and given permission to those already engaged in nursing practice to lay hands on patients. Both are steps toward legitimizing the healing touch, and for that I applaud her.

Perhaps it is because she has one foot in the miraculous world and the other in the halls of science that Dr. Krieger posits possible scientific explanations for her miraculous touch. She speaks of "electron transfer resonance" and wonders whether healers might be altering enzyme activity and oxygen levels. John Thie, author of *Touch for Health*, also tries on scientific-sounding explanations, arguing that his touch works by affecting "neuro-lymphatic and neuro-vascular points" in the body.[14] This nod to science is one thing that distinguishes late-twentieth century miracles from those of earlier ages. But one who gives considerably more than a perfunctory nod toward science is psychologist Bernard Grad.

Grad is at Montreal's McGill University. For a number of years he has specialized in studying miraculous healers under scientific conditions. In one of his studies a well-known healer placed his hands above and below a cage of mice for a period of 15 minutes, twice a day. The mice, and those in a control group, were fed a diet deficient in iodine and were dosed with chemicals that interfere with the absorption of iodine by the thyroid gland. This diet and dosing combination quickly leads to goiter, the enlargement of the thyroid gland, and both the treated and control group mice did develop the disease. But the thyroids of the group in the cage that the healer held grew significantly slower than those of the controls. In other words, without even touching the mice, the healer's hands appeared to offer them some protection against a purely physical disorder.

Then, adding wonder upon wonder, Grad devised a second experiment in which the same healer got similar results, this time without even touching the *cage*. In this experiment he merely held wool and cotton cuttings in his hands. They were then placed in the experimental group's cage while the control mice had to make do with cuttings that were not pre-healed. Again, the thyroid glands of the treated mice grew significantly more slowly than did those of the control group. Grad concludes, ". . . the simplest explanation would seem to be that there is a life force emanating from the hands of people, probably more in some than in others."[15]

When confronted with a conclusion like this, one has to decide whether to accept the evidence as it stands or to reject it. If the latter choice is made, the reasons for the rejection should be made explicit. I am one who does not accept the evidence. I can argue that the experiment needs replication, that there may have been cheating (as has proved true in a number of other scientific studies of miraculous, or paranormal, events), or that the experimenter effect (the researcher manages to find what he was looking for) was operating. But in truth, I reject the evidence because I do not believe it. It goes against my experience of the world and contrary to my experience with healers who claim effects that I just cannot see. I do not believe it.

In another of Grad's experiments, a beaker of salt water was held ("treated") for half an hour by three different people. One was "psychiatrically normal," and the other two were seriously depressed. In a control condition, the beaker was not held by anyone. The "treated" and untreated water was poured over soil containing barley seeds that were then oven-dried and watered from the tap. As the seedlings appeared they were counted and measured. The plants that grew from the solution held by the normal subject were taller and more numerous than either those held by the depressed subjects or the unheld control plants. However, except for two days of the experiment (days 12 and 15) the height difference was not statistically significant, and at no time did the difference in numbers reach statistical significance. Yet despite this very limited support for the healing hypothesis, Grad concludes, "Thus, the prediction that the healer's plants would grow significantly faster than the others was supported by the results."[16] He goes on to say, "In short, it would appear that a positive mood while treating bottles favors a change in the solution which leads to a stimulation of cell growth as compared to other solutions not held by anybody or held by persons in the depressed state." This is not good enough. Grad's enthusiasm for the miraculous has apparently led him to overstated and unlikely conclusions based on very limited data of minimal statistical significance.

Furthermore, his conclusions are not in keeping with ordinary experience of the world. Take my neighbor Alf, for instance. Old Alf hates dogs with a passion only exceeded by his hatred of foreigners. He is depressed and cantankerous and has been for years. Yet he is without doubt the best gardener I know. His peas and beans dwarf those of happier and more "psychologically normal" neighbors on either side of him. He could grow barley seeds in gasoline, but his sour face would stop a clock. I've known too many Alfs to trust Grad's results.

There is one other thing. Whenever scientific experiments whose results support the miraculous are subjected to rigorous investigation, they are invariably shown to be faulty. Either bad design, self-delusion, or downright fraud accounts for the findings. This has been true of the very best psychic experiments in England, Russia, and the United States. Data have been fudged, foolproof mechanisms fooled with, impartial scientists taken in by magicians' tricks. (If you want to learn how these tricks are done, see *The Psychology of the Psychic*, written by David Marks and Richard Kamman and published in 1980 by Prometheus Books.)

For a recent example of such trickery, have a look at the banner headline in the October 23, 1979 *Star*: "Faith Healer Stuns Scientists by Controlling Growth of Deadly Bacteria." Under "strictly" controlled conditions at a radiation laboratory of the University of California, "one of America's most respected faith healers," Dr. Olga Worrall, had "amazed" scientists by controlling the growth of *Salmonella typhimurium* by the laying on of hands.

The experiment was very similar to Grad's plant work, and the scientists who testified to the accuracy of the claims were named in the article, including "Professor Elizabeth Rauscher, a physicist of the Nuclear Division" of the laboratory.

But Elie Shneour, a scientist from the laboratory who was not named, read the article and investigated its claims. The results? First, no such experiment ever took place there. Second, no one named Elizabeth Rauscher ever worked there.[18]

Extraordinary healing comes from need, hope, and determination, not from Jesus, magnetic fluid, the water of Lourdes, or a handful of cotton. The effect may be helped along by a relic or sleight of hand, but it is produced by the sufferer. A relationship is a great aid to healing, both ordinary and extraordinary, and skin-to-skin contact is a powerful ally to a healing relationship.

For me, the power of touch to help and heal is in itself miraculous. True, it is an everyday, ordinary sort of miracle, completely understandable in the material world, a violator of no physical laws. But that only makes it more miraculous, since it is equally available to the simple and the sophisticate, to the atheist and the Christian, to

the earthy and the ethereal. It is fine just as it is. And it is that
ordinary miracle that I am giving away here.

With this plain miracle of healing both free and abundant, why
then have so many insisted on gussying it up with a miraculous
miracle? There are at least three explanations.

For one, many people are drawn to the foreign and exotic; wealthy
Japanese businessmen impress their friends with Mustangs and real
Kodak cameras while Yanks sip Dom Perignon and wear Chanel.
Something as available as the palm of your hand does not offer much
in the way of exotica. Some have added the extra spice of mystery by
conjuring up life lines and heart lines in the palm (see, for example,
*Hands—The Power of Hand Awareness* by Bernard Korman);[19]
others by adding a four-inch miracle-gap between the hand and the
part it is supposed to be touching.

Second, the ability to perform miracles is the traditional test the
healer must pass before being endowed by his patient with the power
to heal him. Psychic healers in the Philippines do it with sleight of
hand and chicken entrails, Father DiOrio with swooning, Dr.
Krieger with non-touching touch. Those four inches of air between
the healer's hands and the healee's skin is the leap of faith upon which
the Krieger miracle is based.

The third reason people seek healing miracles is that some suffer
from conditions it would take a miracle to heal. Having made the
doctor circuit, having gone the health food and exercise route, they
still have an incurable disease and are still unwilling to face death.
Perhaps it would be better were they simply to acknowledge that the
end of life was approaching, but the wish for a reprieve—even a
miraculous reprieve—is understandable to most of us poor mortal
souls, hoping to postpone the shuffle-off just a little bit longer.

But those are extraordinary cases. For the most part, the gussied-
up miracle is not used for anything more unusual than relieving pain
or reducing anxiety—or curing a pulled back muscle. Krieger herself says: "Therapeutic Touch is noticeably useful for two things: It
elicits a rather profound, generalized relaxation response in the
healee, and it is very good at relieving pain."

She goes on: "It may come as a surprise that healing is not mentioned, since that is ostensibly a major purpose of Therapeutic Touch.
However . . . it must be acknowledged that it is the patient who heals
himself. The transfer of energy from the person playing the role of

healer is most usually little more than a booster until the patient's own recuperative system takes over."

And on: "At best, the healer accelerates the healing process."[20]

Given all this, why not just induce relaxation, relieve pain, and accelerate the healing process without bothering with the magic of Therapeutic Touch? The technique's proponents would undoubtedly answer, "Because it works."

Very well, let us assume that it works. Dr. Krieger, after all, is not the first healer to find invisible auras; she is one of a long line who work by the laying on of hands, or even the almost-laying-on of hands that she advocates; and this touching-without-touching is part of the long human history of healing miracles. So maybe it works.

But. If you are sick or troubled or in pain . . . if you long for human comfort . . . if you need contact with a helping person . . . if you require reassurance that this person is concerned for you . . . WOULD YOU RATHER BE TOUCHED, OR ALMOST-TOUCHED?

In short, Friend, other than so you can say you witnessed a miracle, why bother with the four-inch gap? Why not get the real thing?

Listen. Miracles are cheap. People have been getting rich and famous on healing miracles for as long as there has been trouble and pain. Jesus made his reputation on it. The apostles built Christianity on it. Greatrakes, Mesmer, Oral Roberts, Werner Erhard—if you know their names, it is because they can perform healing miracles. You can buy a healing miracle for under a dollar at your local *botanica* or from the neighborhood roots man.

*The real miracle is that by using hands and voice and eyes, we can help and heal each other.*

Try not-touching touching if you want. Try prayer if you like. Try Transcendental Meditation if you must. But in the end, try your ordinary, garden variety, hank-of-hair and piece-of-bone, jes' plain s e l f. The real miracle is that helping and healing are so common-place they go unnoticed until somebody pastes a bloody miracle on them.

## 10

# Touching and Doctoring

The healer I faith is someone I've gossipped and drunk with before I call him to touch me.

—W. H. Auden

In recent years there have been two major advances in medical education; one at the basic level, and the other, more advanced. The aim of both is (or, in some cases, should be) the rehumanizing and personalizing of what has come under ever-increasing fire as the mechanized, technologized, computerized practice of medicine. The basic level advance is the behavioral science course, and the advanced advance is the family medicine program. The former attempts to broaden the perspectives of future doctors, and the latter tries to turn out better family, *née* general, practitioners. The subjects covered in these courses range from poetry to medical economics, from interview skills to ethnic attitudes toward disease. Both behavioral science and family medicine represent the edge of a wedge cutting through what psychiatrist Harold Bourne has called "the corpse-centered medical curriculum." Yet even here there is little or no instruction in the art of the healing touch. Most of the texts used in these courses ignore completely the significance of touch, and those few that mention it do so only in passing.

This lack of interest in touch as a therapeutic skill pervades medical training, both in teaching and texts. I examined every book on the shelves of a major American medical school under the headings of doctor-patient relationship, interviewing, and medical examination. Not one contained any useful information about the meaning or value—or even the abuses—of touch. I have looked at medical curricula from the wild west of Australia to the British Isles, and nowhere have I been able to locate a course, or a significant section of a course, that attends to the subject. The one thing that medical practitioners consistently remember about their training in touching is the injunction not to do it.

There are exceptions. Some students are lucky enough in their later years at medical school to study under a clinician—usually an older man with many years of experience—who knows and understands the importance of touch in medical practice and is able to pass on that knowledge to future doctors.

They are lucky indeed, for the human touch is as important to doctoring as to any of the healing arts, and in one way it is vital. For medicine is one art that *requires* physical contact between healer and patient. There are very few branches of medicine that do not demand skin meeting skin at some point in the diagnostic or therapeutic process. The routine physical, the neurological examination, cardiac massage, dermatology, ophthalmology—all require physical contact of a precise nature between doctor and patient.

Surgery? Certainly. All right then, surgery under anesthetic? Yes, touch plays a role here too. The patient may be asleep during the operation, but both before and after she is in contact with the surgeon in whose hands she places herself. He will either reassure or frighten her, soothe or agitate her. The way he uses touch will help determine which it is to be.

Here's an example. Alan Clarke is Professor of Surgery at Otago Medical School in New Zealand. He is also a gifted and natural toucher. I spent a week following him through ward rounds, conferences with patients, and actual surgery in the operating theater. I noticed that in his pre- and postoperative bedside conversations he invariably managed to find a reason to lay one of his large hands on the patient. With one of them, a woman in her late forties, he slapped his hand on her thigh and said, "Well, Mavis, are you ready for surgery?"

She slapped her hand on *his* thigh and answered, "More to the point, Doctor—are you?"

The comfortable reciprocity in those two slaps told me that they were both ready.

It is not my intention in this chapter to give detailed instructions on the specific uses of touch for every medical subspecialty. That is a job best done by medical specialists in the training of their students. Instead, I shall try to point out uses of touch that are common to all of medicine by looking at selected aspects of a small number of specialties. Since family (or general) practice is the most all-encompassing, I'll begin there.

### Family Medicine

In the literature of medicine, there exists a special sort of article. It is the hail and farewell of a retiring doctor, often a GP, who is passing on his years of accumulated wisdom in what may be his first, and will almost certainly be his last, communication to colleagues through the medium of the medical journal. These living testaments offer advice to younger doctors, and sometimes that advice deals with the importance of touch in medicine. An excellent example is by P.N.K. Heylings, a Yorkshire general practitioner writing in the pages of the august *British Medical Journal*. He called his article "The No Touching Epidemic—An English Disease." True to the traditions of his profession, he began by listing the symptoms of the disorder:

> Its symptoms include a feeling of loneliness and abstraction from one's fellows. Morbid doubts of other people's loyalty, and feelings of insecurity. A fear of unpopularity; an inhibition of feelings. Unusual reaction to others when one is inadvertently touched. Guilt feelings on touching another person. Frigidity. Loss of tenderness and ability to comfort people in distress. A hesitancy and doubt when comforting people in pain. Fear of the dead bodies of blood relatives. Inability to comfort. A strange, inhibited and cold attitude to strangers and foreigners. Solitary toilet habits; a tendency to keep babies in their prams and young children glued to their desks. Antagonisms to physical forms of discipline. Dislike of the involvement of relatives in boxing or wrestling sports. Horror at the sight of courting couples. An inability to communicate with people standing nearby in public places and churches. A tendency for nurses to spend more and more time talking to each other in the side ward rather than tending patients. An antagonism to massage as a form of ther-

apy. Shyness and introversion. A tendency to divorce. An incomprehension of people's needs. Masturbation. Loss of interest in a tango; an exaggerated interest in no touch techniques in dancing. A preference for television rather than conversation.[1]

Dr. Heylings probably did not know it, but his description of No Touching as an English condition is supported by scientific study. In the mid-1960s the psychologist Sidney Jourard took his notebook into cafés throughout the world and recorded how many times per hour family members sitting at the same table touched one another. In San Juan, Puerto Rico, there were 180 touches per hour. In Paris there were 110. Gainesville, Florida, produced two touches per hour. In London, Jourard never made a mark in his notebook. Nobody touched.[2]

The number of times a doctor touches a patient depends on several factors aside from the country in which he practices. How long is the patient in the office? How far from each other do they sit? Is there a desk between them? Is the doctor garbed in a white coat? Does he employ a nurse to do his physical work for him?

Quantity is not the only measure of the effectiveness of a physician's touch; the quality of touch is at least as important. Is human contact always mediated through the steel of the stethoscope, the wood of the tongue depressor, or the rubber of the patella hammer? Does a surgical glove cover the skin of the doctor's hand? Is his touch fleeting or prolonged, rough or gentle, exciting or soothing? Does his touch convey interest in the patient, or does he handle her like a side of beef?

It is worth considering that Dr. Heylings thinks the remedy for the English Disease lies at least partly in the hands of the general practitioner. He writes:

> How do the older GPs, the real artisans, treat this disease? They take a patient's pulse, they pull his eyelids down to see if he is anaemic. They shine a torch into his mouth. They place a stethoscope down the dress or past the shirt buttons. They hold a patient's hand and say, "Now tell me what's wrong with you, dear." They open the door for the patients to go out. They shake hands and pat hands when the patient enters the surgery. They place a hand on the knee that hurts and the belly that spasms.

They pump the hand of a newly fledged father, and accept his cigar and drink his whisky. They sit in an old lady's arm chair and drink her tea. They use their ears to touch their conversation and thoughts, and a soft understanding voice to massage away their fears. They let each person know by tone of voice or action that they are welcome—that he knows they have problems or illnesses or they would not be in the surgery.[3]

Dr. Heylings concludes his article with a question that is both pointed and poignant. "How many of you reading this article," he asks, "can honestly say that they have used their hands in treating or comforting patients?"

Articles like Heylings' and conversations with elderly physicians reveal both awareness of the importance of touch in medicine and concern that younger doctors seem so blind to it. But this is puzzling. Did medical schools in days gone by really teach touch skills better than those today? Or is this a wisdom that has developed over years of practice? I suspect it is the latter. I have seen no evidence that teaching about human contact was better in the past, unless, perhaps, it was the very distant past. Certainly the many middle-aged doctors I've talked to agree that their training in the use of touch was, like their training in human sexuality, limited to a lecture on the dangers and evils that lurked there. And they also agree that they should have been taught more about both.

Many of them have learned on the job what they were not taught in med school—that touch plays a big part in their practice. And not just in the expected ways. One expects to gather information from the physical examination: the patella hammer, tongue depressor, and stethoscope are instruments that require physical contact in order to serve their functions, and most physicians know how to use their fingers as diagnostic instruments for palpating abdomens and the like. But something else frequently happens during the physical examination. A patient who has come to the doctor with a trivial complaint—a slight cold, an imaginary blemish, or a vague pain— will reveal the real reason for the visit only after the skin-to-skin contact of the examination. Only then does the depression, anxiety, or conflict emerge, often accompanied by tears of relief.

Some doctors never make the discovery. Most practitioners learn this function of touch over the years. But on-the-job training is paid for by the patients who arrive before the lesson is learned. Their pain may not be heard nor their fears elicited by the young doctor ignorant of the relationship between physical contact and self-revelation.

The power of the physical examination to elicit emotion-charged material is not confined to parts of the world where touch is readily accepted. From London, home of the No Touch Café, the general practitioner and medical educator Paul Freeling writes, "There have been a number of comments concerning the way family planning doctors in this country have found it easier to elicit from patients concerns about their sexual function, whilst examining them organically."

From another low-touch area, the South Island of New Zealand, comes an example; it is from the files of the family practitioner Ian St. George. A farmer in his mid-thirties called to make an appointment for a check-up, which in New Zealand (and many other places in the world outside the United States) is usually a signal of anxiety. But during the interview, he denied any anxiety in response to questions about family, job, and physical problems. He was then given a routine physical exam. As they sat down together after the physical, the doctor said he could find nothing physically wrong with him. But there was no need for more questions:

> He quite openly volunteered that while he was relieved to know he was physically OK, what he was really concerned about was that he was on the verge of bankruptcy. His farm just wasn't working out, and he'd been worried and sleepless about it. As he talked he came close to tears at times, and this was a pretty tough, strong farmer. I felt clearly that I had been able to demonstrate to him, probably through touching him, that he could trust me and that he could now talk about it.

On the basis of experiences like this, Dr. St. George has drawn several conclusions about the real role of the physical examination in general practice:

> If you examine people—and that means touching them—they'll often open out and tell you things that they quite clearly wouldn't have told you beforehand. Unfortunately, it's a lesson in scientific versus magic medicine. Scientifically, in half the people who come to see you there's really no need to examine them at

all, or at least no need to touch them. By looking down throats and asking questions you can be very clear of the diagnosis without touching people. But it's often important to do what might be called a therapeutic examination, or, more accurately, a trust-forming or relationship-cementing examination. This does involve touch. It tells your patient three things: a) that you're a proper doctor, b) that you can be trusted, and c) that you're not scared to have this sort of contact with people.

Dr. St. George's impression that 50 percent of general practice patients do not require a physical to diagnose their complaint is, if anything, conservative. In the United States there are about 200,000 visits per year to general or family practitioners. According to data collected by the National Ambulatory Medical Care Survey, in a scientific survey of visits to physicians' offices, only about half of these patients show objective evidence of physical pathology. This means of 100 patients walking into the office, only 50 will have an identifiable physical ailment. Of this 50, 35 will have a self-limiting disorder, an illness or injury which will get better by itself, with or without the doctor's treatment. Of the other 50 patients who come through the door—these are the ones without evidence of pathology— five will be there for administrative reasons (such as an insurance claim or a certificate of disability), and another ten for preventive measures (vaccination, contraception, diet advice). The remaining 35 seek help with life problems, usually of an emotional nature. One conclusion that can be drawn from this data is that *the majority of people who visit their family doctor want from him something he was not taught at medical school.*

If these patients are not coming for help with a physical problem, why then are they coming? A most interesting theory comes from one of America's leading medical educators, Dr. Lynn Carmichael, chairman of the University of Miami's Department of Family Medicine. His theory derives from a mixture of his own experience and the observations of scientists like Desmond Morris, author of *The Naked Ape*.[4] Carmichael says:

I rather suspect that the reason people seek the care of a physician has ancient origins and relates much more to our mammalian heritage than to a reasoned assessment of the benefits and hazards of modern medical care. Like other animals, humans come into the world defenseless and require the care of others to survive. This is true not only for infants, but for all ages. We go through life seeking purpose in being through relationships with others. It is not surprising that when problems arise, be they physical illness or emotional distress, we turn to others. This behavior is readily seen among primates and is referred to as social grooming. I think that our need as mammals for grooming, especially during periods of stress, is the major reason patients turn to physicians for care. This care is provided as it is in primates by physically touching the patient. The good doctor is a good groomer.[5]

In another paper, this one written with his wife, Joan, Carmichael describes one form this grooming-by-doctor might take. The paper also distinguishes patients who are streakers from those who are strokers:

> ... it is interesting to speculate that most interaction between the doctor and the patient is but a highly stylized form of social grooming. This has led us to speak of "stroking and streaking in health care"; the streakers being the 15 percent of patients that get all the attention from the medical model, and the strokers being the 85 percent who fill the waiting rooms of family physicians. No doubt touching the patient relieves stress and the reduction in stress results in less disease. Perhaps the "laying on of hands" is not merely folk-lore or mysticism. Reinstituting the back rub as standard hospital procedure may balance the introduction of the computerized axial tomography scanner. In the relational model, the good doctor is a good groomer.[6]

Dr. Carmichael is one who puts theory into practice. Not only does he make it a point to physically touch virtually every patient who comes for an initial examination, but he employs as one of his staff a professional masseur to work with patients who are "strokers."

### Touch the Heart

Since the human heart is an organ completely encased in the body and thus inaccessible to physical contact, one might think it unrelated to touch. One would be wrong.

The health of the heart, and other internal organs as well, seems to be profoundly affected both by human touch and by its absence. Indications of this may be found in studies by cardiologists, psychiatrists, and epidemiologists, many of which have been brought together with new clarity in James Lynch's pioneering book, *The Broken Heart.* Using census and insurance statistics, long-term health studies from Roseto, Pennsylvania, and Framingham, Massachusetts, government reports and international surveys, this University of Maryland psychologist has amassed enough evidence to make those involved in preventing heart disease look again at what they are—and are not—doing. For while they have been concentrating on smoking (right on!), exercise (maybe), and cholesterol (murky waters . . .), they have had almost nothing at all to say about human contact and its relation to the unhealthy heart. This lack of interest has persisted despite signs and symptoms of an important relation indeed. To wit:

- Early statistics from the Framingham study show married couples live longer lives than expected (based on national mortality statistics) and that the lives of single and widowed people are shortened.
- In Roseto, a largely Italian-American town of stable families with a strong sense of community and a pervasive mutual support network, there are one-third as many heart attacks as there are in neighboring towns. This, despite a high calorie diet of precisely the sort that cardiologists warn against and blood cholesterol levels no lower than the towns nearby.
- A 1956 study by Kraus and Lillienfeld concluded that married couples live longer than the single, widowed, and divorced.[7]
- In 1970 Carter and Glick found that premature deaths—those occurring between 15 and 64—were significantly higher for the single, divorced, and widowed than for married couples. This applied to both men and women.[8]
- For every major cause of death—heart disease, homicide, stroke, cirrhosis of the liver, automobile accident, *whatever*—divorced men stand a two to six times greater chance of dying from it than married men. Comparing married and widowed women, the trend is similar.
- Terminal cancer of every type, whether affecting the lungs, the lymphatic tissues, or almost any other site, is more likely to kill divorced men and women than those who are married. A

divorced nonsmoker is in nearly as much danger as a married
pack-or-more-a-day smoker.
- Studies of the recently bereaved the world over show increased morbidity and mortality rates from all manner of
accidents and diseases.
- An Israeli study by Dr. J. H. Medalie involved screening
10,000 adult males who were without symptoms of coronary
heart disease. By the end of five years, those who had suffered
a myocardial infarction were very likely to be the men who
had reported dissatisfaction with their marriages, including
lack of emotional support from their wives.[9]

Taken as a whole, this conglomeration of studies adds up to a
rather impressive sum of evidence. But I must add a double-barreled
cautionary note. While this research points toward the importance of
human relationships for maintaining health, "points" is not the same
as "proves." The subject is worthy of more attention, but it is not a
proven fact. Furthermore, the assumption that these relationships
include physical closeness is my own, and, while it may seem as
sensible to you as it does to me, it has not been scientifically tested. As
a psychologist who drags the clanking chains of science from room to
room, I can only say at this point that I *believe* that enduring human
relationships characterized by physical closeness tend to keep a
heart healthy. Not all hearts, and certainly not all forms of physical
closeness. There is, for instance, a growing suspicion in medical
circles that a surprising number of middle-aged men suffer heart
attacks in the excitement of an extramarital affair. Smoking may be
safer.

If studies on touch and the healthy human heart are still waiting to
be done, studies on animals abound. And many of the best have been
done by James Lynch.

The animals most studied by Lynch and his co-workers are horses
and dogs; the findings for each are both similar and surprising. The
presence of a person has the immediate effect of elevating the heart
rate of both animals, but when the same person pets the animal, the
effect is just the opposite. Petting not only lowers the heart rate, it
sometimes interrupts it.

Changes in both directions can be dramatic. At the approach of a
person, dogs that have been experimentally isolated suddenly
increase their heart rate, systolic blood pressure, and coronary flow

by more than 50 percent. That is an impressive change. But even more impressive, the simple act of petting a dog can slow down its heart beat by as much as 90 percent. This means a drop from 180 beats per minute while the animal is resting to only 20 beats per minute during petting.[10] Newton[11] and Grantt[12] describe a dog that went into total cardiac arrest for up to eight seconds during human contact. Despite this heart-stopping performance, the dog lived 14 years.

Not only does the dog respond with its heart under normal conditions, it does so even when the animal is paralyzed with curare, a drug that blocks all musculoskeletal movements. Furthermore, every animal tested—and that includes rabbits, opposums, guinea pigs, cats, and monkeys—registered the effects of social interaction with humans in their hearts.

These studies may have major implications about the effect of relationships on the human heart, but there is another finding that may have even greater significance to the practice of healing. Experimental animals were subjected to a sudden noxious stimulus in the form of an electric shock. As might be expected, there was an instantaneous increase in the heart rate in response. This is a reaction to pain. When the shock was regularly preceded by a tone that sounded ten seconds before it, the animal learned to associate the sound to the shock, and its heart rate increased as soon as it heard the tone. This is a reaction to fear.

If the animal is a dog, the presence of a person mildly reduces both the fear and pain reactions. Its wildly racing heart slows somewhat although it does not return to resting level until after the shock is over. But when a person pets the dog during the tone and shock, its heart rate either returns to normal or *falls below* resting level. Petting eliminates conditioned fear and pain responses of the heart; in some animals petting even eliminates the reflexive limb flexion response to the shock.[13]

Most people are by now aware of the dangers of generalizing from one species of animal to another. What is true of rats may or may not be true of cats, and even if it is that does not mean it is true of humans too. Even so, the implications of this research finding for the helping and healing trades is enormous. For if it can be shown that people react to human touch as dogs do, then we have proof for what I accept intuitively already—that human touch is one of the great alleviators of fear and pain. And since it is fear and pain that bring most people to the doctor, the implications are particularly pertinent to medicine. The doctor's hands may be his greatest therapeutic tool.

But the question remains, can these findings be extrapolated to humans? There is some evidence already available that indicates that the answer is probably yes. This evidence—which still must be regarded as preliminary—comes out of observations of patients in hospital coronary care and shock-trauma units.

In the 1970s Lynch and his co-workers began exploring the effects of human contact on patients in two types of intensive care units: one for heart disorders and the other for treatment of shock and trauma victims. They monitored the strength and regularity of heartbeats in these patients and in the process made some rather startling discoveries.

One of the first came from the shock-trauma unit. Many of the patients were there as the result of severe accidents, often involving multiple injuries. Such patients are very near death, and the unit is designed to allow the coordination of heroic efforts to save them. Lynch, Flaherty, *et al.* arranged for a nurse to sit at the bedside of one of these patients, take her hand, and say a few reassuring words. This seemed to have a decided effect on the patient's heart rate, usually in the form of a fairly dramatic decrease. What made this change especially noteworthy is that it took place while the patient was curarized, that is, totally immobilized by a derivative of curare (a powerful muscle relaxant) as part of the treatment regime. These effects were by no means minor; sometimes they were of the order of 30 beats per minute.[14]

A second finding was that the hearts of coronary care patients also reacted to human contact and pulse taking. In addition to heart rate changes, Lynch, Thomas, Mills *et al.* noted an increase in the frequency of abnormal heart beats and changes in the conduction of electrical impulses within the heart. Furthermore, these effects were noted whether the patient was awake or in a coma, whether he was recovering or nearing death. What is more, the effects triggered by routine pulse-taking were recorded in a setting of sensory bombardment; the intensive care unit is a cacophony of clicks, beeps, buzzers, bells, hurried footsteps, and whispered conversations.[15] That a touch on the wrist can have any measurable effect in such a setting is a tribute to the power of the human hand to touch the heart.

I must say again, however, that this research is still in a preliminary stage. While major changes in heartbeat have been recorded in individual patients, the statistical picture is less clear. When Mary Mills and colleagues studied 62 coronary care patients in 1976, they found that pulse-taking had significant effects on the number of ectopic heartbeats.[16] But when Lynch, Thomas, Paskewitz, *et al.* enlarged the study to 225 patients, the results were not as great as might have been expected. No significant changes in heart rate during pulse-taking revealed themselves in the larger study although some patients showed a significant decrease in arrhythmia. The research team concluded ". . . the present data clearly indicate that no simple relationship exists between human contact and cardiac arrhythmia. What does seem clear, however, is that human contact is an important stimulus for patients within life-threatening environments."[17]

Or, in the words most frequently used in the social science literature, More Research Is Needed.

But waiting for more research is not like Waiting for Godot. You can take action while you wait. Changes can be made in the intensive care unit before all results are in. All results are *never* in. Those who apply social science research—and doctors are prominent among them—must be able to act on incomplete data. James Lynch, writing with Paskewitz and others in the *American Heart Journal*, points the cardiac specialist toward a shift in thinking based on this admittedly incomplete data:

> . . . there is almost universal acceptance of emotional involvement in arrhythmia, but very little empirical work into the nature of this phenomenon. There are, indeed, few medical phenomena more widely held yet more poorly understood. It is ironic to note how frequently the only treatment suggested to deal with psychological factors is sedation or tranquilization. In many coronary care units in the United States sedation or tranquilization is the exclusive treatment for psychological problems in spite of the evidence that other approaches may be more effective.[18]

The caring touch may yet turn out to be one of the approaches that is more effective.

To get to those intensive care units, many patients come by way of

the ambulance and emergency room. It is to the use of touch in
emergency medicine that we shall now turn.

### Touch and Let Live

The sound of the siren slowly descends from a shriek to a growl as
the white ambulance brakes to a shuddering stop behind the over-
turned Buick. Before the wheels stop turning, the leader of the
emergency squad is out the door. As her trained eyes follow the trail
of broken glass and tire marks leading to the wreck, she spots a man's
leg through what once was the windshield. The leg is bent double,
and the toe of the foot rests on the back of his thigh. A soft, whimper-
ing moan from within the car tells her that the man with the backward foot is alive, afraid, and conscious of his pain. He has to be kept
alive, his leg must be straightened and set, and his sheet-metal
prison has to be cut from around him.

In such a setting, with such obviously high priorities, the niceties of
touch might be relegated to another time, another place. But it does
not work that way. In this life and death situation, the effective use of
touch may be the factor that determines whether the ambulance
heads for the emergency room or the morgue.

Of most immediate importance is the tactile information the
emergency worker gets from her fingers. Is there a pulse, and if so,
how strong is it? Is the man in shock? The feel of his skin will help
decide. Is the victim feverish or hypothermic? The trained hand
knows and knows fast.

At the same time it is collecting this information, the emergency
worker's hand is transmitting equally vital messages to the patient.
Like the ambulance siren, it lets him know that help has arrived.
And if, because of shock or pain or fear, he is unable to take in verbal
reassurance, the hand may be the only way to get through.

These are complex and demanding tasks, and not all touches will
be equal to them. One of the most effective ways of touching in
emergency work is to take the carotid pulse in the neck. Besides
giving direct information about how the body is coping with trauma,
it is a particularly reassuring form of contact. It conveys competence
as well as kindness, it is unambiguously a healer's touch, and it is so
centrally placed as to be directly connected to both brain and heart.
Skilled emergency workers sometimes find themselves keeping
their fingers on the neck long after the business of pulse-taking has
passed.

The effects of this hands-on reassurance are not merely psychological. By reducing anxiety, such a touch may increase the chances of survival. In cases of cardiac emergency, where there has been damage to the heart, the effect can be especially profound. Reducing anxiety slows the pulse rate and lessens strain on the heart. The quicker the coronary system can be returned to a near-normal level of activity, the greater will be the victim's chances of recovering from the trauma of a heart attack. What's more, if additional damage associated with the strains of anxiety can be avoided, the chances of a long-term recovery are improved.

Touching and talking can also reduce pain. That twisted leg in the Buick still has to be turned around, but there is work to be done first. While she has a hand on the accident victim's throbbing pulse, the emergency worker talks to him, initially in a soothing reassuring way; then, carefully describing what she is going to do with his leg. Slowly she moves her hand from the neck to the injured limb, continuing to talk all the while. She lets her palm rest on the leg, and in a few minutes the contact begins to ease the patient's visceral fear that his leg will be hurt further. Working slowly, keeping in physical contact, and continuing to describe what she is doing, the emergency worker is able to rotate the injured limb back into its normal position without the patient being overwhelmed with pain and fear.

Jackie Goff, who is in charge of emergency paramedic* training for the State of Vermont, puts it this way: "Quality of touch is very important in emergencies; in fact, it's one of the first things we teach emergency medical technicians. Establishing contact can be vital in emergency work, and touching is the best way to do it. Holding the head in a spinal injury keeps the neck from wiggling *and* establishes contact."

### Medical Messages

The fact is that touch pervades the practice of medicine. It's just that some doctors never discover it. For example, in response to a questionnaire about nonerotic physical contact with patients, one

---

*"Paramedic" is a widely accepted term, but it is one I detest. "Para" means, among other things, "beside," "beyond," "wrong," "contrary," and "abnormal." Health workers should define themselves, rather than be labeled "para-" anything. So strongly do I feel about this issue that when a hospital where I was an honorary clinician established a "Paramedical Library," I unscrewed the sign from the door and replaced it with one that read "Hospital Library." My sign is still up.

ophthalmologist stated, "I'm too busy to even think about such things. My practice is confined between the upper and lower lids."[19] In this case, the designer of the questionnaire (the psychiatrist Judith Perry) defined nonerotic contact as "hugging, kissing, and affectionate touching," but, as we have already seen, there is a great deal more scope for helpful touching in medicine than that. Another ophthalmologist, Baltimorian Richard Susel, uses touch consciously and conscientiously when treating his patients. "Through touch," he says, "I transmit my desire for the patient to get well. Even if it's nature that is the ultimate healer, your touch tells patients that you're on their side, that you're rooting for them to get well."

Susel is one among many physicians and nurses I've talked to who believes that a therapeutic touch reduces the need for pain medication. There is a further consensus among touch-aware healers that the right touch enhances the effect of pills and potions.

And what is this "right touch"? It is undoubtedly different for different doctors, for different patients, for different disorders, and even for different cultures. For example, touching the head of a Polynesian patient would almost certainly be the *wrong* touch. The head is an area of high *tapu* and should be touched only when absolutely necessary—and then slowly, and with great gentleness. For Dr. Susel the right touch is one that is specific to the area that is causing worry or pain. "This . . . is sinus, and this . . . pain is caused by glaucoma."

For me, the uses of touch that Susel advocates go beyond encouragement; they embody, in an age of scientific medicine, the most ancient art of medicine—that of physician as healer. To the power of antibiotic or analgesic, touch adds the power of the healer, and the combined effect is of a strength never before possible in the history of medicine. If we can regain our knowledge of the use of the self as a clinical tool (in which touch plays an important but by no means exclusive part) and combine it with our relatively new knowledge of the use of biochemical ingredients, we have something to offer patients that far exceeds both the personal power of the Ancients and the impersonal prescriptions of the Recents.

### Uncommon Sense from Dermatology

Dermatology, that branch of medicine that treats disorders of the skin, ought, by its very nature, to have a deep and abiding interest in the phenomenon of touch. After all, its organ of study (and the skin is the biggest organ of the body) is a mass of receptors of touch (as well as pain, heat, and cold), and it is exquisitely sensitive to tactile stimuli. Beyond that, there is some evidence that touch—and lack of touch—is related to certain skin disorders; René Spitz, for example, linked the development of eczema to lack of maternal touch. Yet the journals of dermatology treat touch much as the journals of other medical specialties—they virtually ignore it.

Furthermore, a student of dermatology would appear to have no better chance of learning touching skills than her colleagues in surgery or psychiatry. From talks with dermatologists and their patients, I have the impression that the range of these skills in the profession is enormous. Occasionally they are highly developed, at least occasionally they are simply nonexistent, and the average practitioner has but limited awareness of their importance. As the state of dermatology is reflected in its literature, any creative use of touch stands out enough to draw one's immediate attention.

Thus it is with a technique employed by Professor H. Musaph of the University of Amsterdam. From Spitz' association of non-touching mothers with eczemic children, and from his own observations of the difficulties some mothers have in making contact with their baby's skin, Musaph came up with a neat reversal of ordinary therapeutic reasoning. Under the guise of treating that most common of the minor disorders of infancy, cradle cap, he found a way to treat the parent-child relationship.

> We usually prescribe generously dosed topical therapy in children with cradle cap. However, if we feel that the baby is suffering from tactile neglect by the mother, we recommend that a less effective cream be rubbed into its skin five or six times first. The result is that its skin is stroked much more often, and this has a beneficial effect not only on the skin disorder but also on the child's general well-being.[20]

Other dermatologists have discovered the importance of touch in conveying a sense of all-rightness to adult patients with disfiguring or repelling skin disorders. From the ancient lepers' warning, "Unclean!" to the Heartbreak of Psoriasis, diseases of the skin have been a source of embarrassment and shame. Those doctors who are aware of the significance of these feelings do not just instruct their patients in the application of salve or ointment—they apply the first dose themselves. Then they make the patients' families part of the healing process by showing them how to continue the application with their own fingers. I am willing to bet that a study of self-applied versus spouse-applied medication will show that the latter is far more effective.

But touch-effectiveness is not limited to social or psychological factors in the treatment of skin disorders; it can work in directly physical ways as well. An example of the usefulness of touch in all three spheres may be found in a sensitive and moving article by Warren Johnson, a man who is both patient and professor, sufferer and health educator. The article, entitled "A Personal Experience with Scleroderma," appeared in the *British Journal of Sexual Medicine*.[21]

Scleroderma is a disease of the connective tissue that is degenerative as well as disfiguring. The skin becomes both brittlely hard and terribly sensitive. The process is a sort of slow mummification, eventually resulting in total loss of movement in the afflicted areas. It is generally considered incurable.

Johnson did not cure his scleroderma. But by an aggressive program of massage and exercise, he and his wife were able gradually to reverse much of the mummification, regaining movement and use in body parts that had become literally hidebound. One of those parts was Johnson's penis. The disease had led to a downward bowing of his erections and a severe dulling of sexual sensitivity. Johnson writes:

> By this time, I had already discovered that if abnormal connective tissue development on any part of the body were attacked vigorously with stretching, massage, and oil, its growth could be reversed over a period of time. I therefore began vigorous massage of the penis with entirely successful results.[22]

Sex is part of normal life, and return to sexual function is part of the recovery process. I know that sounds obvious, but in all Johnson's years of illness not one doctor or nurse initiated discussion or gave him advice on the subject. Nor was he able to find any reference to sex in the professional literature on scleroderma. And when he asked a hospital physical therapist if therapy could be applied to a penis in need, ". . . he giggled and made it clear that for that particular treatment, I was in the wrong kind of massage parlor."[23]

Once again, the sex taboo enshrouds the healing use of touch.

We shall look further at this unhappy relationship in later chapters, but it must not remain under cover while we are still on the subject of doctoring. The conflict the doctor feels about sex and touch has been painted in bright colors by the British playwright Alan Bennett. The play is *Habeas Corpus*, and the scene is between a fiftyish GP, Arthur Wicksteed, and his nubile young patient, Felicity Rumpers. He raises his hand to her shoulder . . .

> Felicity: No! Do not touch me.
> Wicksteed: No? How can I approach you? How can I even speak to you? The least thing about you, the spent cartridge of your lipstick, the dry bed of your compact, the fluff in your handbag's bottom, all the fragrant clutter of your loveliness, I am as dirt and vileness beside it. But . . .
> Felicity: But?
> Wicksteed: But speaking thus I speak as a man. And as a man I cannot touch you, but as a doctor . . .
> Felicity: Does that make a difference?
> Wicksteed: Oh yes. As a man I see you as a fresh, lovely, passionate creature. As a doctor, you are to me a machine, an organism, a mere carcass. Feeling does not enter into it. As a doctor I am a eunuch: I touch you—without passion, and without desire. (He puts his arm around her shoulder.)
> Felicity: Yes.
> Wicksteed: Now I touch you as a man.
> Felicity: Yes.
> Wicksteed: Now I touch you as a doctor.
> Felicity: Yes.
> Wicksteed: You feel the difference? So have no fears, my dear young lady, when in a few moments I shall ask you to remove your clothes in their entirety. Because I shall be as far from desire as is a plumber uncovering a manhole. Off. Off.
> Felicity goes off.[24]

. . . And so do we, though we are going only as far as the hospital, to see how the healing touch may be used there.

# R.N., P.T., O.T., M.D.—Touch in Hospital

## 11

> The physician celebrates computerized tomography. The patient celebrates the outstretched hand.
>
> —Norman Cousins

When you are sick enough to be in the hospital, not every touch you receive there is likely to be a rich and rewarding experience. Here is how a New Zealand medical student described his tactile memories of patienthood: "I felt I had lost the privacy of my body. Continually baring my bum for the nurses to stick needles into, doctors fondling my testicles, and no privacy from the rest of the ward in that large room. . . . The most striking thing, and to me the most shocking, was that doctors were obviously a greatly superior class. They did actually touch patients, but immediately washed their hands after the contact."

This student was not the first to discover negative aspects of touch in hospital. Jane DeAugustinis and her colleagues at Rutgers University found that in a psychiatric hospital, fully 50 percent of the time the meaning of touch was misinterpreted by either patient or nurse.[1] And when Leah Cashar and Barbara Dixson, nurse-researchers from Washington State, observed touch in another psychiatric hospital, they recorded the following incidents:

179

- A male attendant fluffed a male patient's hair, then sat on his lap and snapped his suspenders.
- A female licensed practical nurse gently grabbed a young, suspicious male patient by the back of his neck while walking down the hall behind him.
- A male doctor in a standing position leaned close to a suspicious, young female patient who was seated and touched her lightly on the arm as they talked. The patient physically withdrew. The doctor touched her two more times within about a sixty-second period, and she again responded by physical withdrawal.[2]

These are not isolated examples. Because we leave touch-training largely to chance, many of our hospital-based healers do not have highly developed touch skills. When a nurse or doctor does possess a soothing touch, she is remembered by grateful ex-patients as an island of warmth in an unfamiliar sea. For the sad fact is that with one major exception (which we shall come to shortly) even the healing professions that require skin-to-skin contact as part of their daily routine, usually ignore its significance and subtleties in their training programs. If the hospital is to be a place of comfort as well as computerized axial tomography, the education of those who work there must be broadened to include an understanding of the meanings of physical contact.

These meanings are missing from most training programs today. At a seminar held this year, there was unanimous agreement among the participants—all hospital-based physiotherapists—that they had received no instruction in their training as to what touch means to patients. The group included graduates from Scotland, Ireland, New Zealand, and Quebec. One said: "We only learned techniques, techniques for physical effects. We got the message that touching patients was a necessity only. Okay, you had to handle them, but you had to keep your distance at the same time."

A recently graduated American osteopathic physician told me the same thing: "We were well trained in specific uses of massage and pressure, but the effect that our hands might be having on the patient never got mentioned."

What a shame this is, for the hospital is one place where the healing power of touch is desperately needed. It must take many forms there and serve many functions. Foremost among them is the capacity of a touch from a health worker to provide reassurance about life in a setting that the patient associates with illness and death. This can be given in some unusual ways, one of which was inadvertently discovered by a middle-aged American osteopath taking a postgraduate training course in a large metropolitan hospital. Each morning he and his fellow students followed a specialist through ward rounds. One of the patients they visited was a man in his late fifties whom the specialist disclosed was very close to death. For reasons still unknown to him, on the first morning the osteopath waited by the bedside so that he would be the last to move on to the next case. As the others filed out, he reached under the sheets and playfully pinched the man's big toe. Then he joined his colleagues in the next room. He did the same thing every day for a week. To his surprise, on the eighth day he met the patient in the hall outside his room, dressed, packed, and ready to return home. "I've been waiting for you," the man said, "to tell you that it's because of you that I'm still alive."

"What are you talking about?"

"Well, every morning you pinched my toe when the others weren't looking."

"Yes, but what does that have to do with—"

"Nobody," answered the patient decisively, "nobody plays with the toes of a dying man. So I decided I must not be dying after all."

Another kind of reassurance that touch can offer the hospital patient is that of familiarity in a strange and frightening environment. Like the infant emerging from the womb into the world of the obstetrics ward, the adult patient in the medical ward has left the familiar warmth and safety of his home for the dangerous, fear-filled world of the hospital. The smells are strange and chilling; the sounds are of squeaky shoes, whispered voices, and the snores and coughs of strangers. This new world is seen from a horizontal plane, and its inhabitants speak an unknown tongue. Words have new meanings here. "Negative" results are good; "positive" ones, reason for worry. Skin-to-skin warmth in this context can be a powerful source of comfort.

For the nurse, occupational therapist, physiotherapist, and physician, to all of whom the hospital is as familiar as their kitchen, it may be hard to appreciate just how strange the hospital can be for the patient. An illustration from a setting much less familiar than the nurses' station or the operating theater may make the point.

George is a young and successful Maryland neurosurgeon. Last winter he took a week's vacation skiing the deep powder of the mountains of Utah. On the second day George started down a slope that he was afraid was tougher than he could handle. It was. Halfway down the steepest section, in rapid succession he lost his nerve, his balance, and his footing. George took a header and bounced his way down seventy-five yards of snow-covered mountain. Dazed—perhaps knocked out for a moment—he came to feeling almost certain that he had broken his neck in the fall. The feeling grew as he waited, cold and afraid, for the rescue sled, and by the time he had been carried to a bed in the first aid station, George was in the throes of a full-blown, but unspoken, panic. Inside the hut, he ruminated on the implications of his self-diagnosed injury, and his panic grew even stronger. He had still not spoken a word.

There was a nurse on duty in the station. As she passed his bed, she glanced at George's face and immediately changed direction and sat down beside him. Silently, she took his hand and held it in her own.

"As *soon* as she took my hand, I felt the panic lift. I'd never seen her before and still hadn't spoken to her, but the effect she had on me was almost magic. From complete panic to just about total calm in a few seconds. And all from the touch of a hand."

"What happened next?"

"When I got back to work I completely reorganized my approach to patients. I'm from a very un-touchy family, and I'd never been your warm, touching doctor—not many neurosurgeons are. But from that time on I've made it a point to touch most of my patients. I'd seen for myself what it could do. And it's had a tremendous effect on my relationship with them."

"What about your broken neck?"

"Strained muscle was more like it. Never diagnose yourself."

Many hospitalized patients want a chance to talk about their fears, to share them with another human being, to get them off their chest. This need for catharsis is all too commonly unmet by hospital staff, as Kübler-Ross revealed in *On Death and Dying.* Those most likely to be aware of the need are touch-conscious nurses and physiotherapists. The nurse gets to hear the hidden fears in two situations—at night when the ward is quiet and dark feelings emerge, and when she is giving a backrub. The physio (or physical therapist), who is the hospital specialist in hands-on treatment, knows that patients often fall naturally into talk and tears when they are being massaged.

All this would be fine except for some profession-induced problems. Among physios there are several. Of major importance is the fact that many have received no training in counseling techniques. A number of competent, experienced, mature physiotherapists have told me that they discourage patients from talking about their problems and fears simply because they do not know what do do next. They are trained in the body, not the mind, and they're afraid that in their ignorance they will do harm.

This artificial mind/body split has created a number of unfilled gaps in patient care. If *physio*therapists do not talk to their patients, *psycho*therapists do not touch theirs. The split limits the usefulness of both. I am not arguing that physiotherapists need to know by heart every nuance of Freud, Sullivan, and Rogers, but I am saying that neglect of basic listening and counseling skills constitutes a serious gap in their education.

Academic psychologists must bear at least part of the responsibility for this gap. I have seen programs where psychologists have been invited to teach psychology to physio- and occupational therapists and have wasted the opportunity. Such a course should be designed to meet the specific needs of the students, who in this case should be learning the skills of therapeutic listening as they are learning to understand the psychological components of pain, fear, loss, and rehabilitation. Instead, they have simply been given a watered-down Introductory Psychology course. Pity.

Another pity is that many health workers simply do not like to touch. In an informal survey of occupational therapists, Huss found that 60 percent were uncomfortable touching clients.[3] Among physiotherapists the situation is complicated by the growing popularity of ever-more-sophisticated interferential devices and ultrasonic machines. These electronic marvels can create any effect from a slight tingle to a pulsing sensation that makes your spine feel like a cow on a milking machine. But I have yet to see a patient tell *any* machine that he feels old and impotent since his back went out while he was digging in the garden. No patient I know has ever confided to her ultrasonic device that after her mastectomy she felt as though she were no longer a woman.

For doctors, the no-touch problem is at least in part a result of their ever-increasing status. When a healer's status is so far above his patients that there is no physical contact between them, he has been elevated out of some of his potential usefulness. John Bruhn, writing in the *Southern Medical Journal*, believes that diminishing physical contact with the doctor is a source of increasing patient dissatisfaction. His thoughts on the matter are worthy of attention:

> Laying on of the hands in some manner by the doctor is expected by most patients. It is my contention that tactile communication has decreased in the doctor-patient relationship and that this is a source of dissatisfaction for patients. Instrumentation has altered the mode of conducting a clinical examination and has minimized touching of the patient by the physician. New types of health professionals such as physician assistants and nurse practitioners conduct clinical examinations under physician supervision; thus the physician may not "touch" the patient. The type of practice setting may alter a patient's chances of being seen and "touched" by the same physician. These factors are responsible, in part, for diminishing tactile communication between doctor and patient.[4]

More hospital patients are touched by nurses than by any other group of healers. This was demonstrated by Barnett's survey of the utilization of touch by health personnel in two Texas hospitals. Nurses and nursing students accounted for nearly half of the 900 touches recorded.[5] (Her other findings are of interest as well. The hands, forehead, and shoulder were the areas most frequently touched while the fingers, toes, ankles, and genitalia were never touched. Also, the older the staff member, the less likely it was that she or he would employ touch.)

Given the proportionally high level of tactile contact among nurses, it is fortunate that nurse education provides the exception to the absence of touch-consciousness in most other training programs. At least in the United States, young nurses can be expected to have gained both knowledge and practical touch skills as part of their education. The literature of nursing fairly consistently presents useful articles on the ways touch can be employed as an agent of healing. While just two decades ago there was no real mention of touch in standard nursing texts, the 1978 edition of a popular contemporary textbook, Henderson and Nite's *Principles and Practice of Nursing* does a credible job of presenting touch as an instrument of communication and health.[6]

In that same year the theme of the *Imprint* (the journal of the National Student Nurses Association) annual writing contest was,

"The Importance of Touch in Patient Care." The winner of the contest was Susie Meredith, a student from Forth Worth, Texas. Her article nicely summarized the physical and emotional uses of touch in hospital. Of the former she wrote:

> When used by the health care personnel to assess and diagnose, [touch] is called palpation. Without this all-important assessment tool, this tool that requires us to be perceptive in our touch, no patient care could be complete. Enlargements of body organs, lymph nodes, and tissues could easily be overlooked without palpation. . . . All segments of a hospital stay include touch. Physicians' and nurses' assessment of the patient, procedures, transportation, surgery . . . these are all times when touch is an integral part of patient care.[7]

She went on to argue that nurses must be trained to listen to patients, to assist them with problems, to display empathy, and to touch.

> Yes, trained to touch. A touch that shows we feel close to the patient. A touch to show we understand the loneliness. a touch to show we understand the pain. A touch to show we understand the fear. A touch to show we understand the "today" the patient is forced to cope with. A touch to show we are here and ready to help the patient. That touch is an indispensable ingredient in nursing, something a nurse can offer a patient that no other person has the opportunity to do on a day-to-day continuing basis.[8]

Meredith's contention that touch can "show we are here and ready to help the patient" has received some support from an Iowa hospital study conducted by Ruth McCorkle.[9] Like a number of others in the nursing literature, McCorkle's article treads further onto that thin ice beyond the solid base of data than I dare follow. She finds evidence that I cannot accept for some positive effects of touch, but her conclusion—that the use of touch indicates to seriously ill patients that the nurse cares about them—is one I accept without reservation.

A psychiatric hospital study by Donna Aguilera—and because of design problems this too should be considered preliminary rather than definitive work—showed that touch increased verbal interaction, rapport, and "approach behavior" between nurses and patients.[10] Unfortunately, the author does not adequately describe the types of touch involved, and I must add this to my list of touch articles in nursing journals whose main function is to invite further research.

There is one touch-in-hospital study that is not beset by problems of design and description, probably because it was conducted by psychologists. The Connecticut hospital research of Sheryle Whitcher and Jeffrey Fisher has been carefully constructed to minimize all possibilities of experimental error. The study compared the effects of a female nurse's touch on men and women recently admitted to hospital for elective surgery.

All patients were given private pre-operative instruction by the nurse. Those in the experimental group received a touch on the hand at the beginning of the session and a minute-long touch on the arm near the end; the control group received the instructions and the usual nursing care, but without the touch.

The nurse's touch had an effect, but not the effect everyone would have predicted. The interesting result was that women experienced favorable reactions to the touch while the reactions of the men were largely negative. In an earlier study, Jeffrey Fisher and other colleagues also found women more positively affected by touch. But this time men did not react negatively to touch, perhaps because this study was conducted in a library, not in a hospital. Whitcher and Fisher conjecture that men and women attribute different meanings to touch in a context of dependency such as a hospital. What for women was probably reassuring may have been threatening to men. If this finding proves correct, hospital staff will have to be as aware of their patients' sex as their ethnic origins and age. All give valuable clues to their probable response to touch.[11]

### Pulse

As we have already seen, nurses, doctors, and emergency workers frequently make physical contact with patients by taking their pulse. And we have also seen how the simple act of pulse-taking can affect the heart, register through the fog of coma or the clatter of an intensive care unit, can reduce shock, announce that help has arrived, and calm the fears of a trauma victim.

Yet little attention is paid to the potential of this universally accepted form of touch in the training of most hospital workers.

Usually, it is just a matter of finding the right spot on the wrist, checking the watch, and counting.

But it wasn't always like that. Pulse-taking has been as taboo-ridden as any other form of healer-patient touch. In eighteenth-century England, female patients protected themselves from the physician's eyes by allowing only a delicate arm to peek through the bed curtains.

Dutch physicians were taking pulses at least a century earlier, but since watches with minute hands were not yet invented, I suspect that the benefits of the procedure were more therapeutic than diagnostic.

Uroscopy was a diagnostic technique popular in the seventeenth century. The diagnosis was made through eyeball inspection of the patient's urine, and today the practice is usually dismissed as quackery. But as Steen's satirical painting, "The Lovesick Maiden," intimates, the real effect may have come from contact between the patient's wrist and the physician's right hand, and not the vial held in his left.

For traditional Chinese physicians, pulse-taking was the very heart of medical diagnosis. The procedure could take as long as three hours while the healer listened through his fingers to the five humors of the body.

This ancient Eastern medical art is still with us, and it has been beautifully captured in the words of a Western surgeon, Richard Selzer. In *Mortal Lessons* he describes the visit of Yeshi Dhonden, personal physician to the Dalai Lama, to the American hospital where Selzer works. Invited to make morning rounds, the physician prepares himself by two hours of bathing, fasting, and prayer. Followed by an assembly of hospital staff, the berobed healer approaches the bed of a puzzled looking patient. They are briefly introduced, and for some time he simply gazes at her . . .

> At last he takes her hand, raising it in both of his own. Now he bends over the bed in a kind of crouching stance, his head drawn down into the collar of his robe. His eyes are closed as he feels for her pulse. In a moment he has found the spot, and for the next half hour he remains thus, suspended above the patient like some exotic golden bird with folded wings, holding the pulse of the woman beneath his fingers, cradling her hand in his. All the

power of the man seems to have been drawn down into this one purpose. It is palpation of the pulse raised to the state of ritual.... After a moment the woman rests back upon her pillow. From time to time, she raises her head to look at the strange figure above her, then sinks back once more.

I cannot see their hands joined in a correspondence that is exclusive, intimate, his fingertips receiving the voice of her sick body through the rhythm and throb she offers at her wrist.... I want to be held like that, touched so, *received*. And I know that I, who have palpated a hundred thousand pulses, have not felt a single one.[12]

### Problems of Language

Among hospital patients there are certain groups that have specialized needs for touch. An obvious example is the patient who speaks a language different from that spoken by the staff. This can be a problem even when they both speak English, for the patient might think and speak in lower-class English while the staff is limited to middle-class and medical-class speech patterns. But the situation is infinitely more difficult when the patient is a refugee, a recent immigrant, or even a foreign tourist. Translators provide help when they are available; when they are not—and that's most of the time—gesture and touch can be called upon to provide instruction and to give comfort. Staff members who are at ease with their bodies and hands will have an inestimable advantage over those who are not. Those with stone faces and cast-iron fingers will be severely disadvantaged.

There are some patients whom no translator can help. Aphasics and mutes—people who have lost or never acquired the power of speech—can sometimes understand the spoken word but cannot reply; the profoundly deaf can do neither. For those who know sign language, this is the preferred means of communication, and a reasonable size pool of staff members should be at least minimally conversant in it. Touch has a role to play here too, both in attracting attention and in breaking through the wall of loneliness that so often surrounds those cut off from spoken communication.

A moving description of the use of touch in a case of aphasia appeared in the *American Journal of Nursing* under the title, "Touch is a Way of Caring." Written by Nancy Jean Amacher, who at the time was a student nurse, the article describes the growth of a relationship between herself and Sally, a 65-year-old aphasic patient with right hemiplegia. Amacher discovered that the nursing notes on Sally contained an extraordinary—indeed, a classic—observation. For one eight-hour shift the notation in its entirety read, "No verbal complaints." Considering the fact that the patient was physically incapable of speech, her lack of verbal complaints need not be taken as a sign of blissful serenity.

In her attempts to help Sally walk and speak again, and to reinvolve her with the world through a relationship with another person in it, Amacher used every means of communication she could think of. She named objects and had Sally repeat them after her. They practiced sounding out words. Together they worked on an exercise program, and she hugged Sally whenever a small gain was made. As the nurse helped the patient, their growing relationship taught the nurse. One of the lessons she learned was about touch as a communicator:

> Of the many interesting and rewarding experiences working with Sally, the most important was learning to use touch therapeutically. Often, when we could not communicate verbally, I held her hand or hugged her around the shoulders to show I was trying to understand. Soon, instead of waving good-bye, Sally would extend her hand, and I would caress it to demonstrate my concern for her. I felt close to her, for touch involved me as no words could. Now, many months later, I often touch patients in greeting, and do not hesitate to touch them during treatments or examinations of their skin. I feel that touch often reassures patients who have had mutilating surgery that they are still lovable despite their deformities.[13]

### Children in the Hospital

Children, and particularly very young children, are another group with special touch needs. Cuddling, rocking, and other skin-to-skin measures are the best way to meet the most pressing need of children who are in a frantic or fearful state, the need to be comforted. Mothers, be they monkey or human, know this without having to read it, but innate knowledge is not generally accepted in scientific medicine. It takes a controlled study to convince many health professionals that what they feel within themselves, what they see all around them, what, in fact, they already know to be true, really is true. Such a study now exists.

It was conducted at a large, midwestern American hospital by nurses June Triplett and Sara Arneson. Sixty-three children between three days and 44 months old, all patients in the pediatric ward, were divided into two groups on a random basis. When those in Group A showed distress they were given verbal comfort (talking, humming, singing, or making soothing sounds) for five minutes or until they quieted, whichever came first. If they were still distressed after five minutes, tactile comfort was offered as well. Group B was given simultaneous verbal *and* tactile comfort as a first response to distress. Tactile efforts included patting, stroking, rocking, holding, and offering a pacifier.

In all, there were 100 interventions of which 40 were verbal only (Group A) and 60, tactile-verbal (Group B). Of Group A interventions, only seven succeeded in quieting the children. But of the 60 tactile-verbal interventions in Group B, 53 were successful. This is a highly significant difference, and one that led the authors to conclude:

> On the basis of these findings, we believe that the deliberate use of verbal and tactile comfort measures can markedly minimize the distress exhibited by young hospitalized children. After such interventions, children are more able to use their energy for recovery rather than for expressing displeasure. It is also clear that these comfort measures are generally effective within five minutes—a time period that does not appear unreasonable in a nurse's busy schedule. The data clearly demonstrate that tactile comfort is the method of choice, although verbal comfort may be successful with a few children.[14]

### The Geriatric Patient

Elderly patients constitute another group with special touch needs, needs that will come to the fore as more and more hospital beds are occupied by chronic, slow-healing, "medically unexciting" geriatric patients for whom caring is of greater relevance than curing. The major burden and responsibility for this care is in the hands of the nurse. Those hands can be a great asset in rendering such care, and here too the touch-trained nurse will be able to offer more than her untrained colleagues.

Touch is particularly effective with the most difficult—and often least rewarding—elderly patients, those in a state of senility. Physical contact may be one of the few means available for getting and holding their attention. Keeping the senile patient focused on reality for even a brief period can be a trying task, but the task is made easier by touch. It comes as a surprise to many nurses and doctors just how effective resting a hand lightly on an arm or even holding hands can be for keeping a senescent mind attending to the present moment.

In designing programs for such patients the touch factor need not be left to chance. Activities that ensure close physical contact can be built into the daily routine. A morning hairbrushing session is one possibility; a weekly dance is another. At the Lakeview Convalescent Center in Wayne, New Jersey, there is a long-established skin regimen that is regarded as the key to treating the whole person. As described by Jean Hardy,

> This means a general rubdown of the entire back area in addition to massaging other areas prone to dryness such as the coccyx, elbows and heels. Back rubs are given after the morning bath or part of morning care, in the late afternoon as part of P.M. care and again just before bedtime.[15]

The benefits of such a regimen are manifold. On a physical level backrubs stimulate circulation; on a psychological level they act as a tranquilizer and sedative without side-effects. Lakeview staff have found that the backrub also helps establish a personal relationship between nurse and patient: "It provides that sense of touch which is in part responsible for the easy, quick rapport between patient and nurse that could take days if words alone were used."[16]

There is another benefit as well. Massage at Lakeview is done with baby lotion. Besides preventing the dry breakdown to which old skin is prone, the fragrance is appreciated by incontinent patients embarrassed by body odors. The lotion and the manner in which it is applied help them feel clean.

### Touching the Dying

The dying patient is an anomaly in hospital. Our hospitals are designed to restore health, and so is the training of those who work in them. For many, the patient who is not going to get better represents a failure of that training and of themselves as doctors and nurses.

This attitude overlays a much deeper abhorrence of death. Many of the world's cultures respond to the very sick and dying among them by withdrawal and vilification, and these responses find expression in the industrialized world as well as among "primitives." While in the last ten years medicine and nursing have improved remarkably in the treatment of death, even the well-trained practitioner feels an aversion to the dying patient that must be overcome before emotional help can be offered.

This aversion is often expressed by decreased physical contact and increased distance. The same doctor who sits and chats with other patients, stands with folded arms by the bedside of the dying and, as the disease progresses, steps back a little further each day when making his rounds. The nurse's visits are less frequent, and each a little briefer than the one before. The family begins to sit nearer the foot of the bed than the head; they touch their dying relative less frequently and steer the conversation from personal subjects to meaningless pleasantries.

It is in this context that New Zealand surgeon Ivan Lichter and physiotherapist Ellen Smoothy have initiated the TLP Programme. When ordering medication, Lichter prescribes TLP in the same way that he would morphine or antibiotics. TLP stands for Tender Loving Physiotherapy. It is administered by Mrs. Smoothy, who possesses, in addition to a name brilliantly suited to her profession, an easy rapport with her patients. One of her specialities is physiotherapy with the dying patient. TLP with the dying patient serves three functions, the first two of which are short-term rehabilitation and clearing of the chest. These are familiar to physiotherapists, most of whom are well-trained in strengthening postural muscle groups, easing pressure areas, and chest physiotherapy. The third function is not so well known; it is the use of touch as a way of easing the transition from life to death. Here the emphasis is on treating the person rather than the condition. TLP provides a warmth and physical closeness with another person that is all too often missing in the last days of the dying patient in a hospital. It can be performed by the physiotherapist or, even better, taught to the family.

Because it is used mainly as emotional support does not mean that TLP can be performed without regard to technical skills. The exaggerated bony prominences that are part of the wasting away associated with chronic disease should be avoided, and soft tissues should not be compressed onto them. It is better to lift and stretch muscle fibers than to compress them. A smooth, soothing touch is preferable to a deep and penetrating one. Above all, the contact should be used both as a form of comfort and an opportunity for further communication with a person whose days of life are numbered.

Let us end this chapter where we began, with the words of a patient in hospital. This time it is not a medical student but a carpenter in his late forties, a man suffering from leukemia.

"I wished I could tell them somehow just what it was like to be in isolation. My wife and my family couldn't come near me—they had to stand at the door with masks on. The only one who was allowed to touch me was a nurse who had been specially cleared as being in good health. [Patients undergoing chemotherapy are highly susceptible to infection, and even a common cold is potentially lethal.]

"This nurse changed my bedding and kept me clean and all that. But she hated to touch me, or at least it felt that way. Whatever she was doing she did with as little physical contact as possible.

"I wish I could have told them how important touch was. I craved the feeling of flesh on flesh. I craved it! It wasn't a sexual thing—in my condition it was the last thing on my mind—but I really felt I was losing my will to live without that touch. I mean I still wanted to live, to get better, but the reason to keep struggling was slipping away from me. I needed the feeling of someone's skin on mine to help me find it again."

# Touch In Psychotherapy

**12**

I can clearly remember one of my supervisors confiding to me during my training that he sometimes patted his "patients" on the back on their way out of the office. Horrors! If discovered, he may be branded as an infidel.

—E. Fuller Torrey

"Bennett subscribed to the totally inexplicable theory that psychiatrists—who, after all, deal with all that is kinky and imaginative about the human soul: dreams, fantasies, sexual obsessions—ought somehow to comport themselves like accountants."[1]

In this one sentence, Erica Jong captures the paradox in which many psychotherapists find themselves; their lives are devoted to the irrational, and they live them like Victorian bank managers. But the reason is not "totally inexplicable"; it is the same as that which provokes healing masseuses to distance themselves from the massage parlor: the work of both masseuses and therapists brings them into daily contact with that which is taboo, and their upright, uptight posture is an attempt not to be contaminated by it.

Like the masseuse, the therapist's concern over image is not a new one. In 1931 Freud implored his student Sandor Ferenczi to desist from the practice of bestowing motherly kisses upon his patients. He pointed out that what started as a kiss might turn to "pawing," from pawing to "peeping and showing," and from there to open slather. Freud regarded the kiss as a danger that would increase the "calumnious resistances against analysis" and warned Ferenczi that ". . . it seems to me a wanton act to provoke them."[2]

Unfortunately, the struggle for public respectability often limits one's usefulness; we have already seen how the specter of illicit sex has haunted legitimate touch. But the problems of respectability are not limited to touch and sex. As this is being written, American academic psychiatry is turning away from "all that is kinky and imaginative about the human soul" in favor of neurology and neuro-transmitters and norepinephrine. Whatever else motivates the turn, a major incentive is the desperate desire of psychiatrists to be regarded by their medical colleagues as Real Doctors.

It will not work. Even if they lock themselves in the laboratory forever and wear a white coat like a second skin, psychiatrists will remain tainted by madness. And the respect they seek may lie else-where. After flunking a psychiatrist on his State Boards, one South-ern physician said with disgust, "I'll bet he's never even *touched* a patient."

He may have been right. The anti-touch tradition in psychiatry has outlived Freud. In 1958, Karl Menninger, one of the world's leading psychoanalytic theorists, advised analysts not to shake hands with patients "unnecessarily." Of touch beyond the handshake, he said, "I shall only mention more serious transgressions of the rule against physical contact as sometimes occurring, but as representing *prima facie* evidence of the incompetence or criminal ruthlessness of the analyst."[3] Either through prudery or revulsion at the thought of physical contact between therapist and patient, Menninger did not distinguish between therapeutic, sexual, and aggressive touch. All were apparently the mark of the ruthless criminal.

Nine years later, Lewis Wolberg, a renowned professor of psychia-try and teacher of therapeutic technique, wrote, "It goes without saying that physical contact with the patient is absolutely taboo." Unlike Menninger, Wolberg did spell out the types of contact included under this "absolute taboo." "Touching, stroking, or kissing the patient may mobilize sexual feelings in the patient and therapist, or bring forth violent outbursts of anger."[4]

Very true. Touch may lead to sexual or angry feelings. It may also express sympathy, elicit feelings of tenderness, mobilize or disinte-grate resistance, and have a number of other effects. The meaning of touch is not the same for all people nor even for the same person in different situations. Most patients know this; Wolberg apparently did not.

This lack of discrimination goes on today. In an article on sex between patient and therapist, psychiatrist Virginia Davidson mentions a well-known study by Kardener, Sheldon, and colleagues entitled, "A Survey of Physicians' Attitudes and Practices Regarding Erotic and Nonerotic Contact with Patients." The study revealed that among the psychiatrists in the sample, five percent admitted that they had sexual intercourse with patients. But 71 percent of the psychiatrists (and 74 percent of the physicians) in the sample indicated their belief that *nonerotic* hugging, kissing, and affectionate touching of patients might be beneficial to their treatment. Despite this belief, only 55 percent of psychiatrists (and 59 percent of physicians) engaged in such practices.[5]

Davidson views the distinction between erotic and nonerotic touch with profound disbelief. She writes:

> The most interesting aspect of this study is that Kardener clearly implies that there are kinds of kissing, touching, and affectionate hugging between patient and psychiatrist that are *non*erotic. . . . How kissing, hugging, and touching (however affectionately labeled) within the context of the psychiatrist-patient relationship can be considered nonerotic requires a certain amount of imagination—or a determined lack of it.[6]

I confess to either or both.

Still, Doctor Davidson is not alone in her concern about touch. In an excellent unpublished 1979 study, Jill Bourdais de Charbonnière wrote to 15 therapists who had previously discussed touch in the psychotherapy literature. Of the nine who answered, only two (Elizabeth Mintz and myself) stood by the pro-touch stands taken in their articles. One strong advocate of nonerotic touch had reverted to orthodox psychoanalysis; another touched less than he used to, and, most disturbing, another regretted having published anything on the subject because some of his colleagues and students had used his words as license for manipulation of their clients. The others in this follow-up study maintained either their limited endorsement or, in one case, firm opposition to touch in therapy.[7]

There is no doubt that touch can be used manipulatively, wrongly, clumsily, and at the wrong time—the penultimate chapter of this book is dedicated to exploring these and other limits of touch. As the reader will by now be aware, I take seriously indeed any misuse of the healing touch. But at the same time it must be remembered that the roots of opposition to touch in psychotherapy run very, very deep. The best analysis of this opposition may be found in two erudite articles by Elizabeth Mintz—the same Elizabeth Mintz who, with me, remains an advocate of touch in therapy. In "Touch and the Psychoanalytic Tradition" she examines the factors that have led to the taboo against touch in psychoanalysis. Important among them are:

> ... Victorian sexual prudery; the desire of the early analysts to establish themselves as scientists, divorced alike from magic and from religion; and Freud's rejection of his own early use of therapeutic massage, stroking and his experiments with the recovery of memories through hypnosis.[8]

She reminds us that Freud's followers were regarded as both sexual perverts and a danger to the community while Freud himself was forced to resign his neurology appointment in London after asking about the sex life of a patient. It is more than likely that incidents like this led Freud to abandon his early experiments with what he called the "pressure technique." We know that he adapted it from a hypnotic technique used by Bernheim and that he abandoned it sometime before 1904. Although he first employed it with patient Fräulein Elisabeth von R., Freud's fullest description of this use of touch is to be found in the case history of Miss Lucy R.

He began with the assumption that everything with any significance to the neurotic disorder was already known by his patients; thus, when his question about the origins of the symptom was met with the answer, "I really don't know," Freud applied the pressure:

> I placed my hand on the patient's forehead or took her head between my hands and said: "You will think of it under the pressure of my hand. At the moment at which I relax my pressure you will see something in front of you or something will come into your head. Catch hold of it. It will be what we are looking for. —Well, what have you seen or what has occurred to you?"[9]

Freud was delighted by the success produced by this laying on of hands. He wrote, "On the first occasions on which I made use of this procedure . . . I myself was surprised to find that it yielded me the precise result that I needed. And I can safely say that it has scarcely ever left me in the lurch since then."[10]

Furthermore, Freud saw this form of touching as an important psychoanalytic tool: "It has always pointed the way which the analysis should take and has enabled me to carry through every such analysis to an end without the use of somnambulism."[11]

Despite his early enthrallment with the pressure technique, when Freud deserted touch so did most of his followers. These followers became known as psychoanalysts, an early and specialized group who have powerfully influenced the direction of psychotherapy. So great has been the analysts' influence that, particularly in North America, their strong taboo against touch has permeated most other sorts of therapy as well. It has been said of Catholicism that the Italians make the rules and the Irish follow them; in psychotherapy, the analysts make up the theories, and the social workers believe them. The influence of psychoanalysis on the practice of psychotherapy would be hard to overestimate.

Much of the analysts' disdain of touch is based on tradition, but as Mintz points out, there are two principles of psychoanalytic *theory* that might preclude physical contact between therapist and patient. The principles involved are the *rule of abstinence* and the concept of the *analyst as a reflecting mirror.*[12]

In psychoanalytic therapy, abstinence simply means that the analyst is not there to provide gratification for the patient. If the patient loves him, he does not love back; neither is anger met with anger. Analysis is what the word implies and nothing more; the analytic patient has to find gratification elsewhere in life. But, as Mintz notes, the prohibition of physical contact makes sense only if its primary purpose is to gratify the patient. In fact, one would be hard pressed to find a therapist today, touching or non-touching, who believes that the therapeutic relationship in itself should satisfy the patient, meet his needs, and make him happy. (I have found one. Malcolm Brown, a California therapist, says that he ". . . practices a style of body psychotherapy grounded upon the premise that the healing process centers around providing the patient with real here-and-now satisfaction of previously unsatisfied needs for love and caring attention.")[13]

The therapist-as-mirror means that the analyst's personality and beliefs, her feelings and attitudes, should be minimized in order that the transference relationship can develop purely from the patient.

I encounter this argument whenever I speak to psychiatric groups on the use of touch in psychotherapy. Inevitably, an analyst will rise to his feet and with a trace of annoyance in his voice, as though having to point out something extremely obvious to someone who really should know better, will explain to me that touching complicates the transference relationship.

And I inevitably agree. Touching does complicate the transference relationship. But it is just as true that *not* touching complicates the transference relationship. As Michael Argyle points out in *Bodily Communication,* ". . . the absence of a nonverbal act, for example, a refusal to shake hands, may constitute an extremely important social act."[14] Yet strange as it may seem to the uninitiated, there is many an analyst who will not shake hands with a patient during the two or three or eight years of analysis for fear of adding an artifact to the transferential material. I have known analysts who make a point of crossing the street rather than having to meet their patients outside the four walls of the office. Anyone who thinks *that* is not adding material is simply wrong. Everything an analyst does or does not do can become the subject of transference, even unto the pictures she hangs on the wall. Even if she does not hang pictures on the wall. As analyst Melitta Schmideberg put it, "Actually, it is well-nigh impossible to denude the physical surroundings of the analyst's office of significance completely. If he refrains from hanging pictures on the wall, the patient observes the fact in one way or another."[15]

To leave the wall and return to the fingers, there are a number of good reasons aside from transference considerations *not* to touch a patient in therapy. They include:

1. Because you don't want to.
2. Because you sense the patient doesn't want you to.
3. Because, although you want to and sense the patient wants you to, you do not feel that this is the most effective therapeutic maneuver.
4. Because you feel you are being manipulated, conned, or coerced into a touch.

5. Because you suspect that you are going to manipulate, con, or coerce the patient by your touch.

There are also categories of therapists and patients who should not touch or be touched. It is unlikely that the compulsive, withdrawn, intellectual therapist is going to be comfortable with touch or any other sort of intimacy in a therapeutic relationship. It is not for him to pretend such comfort, for his touch will be felt as insincere and will be more likely to raise anxiety than lower it. Some patients should almost never be handled. Touch a paranoid and risk losing a tooth; touch a seductress and risk losing your license. Touch a violent patient with a short fuse and risk losing everything.

All that said, there are very good reasons therapists should strive to become comfortable with physical contact. Most of them are identical to the reasons doctors, nurses, and physiotherapists should be comfortable with touch. It is an ancient and worldwide healing practice. It recapitulates the healing bond as between mother and child. It is a source of comfort inherent in our mammalian heritage. It works.

In psychotherapy there is another reason as well, and one that many therapists are still reluctant to face. The reason is this: for all the rules and prohibitions laid down by one school or another; for all the limitations on the length of the hour or requirements for the length of the training; for all the traditions of doing it this way and not that way because Our Founder did it this way and not that way—for all of that, there is an ever-growing body of evidence that psychotherapy does not work for the reasons psychotherapists think it works. Those who spend years learning techniques are learning one of the least important elements in effective treatment. Those whose ambition it is to become a Freudian as opposed to a Jungian, an Existentialist rather than a Gestaltist, are spending their time on theories that often have little to do with practice and even less to do with whether patients get better.

Professor Jerome Frank was one of the first to argue this heretical line. After years of research on the effectiveness of psychotherapy, he concluded that techniques and theories were not the healing factors in the therapeutic process. What did heal was:

1. The personal relationship between therapist and patient.

2. Emotional arousal.
3. Positive expectation.
4. Enhancement of the patient's sense of mastery or control.[16]

There were other blows to the therapy-as-specialized-technique theory as well. With the exception of behavior modification for circumscribed phobias and other highly specific complaints, no one has been able to show that one technique of psychotherapy is any better than another. Yet these same studies show that there are great differences between individual therapists. Truax and Carkhuff have shown that the most successful therapists are those who combine the qualities of empathy, genuineness, and nonpossessive warmth.[17] Whitehorn and Betz concluded that, in the treatment of schizophrenics, active therapists who offer personal participation get better results than those who are more impersonal and distant.[18]

Each of these body blows took its toll. But the uppercut to the jaw of technique theory came wearing the glove of *The Handbook of Psychotherapy and Behavior Change.*[19]

This is the holy book of scientific research on psychotherapy. It would be hard to overstate its respectability or the reverence with which it is held by serious psychologists. The *Handbook* contains over 5,000 well-researched references. In its Second Edition this standard of scientific conservatism states the following:

> Interpersonal and nonspecific or nontechnical factors still loom large as stimulators of patient improvement. . . . It appears that these personal factors are crucial ingredients even in the more technical therapies. . . . This is not to say that techniques are irrelevant but that their power for change pales when compared with that of personal influence. Technique is crucial to the extent that it provides a believable rationale and congenial modus operandi for the change agent and the client . . . these [personal] influences, when specified, may prove to be the essence of what provides therapeutic benefit.[20]

I once tried to specify four factors that can enhance or inhibit these influences in an article entitled "Four Taboos that May Limit the Success of Psychotherapy."[21] The article included what I call a *psyku,* a short, nonrhyming poem with psychological significance. My psyku goes like this:

Touching                    Not-touching
is not a                    is a
technique:                  technique.

The next section of this chapter is about specific uses of touch in psychotherapy.

There are times when a therapist wants one statement to stand out from the rest; whatever else is said that day, these are the words she wants the patient to hear. A light touch can set the therapist's words in capital letters, can announce that this is more important than what has been said before. The touch acts as *penetrating oil* for the communication. Which touch is used here depends both on the relationship with the patient and on the nature of the statement. Fingers resting lightly on the back of his hand will sometimes be sufficient, but if the patient is one who is easily bruised, or the message is wounding or hurtful, placing both hands around one of his may be more appropriate.

A related use is touch for *holding attention*. Borderline patients, people who walk the earth with tentative steps, sometimes get just as out of touch with their therapist as they do with others in their lives. When I sense that such patients are attending more to clouds in the sky than to what's going on between us in the room, I bring them face to face with me by a light touch on the cheek or by turning their chin with my fingertips.

With patients who are in a genuinely mad state, holding attention is not enough. Here, physical contact can be used as *ground control* for bringing a high flyer down to earth. The example that follows illustrates not only this function of touch but something about medical attitudes and reciprocity as well.

The patient involved was a young woman in her twenties who was floridly psychotic, i.e., mad as a snake. I interviewed her in a psychiatric ward in front of a one-way mirror; behind it were ten advanced medical students. The patient was very bright as well as very crazy and explained to me with convincing detail that we were actually in India where she had just arrived from outer space. As we talked she seemed to be rapidly returning to orbit. At one point I asked permission to take her hand. She said I could, and when I did it had a noticeable effect on her. Within three or four minutes she was no longer in Bengal or the Milky Way but was back in the room with me. I let go of her hand, and very slowly she went over and out again. Once again I took her hand, but this time without asking permission. She stared evenly at the back of my hand resting on hers, and then, with a look of utter disdain, removed it. She managed this without ever coming into contact with my flesh. With her finger and thumb-tips she gripped the identification bracelet I was wearing, fastidiously avoiding contact with my skin. She looked upon my hand as though it were a dead mouse that required removal, and it was thus that she placed the whole nasty thing back in my own lap.

I got her message: It is important to have permission before you touch. If you can't get permission, make sure you get the message that follows.

The rest of the interview went reasonably well, and afterward I walked her back to her ward. She said a couple of last words to me, and then I went back to the students. I walked into the room and was met with total silence. In my years of teaching medical students I have learned that total silence can mean only one of two things: 1. "That was the greatest demonstration of clinical skills we've ever seen, Dr. Older." (I've never experienced this one.) 2. "You've just done something so awful that we can't even talk about it." (I was experiencing this one now.) I implored them to tell me what I had done wrong.

"Surely, Dr. Older, you know what you've done."

"No. Tell me."

"You touched the patient!"

"True. Now tell me your objection to that."

"Surely, Dr. Older, someone with your supposed experience would know that touching a patient has all kinds of effects on transference, not to mention countertransference. This woman is either going to be, a) touch-starved from now on so that everyone has to touch her, b) so emotionally dependent on you that neither her real therapist nor anyone else will be able to do anything with her, or c) most likely she'll fall totally, hopelessly, and eternally in love with you."

In my dealings with medical students I have learned to keep an ace up my sleeve. I had one this time, because I knew something that they did not. My ace was the patient's last words to me, and I repeated them now to the students. They were not, "You're the only doctor who's ever understood me." They were not, "You're the only man who can help me." They were not, "I love you." The patient left me with two words. The words were, "You're OK."

I took them as a compliment. Those two words reassured me that accurate meanings can be conveyed through fingers as well as voice.

A little later I had an urgent request from the medical superintendent of a large psychiatric hospital to initiate therapy with another young woman. She was a teenager who had been shot in the head by her father before he killed himself with the same gun. Somehow, the bullet did not kill her though it was still lodged in her brain. As a result of the emotional and physical trauma she had undergone, Sarah was in a very serious condition. She was somewhat disorganized, her memory was impaired, she walked unsteadily, was blind in one eye, and (I assumed) she had great reason to distrust anyone who might in any way remind her of her father. If Sarah did not recover soon she faced the prospect of lifelong hospitalization. Because of her situation I thought it important to establish a trusting relationship as fast as possible. The episode recounted below was an attempt to *build trust quickly* with a patient in a desperate condition.

Our first meeting was spent talking while we slowly walked together around the hospital grounds. We met a second time a few days later. We had talked about twenty minutes when I rolled up both my shirt sleeves and said to her, "Sarah, I want you to feel my arms."

Looking a little puzzled, she did as I asked. I encouraged her to go beyond her first, tentative touch and really get the feel of me. She kneaded my arms, felt my muscles, and got the sense of my skin and hair.

"How do my arms feel, Sarah?" I asked.

"They feel strong. They feel like they could take anything."

"They can, Sarah. And so can I. Anything you have to tell me, anything you think or feel. My arms can take it, and so can I."

I am confident that this combination of body contact and reassuring words helped build the trust she did have in me and that this trust was an important factor in keeping Sarah out of the institution for the next three years.

I have rediscovered for myself what Freud discovered in his early practice—that skin-to-skin contact is an effective way of *releasing repressed material.* This is such a dramatic process that its description is usually followed by the words, "And after that, therapy really began." An example is psychologist James Linden's description of a relatively unsuccessful engagement in psychotherapy with a profoundly depressed 32-year-old woman. After more than 25 sessions, which were characterized by lack of emotional involvement and no real change in the depression, Linden tentatively took her hand.

> A few seconds passed and Colleen began to weep for the first time since I had seen her. A few more seconds passed, and she pulled her hand away and began sobbing. Then she screamed so violently that therapists in offices down the hall asked me afterward what had happened. Colleen sat there with her hands over her eyes and she yelled like a small child: "I hate everybody! I hate the world! How can they be happy? They don't know anything! No one understands me! Why can't I be like everyone else? I want to be happy! I hate everyone! Why, why, why . . ." Her outburst lasted for about five minutes, during which time she also repeatedly said "I'm sorry," and apologized for crying. I stood up and put my hand on her shoulder and told her that it was OK to cry. When Colleen eventually stopped crying she looked up at me and said softly, "I want so badly to change."
>
> At that point, her therapy really began. It was that session, she reported later, which most facilitated her expression of sexual, affectionate and angry feelings toward me, and subsequently toward other people in her life.[22]

The journal in which Dr. Linden presented his paper followed it with a discussion paper by Carl Christensen, M.D. In it Dr. Christensen refers to Linden as a "paramedic" and dismisses his patient's behavior as "acting out." He states his belief that emotional displays accomplish little and (you've heard this before) ". . . merely complicate an already complex process." His dismissive patronizing continues throughout the discussion, the tone of which is neatly captured by his observation, "Dr. Linden might have produced a positive response without all the histrionics and by using a different technique."[23]

Linden's touch burst a bubble that had been swelling inside Colleen, a bubble of hatred. Fear can be another deeply buried emotion. An example of the power of touch to release repressed fear appeared when the same journal printed an article by its editor, Vin Rosenthal, on the subject of holding in psychotherapy.[24] Rosenthal's patient spoke in a flat, controlled monotone even when she was talking about sadness and anger; she "talked about" rather than "involved herself in" both therapy and the rest of her life. Needing to break through this isolating membrane, the therapist held her in his arms. Only then did her tears start to flow. She wept a torrent, and when it finally abated, she suddenly began to vent her anger and sadness. Finally, feelings of fear exploded from her as she spoke for the first time of her dread that she would develop the same sort of cancer that killed her mother.

As Linden and Rosenthal discovered, touch can help the hopelessly blocked patient begin real therapeutic communication. Rosenthal's article is unusually useful in that it describes in some detail just how the therapist makes contact with his patient. His description follows:

> Here is how I hold. Usually with legs crossed, sometimes with one leg down and my foot on the floor. I sit nestled in one corner of the couch, my back firmly supported by pillows. Another pillow covers the area from my groin to my chest. The person lies down on his side facing the back of the couch; his head resting on the pillow at the level of my chest, his legs pulled up as far as is comfortable, his arms circling me loosely. My arms embrace him, encompassing his upper body; sometimes gently, sometimes firmly, he is fully supported. Often I will stroke the person's head during the Holding. I follow the language of his body in deciding whether to rock him, talk, encourage him to talk, or just let us be there together. The pillow serves as mutual protection and to filter body movement communication of the person. Any feelings which emerge from the Holding are all right and may be shared or experienced privately. There is no explicit sexual contact.[25]

I'm emphasizing touch as a recoverer of repressed material because that uncovering process is the essence of classical psychoanalytic therapy. For a therapist to deny herself the extremely useful tool of physical contact is like skiing a slalom without poles: you can conduct therapy without touch and get down the course without poles, but the champion in either endeavor uses everything available.

Here is a third example of touch as an uncoverer, this one from my own practice of family therapy. The incident took place in a New York social work agency where many clients seemed to run the sort of low-grade psychic fever that is strongly resistant to treatment. This family was no exception; they were there because their son was having trouble at school, and the school authorities had insisted that they get help. Their limited involvement in the therapeutic process revolved around their son, and, despite my suspicion that there were unspoken issues between the parents, I could not break through their mutual agreement that everything was just fine. After weeks that seemed like months, then months that seemed like years, we were going around in an increasingly boring circle.

During a particularly droning session on an especially hot day, I was suddenly seized with an idea. I stopped whatever they were talking about, and, after a moment's silence, took the woman's hand. I instructed her husband to take the other. Then I turned to her and said, "You're in good hands. Now tell me, *what* is going on here?"

To my amazement, she did. She spoke of how their child was adopted, an event that left her feeling incomplete as a woman and a failure as a human being. She felt her husband had somehow been cheated because she had not experienced the pain of childbirth. Incompleteness, birth, pain . . . this is the stuff of psychotherapy, the sort of material that gives us shrinks the courage to go on. Nothing like it had ever been said in our sessions together or between the two of them at home. The touch of our hands had actually transformed marking-time-and-calling-it-therapy to real, honest-to-goodness work.

This experience both excited and unnerved me. So strongly ingrained was the taboo against touch that I did not report it to my supervisor; instead, I arranged a demonstration. When it was my turn to present in front of the one-way screen to my supervision group, I brought in another patient, a very difficult woman in her fifties. She was a widow harboring injustices that began the day after she was born. Her father had been awful to her, and so had her brother and her husband. Now her son was being awful to her as was the man who sat next to her in the subway, her boss, and, most especially, me. In therapy we were stuck at the level of her being the victim of so much awfulness.

We were having our usual awful session in front of the mirror when I decided to do something *really* awful. I said, "Give me your hand." She did. "You're in good hands. Now tell me, what is going on here?" And she *did!* Just as with the family, new material emerged that was exciting, frightening, and above all, therapeutic.

When my patient left at the end of the hour, I asked my colleagues for their thoughts and feelings. My fellow therapists were impressed and a bit frightened by what they had seen. My boss, a social worker who was both an exquisite diagnositician and a brilliant therapist, made what I believe was one of her few mistakes in the years that I worked with her. She said, "What you did was good, but now you must learn to touch without touching."

I knew what she meant—you can genuflect mentally when you enter a church without getting down on your knees, and you can touch people with your eyes and your voice without ever laying a finger on them. But the other message that I got was, Don't Touch Anybody. And for several years I did not. During that time I lost a powerful tool in that most difficult trade, psychotherapy.

There is another, very different use for touch in family therapy, one that I have employed only occasionally. A persistent problem when seeing families is one family member (more often than not, the mother) not letting another (usually a child) speak for himself. Usually the therapist responds in one of two ways: either she hesitantly repeats what she has already said a hundred times before, "Ah, Mrs. Levy, everyone is allowed to speak for himself, you know . . ." or, finally enraged, hollers, "Shut up! Let the kid talk!"

I find both these responses embarrassing and much prefer to use touch for *silencing a disrupter*. My usual intervention is to place the flat of my hand on the disrupter's thigh and leave it there for about five seconds. The effect is almost always instantaneous. The appropriate silence usually commences at once. On those rare occasions when this is not enough, I switch to my second response, which is simply to place my hand gently but firmly over the interrupter's mouth. Touch wood, I've never been bitten yet.

Some families hold secrets too awful for them to talk about. Such secrets often involve touch. One family may have the unspoken fear that physical contact will lead to incest; another, that it may end in murder. The touch-skilled therapist can, by his own behavior, provide a *model* that demonstrates that affectionate touch can be benign, that it need not lead to disaster. With the inarticulate or taboo-ridden family, gesture and model may provide the only means of therapeutic access.

There is another form of physical contact that from time to time serves a valuable function in both family and child psychotherapy. The use of the therapist's body as an *agent of control* is not often described in the literature, but it sometimes snatches therapeutic success from the jaws of premature termination, especially when working with children 17 and younger. Many therapists of children and teenagers engulf a tantruming kid in their arms until he finds his own control.

A time when I used this sort of contact successfully involved not a child but a medical student in her early twenties. She had successfully turned my Workshop on Emotions into an encounter group, and, having done so, asked her fellow students how they felt about her. She got decidedly mixed reviews from her classmates, and, after hearing one too many negative comments, she suddenly bolted for the door in tears. But I was seated between her and the door, and when she leapt to her feet so did I. I moved into a position where a direct path to the door would take her right into my arms. This is just the path she chose, and I simply held her while she struggled against me for a moment, then calmed down and returned to her seat. If she had left the room, the whole group would have felt terrible, but by staying she transformed the session into the most important and meaningful of our meetings.

Note that I say she "chose" the direct path which led into my arms. She could easily have avoided me or knocked me down as she went through. I've seen this sort of choice illustrated dramatically a number of times, such as when a large and violent male patient allows a 97-pound female nurse to restrain him with her arms and body. I have experienced the same thing with enraged teenage patients who can only let themselves be hugged when the hug is disguised as restraint.

One of the most difficult tasks of psychotherapy is opening the eyes of people who feel worthless to their true value. Put another way, it is the process of letting patients who feel unlovable realize that they are *worthy of love.* I have written about some of the complexities of this task under the title "Interpersonal Testing and Pseudotesting in Counseling and Therapy,"[26] but I didn't realize then how vital a role touch can play in the process. I do now, partly through my own experience as a therapist and partly through a courageous, self-revealing article by another therapist, Althea Horner. Dr. Horner's article says so much, so well, that I want to quote it at length:

> I was born to a mother who could be tender and demonstrative toward the helpless baby, but who withdrew love when the child's developing will led to the first "no." Driven by a strong need for autonomy, I sacrificed maternal affection at an early age. I do not remember the last time I was held affectionately in my mother's arms. I grew up convinced that she did not love me, and questioned my lovability. Then I married a kind but undemonstrative man who grew up in a home where open affection was not shown. My need for touch, for "stroking," for contact comfort, was once again thwarted. My self-image became more and more one of "untouchableness."
>
> As a graduate student I went into psychotherapy where, from time to time, I would express my longing to have the therapist hold me. Each time I was told that my problem was that I wanted gratification instead of therapy. Now I had learned something new about myself. Not only was I untouchable, but my wish for contact comfort was "bad."
>
> A few years later, facing a personal crisis, I had occasion to see another therapist for a short time. Undoubtedly in order to protect myself from being rebuffed once more, I told him at the start about my previous experience and wondered what he would do were I to express such a wish. He shared openly with me his feelings of anxiety at the prospect. I smiled and reassured him that this would not happen. But now I had learned still more about myself. I made people uncomfortable. My wish for contact comfort was frightening to others. It might drive them away from me. I was now not only untouchable and bad; I was also a danger to others.[27]

Later, Dr. Horner spent a week at the Esalen Institute at Big Sur and found herself in an environment in which physical contact was valued and encouraged. During that week she was gently held in the arms of men and women: "Tentative at the start, but at the very end crying as another woman held me close, the whole structure of my negative self-image came crashing down.... Men—women—it made no difference. The need for the kind of contact that says you are not untouchable, bad, or dangerous has no sex."[28] Writing nearly a year later, Dr. Horner felt that the changes had been maintained and were now a part of her:

> And, not so surprisingly, my inner transformation has affected my approach to others. Being less guilty and anxious over taking the initiative in an encounter, I could allow myself greater openness and spontaneity. I took greater risks, but then I also reaped greater rewards. For, equally predictable, the response of others to me was also changed, including that of my husband and my patients.[29]

There are other uses of touch in therapy that parallel those discussed in earlier chapters. An enfolding hug eases the sorrow of a patient who is grieving the loss of a parent. A firm and prolonged hand hug allays the fears of a patient entering a hospital. Some therapists find that shoulder massage can be an unthreatening way of establishing human contact with a patient cut off from the rest of humanity. And in therapy as well as the general hospital, touch can be an important diagnostic tool.

Of course, you have to use the tool carefully. I became a therapy patient while still a graduate student. When my therapist shook hands with me as I entered his office for the first time, he said, "You must be anxious. Your hand is moist."

"No," I replied, "you've run out of towels in the bathroom."

There is one other use of touch in therapy I want to discuss, and, because it is extremely controversial, I want to talk about it at length. This is the use of touch as a reinforcer. Little controversy exists when touch is used as a positive reinforcer; as previously mentioned, behaviorists have found that many retarded and autistic children learn new behaviors more effectively when they are followed by a friendly rub on the head rather than the traditional reinforcer, a piece of candy popped in the mouth. The controversy develops when touch is used as a negative reinforcer or punishment. I call this the *hard touch*. The most famous (or infamous) advocate of hard touch is psychologist O. Ivar Lovaas. When working with autistic children, he does not hesitate to shake or even slap them to bring their attention away from their inner dreams and back to the person in the room with them. Many psychologists—though not many parents of autistic children—strongly object to such treatment. Since the therapeutic failure rate with autism is notoriously high, I believe the carefully restrained use of Lovaas' technique is justified. These children require some form of sharp intervention, and the consequences of autism are considerably worse than the brief shake or slap.

But if some flinch at the idea of a slap, almost everyone recoils from another of Lovaas' techniques, the use of electric cattle prods on young children. The very thought of such apparently sadistic behavior brings on feelings of repulsion and disgust. But there is more to the story.

The children Lovaas shocks are self-mutilators. These are children who physically maim themselves, even to the point of repeatedly gashing their faces or biting off their own fingers. They do this whether they are hugged or ignored, praised or punished. The usual treatment is constant physical restraint in the form of a straight jacket, for as soon as this is removed they begin the self-destruction anew. It takes Lovaas but a few shocks to extinguish the behavior, and it does not return for a considerable period.[30]

Is this drastic sort of intervention justified? I believe it is *in this situation*. What worries me is that when a drastic technique proves of use in treating an even more drastic condition, it may be used in situations where it is neither needed nor justifiable. There have already been cases where institutional staff have shocked children as punishment for misbehavior. *This* is what I would call "criminal ruthlessness," and I would also call the police. Here are my guidelines for the use of hard touch.

1. The pain or danger caused by the condition must be considerably greater than the pain caused by the touch.
2. Painless methods must have been tried and exhausted before painful ones are considered.
3. Fully informed consent must be obtained from the patient or the patient's guardian before the procedure is employed.

When people hear about a psychologist who uses cattle prods on young children, they naturally want to know what he's really like. So, what is Lovaas like? He is a very fit, athletic, high energy, Norwegian-born Californian. While echoes of the fiords remain in his speech, his actual words owe more to Los Angeles than Oslo. When he praises an autistic child for responding appropriately, he doesn't just say, "Good." Lovaas says, "*Good city!*"

Lovaas's mother had a fiery temper, and his own upbringing included a fair number of switchings from a branch of the birch tree that grew outside her door. He considers his own upbringing too strict and has made it a point not to be so quick to hit as was his mother. Still, like 80 percent of Americans, Lovaas did use physical punishment in the raising of his own four children. If one of them was causing a commotion at the Sunday dinner table, rather than being sent to his room for "time out," he was given a quick pinch under the table from his long-armed father.

In his work, Lovaas no longer uses cattle prods except in the rarest of instances. Instead, he uses his hand in the form of a slap on the thigh or buttocks. He prefers this because it is more in keeping with traditional American child-rearing practice; I prefer it because it is closer to skin-to-skin contact. The further we get from that, the more I worry. I am much more concerned about the effects of cattle prods or shock generators or even birch branches than I am about the use of the human hand as an instrument of hard touch. If hard touch is to be used, I want as much human contact as possible in it.

Lovaas was by no means the first to use punitive touch to alter behavior. The parent's spank, the schoolmaster's cane, and the policeman's billy club have all been deployed toward the same goal. And there have even been times when what would seem like punitive touch has been demanded by the patient. In the early eighteenth century the Convulsionaires of St.-Médard gathered in great numbers around the tomb of St. Paris for a most unusual healing ritual, a ritual during which they offered their bodies to the most extraordinary amounts of pain. Many enjoyed being trampled and beaten. Mackay describes one woman who

> . . . was so enraptured with this ill-usage, that nothing but the hardest blows would satisfy her. While a fellow of Herculean strength was beating her with all his might with a heavy bar of iron, she kept continually urging him to renewed exertion. The harder he struck the better she liked it, exclaiming all the while, "Well done, brother, well done! Oh, how pleasant it is! What good you are doing me! Courage, my brother, courage; strike harder, strike harder still!"[31]

This, not Lovaas, marks the high tide of the use of hard touch in healing.

I have used hard touch only once, and that was not in the usual confines of a therapeutic relationship. It actually took place in prison, in the Women's Prison of New Zealand, to be precise. I'd been a regular visitor there. Since I had a weekly radio show at the time, I always went as a disc jockey rather than a psychologist. I figured that when it came to establishing a trusting relationship with a prisoner, the odds were about 10 to 1 in favor of the d.j.

A big day came when Foxy, one of the smartest women in the prison and a regular recidivist, was released. But the good feeling didn't last long; a week later I got an urgent message at the medical school that I was needed at once in court. The message came from another ex-con who said she would meet me on the courthouse steps. I leapt upon my trusty ten-speed and raced through the downtown streets. I stomped on the brakes and stumbled up the courthouse steps only to be told that I was too late—the hearing had just concluded, and Foxy was going back to jail. She'd been caught walking out of a department store with a couple of suits that the store hadn't intended giving away. She had wanted to use me as a character reference, but the judge said she was going to have to stand trial. In fact, she was on her way to a solitary holding cell now.

Because I'd been a pretty steady visitor, the screws knew me well enough to be sure that I was not about to stage a jailbreak, and Foxy's guard asked me if I wanted to take her to her cell. I did indeed. Foxy was all sheepish and apologetic as we climbed the stone stairs to the holding room. She kept looking back at me to see if I was angry with her. My face betrayed nothing, and I didn't say a word, but when she reached the landing and started into the cell, I came up behind her and booted her squarely in the ass with the side of my foot.

"Hey, what was that for?"

"That was for knocking off a department store one week after you got out of prison."

"Oh."

I want to point out that: a) I used the side of my foot and not a steel-tipped toe, b) this somewhat unorthodox therapeutic touch took place in the context of an already established relationship, c) the concern that propelled the foot was clear to the person who received it, and d) I stayed and talked with her for an hour afterward and came back for another hour that evening.

Foxy wrote me from prison to say that she was going to send me a tape about her life and where she thought it had gone wrong. But she never did, and she has been in and out of Her Majesty's Hotel several times since. Sometimes it works, sometimes it doesn't.

### Some Last Thoughts on Touch in Therapy

• I offer you touch as a useful addition to the repertoire of therapeutic skills, not as a cure-all. Touch skills alone cannot transform an incompetent therapist into a champion, nor can they heal all of the walking wounded.

• When I hold someone's hand in family therapy, I *always* give the hand back to the spouse. Then I move my chair back, leaving them together with each other and slightly apart from me. Whenever possible, the therapist's job is to help strengthen the positive bonds in the family. It is not the therapist's job to be the good spouse in contrast to the inadequate slob in the next chair. Give the couple back to each other.

• People sometimes worry that the informed touch is a calculated touch. It is not. Psychotherapy is the art of keeping your balance on a highwire when one tip of your pole is weighted with spontaneity and the other, with maneuver. Touch is part of that. I have never made a "calculated" touch in psychotherapy, ever. I haven't always touched when I felt like it, either.

• Becoming a therapist does not diminish in the least your potential for sexual arousal. Patients who are young, intelligent, attractive, articulate, and of the opposite sex often convert this potential into actuality. Because therapists find this group of patients so fascinating, it may be wise when first experimenting with touch to make your beginnings with patients who do not fit this description. Those who are either very old or unattractive usually need it more, anyway.

• When practicing therapy in a culture with a strong touch taboo, the touching therapist must be especially sensitive to the feelings of the patient. While you may have gone through 23 encounter groups, 11 marathons, and a Rolfing, your patient may not. On the other hand, touch in an unexpected situation is particularly powerful as a releaser, a comforter, and a change agent.

• Many therapists worry about the possible consequences of touch. They fear sanctions from their bosses, their peers, and even from the law. We live in a strange time in which it is perfectly acceptable to induce convulsions in a person with electricity, yet it may be illegal to hold that same person's hand.

- And once again,

> Touching
> is not a
> technique:
> Not-touching
> is a
> technique.

# The Body Therapies

## 13

What is it, then,
this seamless body-stocking,
some two yards square,
this our casing,
our facade,
that flushes, pales,
perspires, glistens, glows,
furrows,
tingles,
crawls, itches,
pleasures,
and pains us all our days . . .
—Richard Selzer

Body therapies are those forms of treatment that deal with the same problems as the psychotherapies—problems like schizophrenia, neurosis, and character disorders—but which conceptualize and treat them somatically as well as psychologically. Rather than rely on talk, body therapists prod, palpate, massage, manhandle, exercise, examine, hug, and occasionally hit their patients. Whatever the problem, the body is part of it. And the body can be the "royal road to the unconscious" every bit as much as dreams and slips of the tongue.

In his book *Character Analysis*, Wilhelm Reich observed that neuroses are carried in the muscles as well as the mind. Shallow breathing, stiff posture, and an awkward gait reveal as much about a person as do fears and fantasies.[1] Body therapists deepen the breathing, rearrange the posture, and smooth the awkwardness as a way of revealing and releasing inner conflicts.

To understand the body therapies one has first to come to terms with Wilhelm Reich. Understanding Reich is no easy task, for he is one of the most complex figures in the history of psychology, having been in his lifetime a visionary and a madman, a social democrat and an authoritarian tyrant, a masterful clinician and an ass. Reich was writing about mystification before Laing, plotting sexual response curves before Masters and Johnson, advocating holistic medicine before Pelletier, describing the psychology of fascism before Adorno, and denouncing patriarchies long before the women's liberation movement.[2]

A Marxist in his early years, he was thrown out of the Communist Party. A psychoanalyst in his early and middle years, he was drummed out of the psychoanalytic movement. An internationally famous psychiatrist, he was kicked out of a number of countries. And most ironically of all, this impassioned advocate of freedom ended his days inside the walls of an American federal prison. Toward the end of this seesaw life of his, Reich believed that the Russians were after him, that he could make rain and divert hurricanes, that he had discovered new forms of energy, that the earth was being invaded by spacemen with whom he fought nightly battles—and he was able to convince a substantial number of followers that all these things were true. (For an insider's view of these years, see Ilse Ollendorff Reich's *Wilhelm Reich: A Personal Biography.*)[3]

Reich is of interest to us here because he is the putative father of touch in psychotherapy. (It could be argued that Ferenczi or even Freud first sired therapeutic touch, but the former's influence has never been great, and the latter denied paternity through most of his life.) After several years as an orthodox analyst and a member of Freud's inner circle, Reich devised character analysis, a type of therapy that was a departure from the rigid psychoanalytic tradition. (The tradition was then even more rigid than today. Nic Waal, a prominent Norwegian psychiatrist, described the clinical movement in the 1930s: "... it was, in fact, a horrible offense even to touch the patient. It was to break all basic rules and basic thinking on transference. It seemed to seduce the patient."[4] Of her first analyst, she wrote, "He did not take my hand, he hardly greeted me, he stood at a four-meter distance when I entered the room."[5] Her second analyst was almost the same: "He stood at a four-meter distance, did not take my hand, and his comments were 'yes' and 'no.'")[6]

Unfortunately, we have very little direct information about what kind of touching Reich actually did. He makes passing references to pressing muscles, palpation, and loosening character incrustrations, but beyond that there is little to go on. What is worse, the very detailed description of the evolution of Reich's work by his biographer and admirer, David Boadella, merely tantalizes. He tells us what Reich did:

> Reich began to use his hands directly on the bodies of his patients in order to work directly on the tense muscle knots. He was at great pains to point out that this was quite different from a physiological massage or manipulation since it was necessary to understand the role of each tension in the total armoring of the patient. In vegetotherapy [one of Reich's early names for his method of treatment] he was guided always by the *emotional function* of the tensions.

But he doesn't tell us how he did it:

> If this was not grasped, mechanical pressure and muscle groups had only very superficial effects. For this reason no time will be made here to describe vegetotherapeutic techniques in greater detail.[7]

When I asked Boadella if he could point me toward some documentation as to Reich's use of touch, he replied, "There is no published account of Reich's style of touch. This is taught by example."[8]

I am not alone in my frustration at this determined lack of detail. In his penetrating critique of Reich's work, *Reich*, Charles Rycroft takes him to task for his failure to describe the reactions of therapist and patient to nude physical contact. Rycroft observes:

> Characteristically, Reich remains silent both about the patient's physical and psychological responses to being looked at and touched by his therapist, and about the therapist's responses to

the increasing relaxation, trustfulness and overt sexual behavior of his patients. He writes, as 25 years later Masters and Johnson have done, as though it were possible for a therapist to remain objective, unmoved and yet human when confronted with the overt sexual reactions of his patients. As a result it is impossible to decide to what extent the effectiveness of such direct onslaughts on sexual inhibition depends on the therapist's correct understanding of the psychological and physiological principles involved or on some charismatic factor in his personality which enables him to bless the patient sexually by a secular, pseudo-medical form of the religious ceremony of Laying On of Hands (Confirmation).[9]

We do not learn much about Reich's style of touching from his most famous student and analysand either. Like so many of Reich's disciples and students, Alexander Lowen is heavy on praise of his teacher but very light on detail.[10]

The same problem applies to his own work. Lowen is the founder of Bioenergetics, a therapeutic school that directly derives from Reich many of its tenets but which has been molded by Lowen into its own form. Bioenergetics is today a major force in the realm of the body therapies. Unfortunately, Lowen is as coy about his own touch technique as about his mentor's. For example, after describing a case in some detail, he concludes, "That the character was finally broken though was due to the use of a technique which could circumvent the rigid exterior to reach the biological core." And that is all the reader learns!

The careful reader is at best able to piece together some bits of information handed out in passing. We know that Lowen sometimes presses a patient's throat:

As she lay on the couch during the second session I could sense from her breathing a catch in her throat. Palpation revealed a powerful spasm of the throat musculature. A quick pressure on these muscles produced a scream of fright which was followed by deep crying. The traumatic incident flashed into her mind.[12]

We know that he does something to jaws:

At the first session with an attractive young lady, I was struck by her strong jaw and the set of her head. The impression this jaw gave was one of grimness. It is only a matter of degree from a determined jaw to a grim one but I did not doubt my impression. . . . While I worked on the total body attitude I spent time each session softening the jaw and releasing tensions at the back of her neck. Each time I worked on this region she would cry softly, following which she brightened perceptibly.[13]

And it appears that Lowen's patients wear little clothing in their sessions with him:

During the subsequent therapy we both realized that he did not face the problems of his life. One day he became upset and nauseous and had to throw up. As he did this we were both shocked to see a yellow streak appear on the midline of his abdomen. The expression "yellow bellied" flashed into our minds simultaneously. One tends not to take such phrases literally, but here was a visual demonstration one could not ignore. The yellow coloration disappeared when his stomach was empty.[14]

Despite the reticence of Reich and Lowen to describe what they do with patients, we do have reports by others of the kinds of contact that occur in Reichian and Lowenian therapy.

In a long article entitled "The New Body Psychotherapies" Malcolm Brown tells us that orthodox Reichians usually ask their patients to take off all their clothes and lie on a bed or couch for most of the session. The session begins with patients doing deep breathing exercises while the therapist looks for tensions, blocks, and spasticity in the muscles as well as shallowness of breathing.

A . . . very common alternative is for the therapist to actively begin to manipulate the patient's body with two hands, placing them in such a way as to either further the process of organismic relaxation set going by the deep breathing or else to give relief and release to those parts of the body which seem resistive to the whole relaxation process. What little talking is engaged in is highly selective, there being a certain obligation on the part of both patient and therapist to confine themselves to bodily-related phenomena.[15]

Brown says that, by contrast, Lowen uses much less direct body contact, relying instead on stress positions, activity exercises, and verbal techniques designed to increase and release feelings. Patients keep their clothing on unless they request nudity, and the breathing exercises at the beginning of the session are done with the patient standing or arching backward rather than lying on a couch. Bioenergetics usually combines talk and advice (much as you would find in ordinary psychotherapy) with work on breathing, posture, and musculature. Using breathing exercises, tension-producing postures, the gag reflex, and finger attacks on tight and spastic muscles, Bioenergetics attempts to get patients in touch with repressed or locked-in feelings. Muscle palpation is sometimes followed by a wail, a flood of tears, or a sudden feeling of fear.

For about three months I was a participant-observer in a Bioenergetics group. Unfortunately, the experience did not allow me to write directly about the uses of touch I observed, for I observed almost no touch, either between therapist and patient or among group members.

In his study, *The New Group Therapies*,[16] Hendrik Ruitenbeek describes some physical contact in Bioenergetics, but his description is so brief that I suspect he has read more than he's actually seen. Ruitenbeek says that during a dramatic moment in the group Lowen's patients (or subjects, as Lowen prefers to call them) sometimes embrace each other. Between therapist and subject the contact takes two forms. One is what Lowen calls the laying on of hands and appears to be a kneading massage of tense and spastic muscles. The other is a simpler form of contact, such as holding a distressed patient or embracing a joyful one. Ruitenbeek, himself a therapist, argues that the main difference between Lowen and others is that Lowen writes about his uses of touch (though, as we have seen, in no great detail) ". . . whereas many other therapists consider these actions as something between them and their patients and prefer to keep it that way."[17]

Ruitenbeek concludes:

The value of Lowen's bioenergetic groups and the encounter groups that employ touch and physicality in their sessions is that they essentially bring back to the patient a long-lost desire to express his feelings in a physical way. Anger can be expressed verbally (and most of the time it is) but it also can and should be at times expressed physically. So it goes for affection, words are often not enough to express warmth, human consideration and concern, or simple affection, and the body then has to become involved.[18]

Reich's most energetic child may be Lowen, but his most prolific offspring is not a person but—appropriately—a movement. Like a prize bull whose frozen sperm keeps his characteristics alive long after he is gone, Reich posthumously sired the human potential movement, that lovely flower child of psychology that was born under the redwoods in the Big Sur. (Reich was not the only bull in the paddock. Some of the relations look a lot like Gurdjieff, Lewin, Moreno, and Maslow.) The HPM has a thousand children of its own now, and they are a widely traveled lot. You have to leave California and even the United States to realize just how far-flung the family is. You can learn psychodrama from a master in Western Australia. You can study advanced Gestalt psychology in the southernmost city of New Zealand. You can find patients playing growth games in a London psychiatric hospital. You can take *est* in Bombay.

The human potential movement is a child of the 60s. It was always an unruly kid, so that even now, two decades (two decades!) later, it is still difficult to categorize and define. And that would suit the human potentialists perfectly. As good a definition as any comes from Jane Howard, a journalist who devoted a year of her life to participant-observation of the movement and described it in an engaging book, *Please Touch*. She defines the HPM as

> ... a loosely organized force which resists labeling but which for the sake of convenience is often called the human potential movement. The movement is many things. It is a business, a means of recreation, a subculture, a counterculture, a form of theater, a philosophy of education, a kind of psychotherapy, and an underground religion, with its own synods, sects, prophets, schisms and heretics ...

> Some of them don't even know who the others are. They all, however, share an unwritten credo. They all believe that you don't have to be sick to get better, that you needn't stop growing just because you are chronologically an adult, and that the best place to achieve growth is among other people also engaged in growing.[19]

Whatever else the movement may be, it is the greatest source of physical contact in post-Freudian psychotherapy. The nicknames by which it is (sometimes derisively) known tell the story: Group Grope. Touchy-Feelies. And for insiders, the "All-purpose cop-out Esalen hug."

The HPM is very much oriented toward touch. Common activities include backrubs, massage, hands-on relaxation exercises, trust exercises in which one person falls back into the arms of another, love baths in which everyone in a group hugs one another, and blind walks.

The blind walk is really designed as another trust exercise—one person leads a blindfolded partner on a walking journey—but it is also an excellent teacher of tactile discrimination. Jane Howard describes it well:

> We were supposed to join hands and introduce each other to the widest possible variety of tactile experiences. The idea was to "feel the world, for a change, instead of seeing it," and in the process to sense how it was to be dependent. I guided the Lady Notary Public to smooth marble table tops, prickly horsehair upholstery, offensive plastic plants, tinkly crystal lamp pendants, and a trunk hidden away in the storage room. She barely touched any of these surfaces, reaching out tentatively and quickly withdrawing her clear-polished fingertips.[20]

In my work as therapist, counselor, and teacher, I have borrowed heavily from the human potential movement and found many of its strategies and games to be useful ways of translating concepts into personally experienced reality. (I have written about experiential teaching in *Teaching of Psychology*.)[21] But I do not accept all the ideas of the movement, and some I explicitly reject. The 1960s Gestalt ideal of "You do your thing, and I do mine, and that's it, Baby" is for me the perfect prescription for divorce. The HPM's 1970s journey into mysticism is something I regard as a failure of an earlier ideal of here-and-nowness. I have always valued the movement's earthiness, and these more recent travels into the world of the occult is a trip I will not take.

But the blind walk is one I gladly will, and often have taken. Whenever possible, I try to hold blind walks outside. I have led

Australian family practitioners through tropical gardens and New Zealand psychology students along campus paths. The blind walk is one of my favorite ways of teaching touching, a subject we will explore in the next chapter.

Another perspective on the HPM may be found in *Touching*, a novel by Gwen Davis (based, I believe, on Jane Howard's *Please Touch*). The action takes place at a nude marathon held in and beside a private, heated California swimming pool. As you might suspect, there is no shortage of physical contact, therapeutic and otherwise. Here's a sample:

> His fingers moved to the side of my neck, and they were warm; he worked the anguish loose from the tight muscles around my collarbone. The back of his wrist tilted up toward my face, and I leaned my head so my cheek could touch it. And God, it was soft. So manly, surprising soft. And his fingers were moving up to my face, tracing it, lifting my lids so I would see him, really see him. "You're so afraid," he whispered. "So afraid."[22]

Ms. Davis' passionate prose notwithstanding, "touchy-feely" is in some ways an unfair appellation for the movement, one that reveals more about the society that uses the term than the group that it supposedly describes. While there is some touch purely for the sake of sensory pleasure in the human potential movement, what really distinguishes it from ordinary group therapies is the allowable use of touch as part of the healing process. Put another way, therapeutic maneuvers are not dismissed or forbidden simply because they include some form of physical contact. And many HPM games do. In the well-known Break-in game, a person who feels like an outsider in life or in the group is encouraged not just to talk about it, but to physically break into a circle formed by the other group members linking hands. Similarly, a person feeling trapped in relationships struggles to break *out* of the circle.

Arm wrestling is almost ubiquitous. It constitutes an energetic, harmless way of expressing competitive feelings. Other feelings are brought into awareness by the Approach game in which two group members walk slowly toward one another from opposite sides of the room and express their immediate feelings about each other—without words—when they meet. Occasionally the therapist is one of the participants, and the exercise is used to create awareness of transference feelings. But sometimes the therapist learns more about himself than about the patient.

It happened to me. When I was a student therapist one of my first patients was a somewhat obsessive and compliant young man whom I saw for several years in individual therapy. We discussed in the fullness of time nearly every issue that is associated with analytically oriented psychotherapy, usually with a degree of detachment that was in keeping with *his* use of isolation-of-affect as a defense against anxiety and *my* fear of letting things get out of control. In our third year together, he and his wife joined a couples group I was running. By now I had started to experiment with variations on the psychotherapy techniques I was learning in graduate school. At one group meeting I had him stand facing me in order to intensify and express a feeling he was struggling with. Standing there with him in the middle of the room, I asked him what he was feeling toward me at that moment. I expected him to say that he wanted to hit me. Instead, he said quietly, "I want to kiss you." I nearly fainted—literally. My knees grew weak, my breathing rapid. I mumbled a few pseudotherapeutic words and sat the both of us down before I fell down. Oh, I could deal with homosexuality—as a topic; but I could not begin to handle the idea of another man wanting to kiss me.

That experience may have been one of the choice points of my life. It wouldn't have taken much for me to renounce experiments in psychotherapy and return to the safe, charted territory of orthodox methods. Had I made that choice I would have tacitly accepted the reigning dictum that those who deal with the mind must never touch the body. I don't know whether it was God or Devil who saved me from making that choice, but whichever it was, I humbly thank Her.

Those who do not draw an iron curtain between psyche and soma, who use physical as well as verbal measures in the struggle for health, risk the disapproval of their peers. So imbued are most therapists with the no-touch mentality that they feel guilty about body contact even when they haven't been criticized. For many of us, the ghost of Freud or Skinner or our first supervisor perches like a raven on our shoulder, digging in its talons in response to any impulse to touch a patient, and admonishing, "Nevermore!"

I saw this graphically illustrated at England's most prestigious psychiatric institution, the Maudsley Hospital. During a seminar on touch and psychotherapy, a senior psychiatrist in his mid-forties confessed that he had been holding a patient's hand in their weekly sessions for over two years. I say "confessed" because that is how it felt to him; although the hand holding was effective, supportive, and devoid of sexual overtones, he had never told a soul about it.

When I asked him who was sitting on *his* shoulder, he laughed ruefully, shook his head and mumbled a name I didn't quite catch.

"Who?"

He paused and smiled once more. Then he spoke:

"I said that the disapproving conscience on *my* shoulder is none other than Maudsley himself. Beard and all!"

The English psychiatrist's reservations about his own use of touch fits a pattern I have observed among the helping professions. Psychiatrists worry that touch is somehow a breach of propriety; they fear that to touch a patient is to violate some unspoken medical code. Psychologists fear the law suit; their fantasy is that a litigious patient will haul them into court as the result of a misinterpreted touch. Social workers don't fear their patients—they fear their supervisors. Their fantasy is that they will come to work one morning and find themselves fired for having hugged a patient.

It is not always fantasy. A Massachusetts social worker did come to work one morning to find himself fired for hugging a patient. In January 1981, a 55-year-old psychiatric social worker named Daniel Murrow was dismissed from the hospital where he had worked for a number of years for "improper conduct." The psychiatrist who sacked him described the hugging to journalist David Arnold as "overt acting out" and worried aloud about "medical malpractice suits stemming from situations of deviance." It seems that the social worker made a practice of hugging his patients and that he had already been warned to stop his "indiscriminate hugging." When he hugged once more, he was given the boot. Murrow's patients responded by sponsoring a Hug-In at a large public hall and by planning their own Human Development and Resource Center with Murrow at its head.[23] As I said in the last chapter (and before that, in 1977), we live in a strange time. Psychiatrists regularly electrify their patients' brains without a trace of concern over legal consequences, but a hug from a social worker arouses fears about lawsuits for malpractice.*

---

*I had better make clear my feelings about electroconvulsive therapy. I regard it as an effective treatment for certain types of depression. I also think it is widely abused through overuse in understaffed, underfunded madhouses throughout the world.

If sexless body contact leads to such disapproval, real and fancied, imagine the levels of censure associated with explicit sexual contact in the name of therapy. Such contact does exist, and so does its condemnation. The contact usually involves a *sexual surrogate*, a woman or (less often) man who trains patients in social contact, sensual awareness, and sexual technique through direct experience. The use of sexual surrogates has been denounced as everything from sin to medicalized prostitution. This lively issue at last brings us back to that happy land where all conflicts are reconciled, the sexual dysfunction clinic.

Well, *almost* all conflicts are reconciled. One that remains very much unresolved is over the role of surrogate partners. Masters and Johnson—the team that pioneered the use of surrogates—no longer use them, perhaps in response to criticism from more conservative colleagues. But other sexual dysfunction clinics continue to employ sexual surrogates, notably the Center for Social and Sensory Learning in (where else?) Los Angeles.

Before I knew anything substantial about the CSSL and its surrogates, I disliked both instinctively. Serviced sex . . . surrogates . . . Southern California . . . Social and Sensory Centers . . . the whole thing was just a bit too sibilant for a bashful, barefoot boy from Baltimore. Anything that originates south of San Luis Obispo and west of Wyoming is automatically suspicious.

Reluctantly—most reluctantly—I've changed my mind. After considerable reading I have had to face the fact that for many people with sexual disorders the use of surrogates makes plain, common sense. After all, by disallowing surrogates, you automatically eliminate from treatment all those whose problem is that they can't relate well enough to another person to find a sexual partner in the first place. Well represented on this long list of troubled souls are those sexual criminals who do nasty things to unwilling victims at least in part because they don't know how to relate to appropriate partners in a straightforward way. And while Baltimorians don't much care for the idea of rewarding sex offenders with a delightful sexual experience, even we have to admit that trying to cure them makes infinitely better sense than locking them away for a few years and then releasing them with all the new tricks they've learned inside.

There were at last count about 100 sexual surrogates practicing in the United States, the majority living between Fantasyland and the

Queen Mary. And it is in Los Angeles (where else?) that the International Professional Surrogates Association has been formed. It is in every sense of the word a professional body. The Association concerns itself with setting up standards for training, writing a rather strict code of ethics, and defining standards for therapeutic work. Some might think it a Californication of the language to call what is obviously one long, hot sexual encounter "work," but in fact, sexual intercourse accounts for very little of the time spent with clients. Typically, sessions are held once or twice weekly for a period of 12 to 15 weeks. As to whether it is actually work, one sexual surrogate had this to say to interviewer Robert Edward Brown:

> I wouldn't call the process of the therapy itself all that pleasurable. It takes a hell of a lot of energy and so many times you have a client who doesn't know how to communicate sexually, or any other way. Even when you teach the techniques, you can't put magic there and pretend you're relating. Nothing turns anyone into a great lover overnight. Some of them you enjoy more than others, but you always have to be aware of where they are and what they need and you still have to be real. That's a hard job.[24]

She added, "I juggle spontaneity and therapeutic intent." That sort of juggling act sounds remarkably like my own feelings about therapy as a highwire performance, and it convinces me that we are talking about the hard work of healing, not licentiousness.

If sex isn't all there is to it, what more is there? This depends in part on the orientation of the therapists. Masters and Johnson spend a lot of time in conversation with their patients eliciting detailed sexual history, much as would a psychotherapist. But at the Center for Social and Sensory Learning, the emphasis is much more on touch. Many of the Center's clients meet as a group for 12 weekly classes; their lesson plan is a progression of sensual experiences, most done with a partner of the opposite sex. Touch begins with a caressing of each other's hands. As Barbara Roberts, director of the Center describes it:

> They are asked to tune in directly to the sensations, closing their eyes to screen out other input, and to concentrate totally on how their hands feel. Surprises are frequent. Upon opening their eyes they may be shocked to discover they have experienced a

considerable amount of pleasure with someone who, at first, did not attract them at all. It may even have occurred with one who had earlier repelled them . . . this unexpected pleasure forces the recipient to re-evaluate his old belief. Previously, he may have believed that he could only receive pleasure from caressing a particular type of woman, a woman he finds attractive. But now he is aware that he has gotten pleasure from someone he had found unattractive. The door has been opened for growth. And as this new data is integrated in his mind, the separation of mind and body has begun to heal.[25]

The surrogate work also begins with nonsexual touch. Barbara Roberts describes it (again, to Robert Edward Brown) as follows:

We begin with the sensate focus exercises which help the client become more comfortably in touch with his body. This program includes touching exercises for various parts of the body, such as hands or face or feet. Touching genitals is deliberately played down because there is usually too much anxiety focused there. Other exercises include ways of helping the client sensitize his entire body, such as showering together. The exercises are not designed to be specifically erotic, but to make the client aware of the sensations of touch. Many clients have developed an anesthetic reaction to touch.

The surrogate and the client take turns, so he learns what it's like to give and to receive pleasure with each exercise. We also use body-image exercises so that the client can begin to understand how he really feels about his own body, and about the bodies of others. Then we use massage methods and relaxation techniques to loosen both muscular and emotional tensions, and to reduce anxiety.

The "sexological" examination is the most dramatic and educational exercise. It involves the client and the surrogate completely examining each other's genitalia. Most men and women have never done this. It gives them the opportunity to see as well as feel the sensitive parts of their partner's sexual apparatus. The client learns exactly what spots respond to sexual stimulation and what parts do not, lessons that most women—even liberated ones—are reluctant to give.[26]

How does one judge the worth of the body therapies? I'm afraid that, as with so many other forms of healing, individual responses differ so markedly that generalization is almost impossible. I would advise prospective clients to avoid any form of therapy that makes outrageous claims of success, any therapist who demands that his theories be treated as ultimate truth, any group that insists on absolute conformity. Beyond that, it's a matter of individual choice, which, in the case of the body therapies, means literally, Different strokes for different folks.

# Limits to Touch

**14**

We have to cure ourselves of the itch
for absolute knowledge and power.
We have to close the distance
between the push-button order
and the human act.
We have to touch people.

> —Jacob Bronowski

What have we here?

The Widow is well dressed, well bred. She is over sixty, but her brave, erect posture and careful grooming—dignified but not ostentatious—create an impression of someone younger. Yet, despite her rectitude, she looks worried as she gazes out the window. She sees not, for her thoughts are turned inward.

The Widow's introspection is cut short by a disembodied voice, whose pitch and timber form an exact auditory counterpart to her appearance. It is a male baritone, smooth as honey but with no trace of oiliness; rather, it conveys concern without distress. It is the Voice of Authority.

The Voice is one she has heard before, and it stirs long dormant memories. (It is, in fact, a perfect composite of the voices of her father, the family doctor when she was a girl, her late husband, and an oft-imagined airline pilot.)

The Voice asks her a direct question: "What's the matter?"

The Widow looks embarrassed and does not speak.

The Voice speaks for her, uttering her silent thoughts with a mixture of clinical coolness and sincere compassion. It needs say but a single word: "Constipation."

The Widow remains silent, but her face expresses grateful acknowledgement that the right word has been spoken, that her problem has been understood.

She feels relief.

The Voice moves on. Having understood her, having accurately diagnosed her condition, it issues her a command: "Give me your hand!"

Caught between her natural reticence and a feeling of total trust in her unseen companion, the Widow hesitates for a moment, then holds out her right hand, palm turned toward heaven. From somewhere above—from Somewhere Above—she receives a tablet of Ex-Lax.

Ex-Lax?

Ex-Lax. Terrific. She's put her complete trust in this mysterious healer; then, as a sign of both her trust and her need, she has given him her hand. And all she gets in return is Ex-Lax. While this may not be the best thing that's ever happened to *her*, it's just wonderful for the Company. This commercial is going to sell a lot of laxative. Like the Moonie in the airport who first shakes your hand and then shakes you down, it illustrates a use of touch that is good for the toucher but not for the recipient.

This is *exploitive touch*. Skin-on-skin is a powerful means of human contact, and the effects of its misuse are much worse than those of weaker forms. Because exploitation is not always so easy to define as the desire to make a lot of money selling laxative, it is not always easy to avoid. The healer must often ask herself the difficult question, Is what I am about to do for the patient's benefit or my own? And sometimes she still doesn't know.

For example. I have tried to show how touch facilitates talk, brings back memories, opens up areas of embarrassment. While this uncovering process can be the essence of a healing relationship, there are times when such disclosure is premature. In the realm of sexual behavior there is somewhere a dividing line between consent and seduction. Premature disclosure is like seduction: both can be exploitive, both extract a price that will be paid later, and both are aided and abetted by touch. In psychotherapy, getting the patient to disclose secrets against his will may make the therapist feel like a brilliant detective-clinician, but it may also bring with it a resentment that dries up progress or even leads to premature termination of therapy.

The words "sex" and "exploitation" go together like baked potatoes and sour cream, and I have talked about the two so often, in lectures, seminars, and in this book, that I'm beginning to feel like the psychologist who was giving a patient an ink blot test. "What do you see in this first card?" he asked.

"Tits and bums," answered the patient.

"And in this one?"

"A penis and a vagina."

"Ah, yes. And in this third one?"

"Two couples screwing."

By the time he had reached the tenth and final card (on which the patient saw seven rows of breasts and a pair of balls) the psychologist felt reasonably certain of his diagnosis. "You seem," he said, "to have something of a fixation on sex."

"Me?" said the patient with obvious surprise. "It's *you* who keeps showing me dirty pictures!"

Touch is associated with sex, and not only in pictures. Because of their association, and because breaking one taboo can lead to breaking others (one of the few truths in the marijuana-leads-to-heroin theory), so long as therapeutic touch is surrounded by taboo, I believe that the subject needs repeated discussion. The few times I haven't brought it up, someone in the audience has. Healers, be they therapists, general practitioners, or masseuses, worry immeasurably more about touch leading to sex with their clients than does the general public. And for good reason. From their experience they know much better than the public that when two people share a private room for a relatively long period of time, and one talks about intimacies and secrets while the other tries to comfort or help, there is already something sexual about the experience even without the added closeness of flesh meeting flesh.

Indeed, a follow-up study by Kardener and associates of their survey of physicians' attitudes toward physical contact with patients showed that ". . . the freer a physician is with nonerotic contact with patients, the more statistically likely he is to engage in erotic contact."[1] What does this finding mean? Kardener's brief discussion cites Freud's 1931 warning to Ferenczi that the advocacy of even nonerotic contact would lead to the breaking of proper limits, ending in debauchery.

Kardener thinks his data show that Freud was right. I'm not so sure. When teenagers try marijuana and discover that the dire outcomes predicted by their parents, their principals, and their government just don't exist, they are more likely to try another drug that is forbidden but that carries real risks. When physicians, whose training has forbidden them any physical contact with patients beyond the minimum needed to palpate an abdomen and take a pulse, try it anyway and find that instead of disaster they get better results, they too may be tempted to move on to riskier things. Those who do sometimes meet with professional and personal disaster, and I have found no evidence that their patients are benefited.

There are a number of reasons for my belief that the sex taboo between healer and supplicant should be maintained. Their relationship is not one of equals, and the imbalance always carries with it the possibility of exploitation. The situation is further aggravated by the echoes of the parent-child relationship. The patient tends to be dependent and in need of help; the healer, authoritative and relieving. This increases both the patient's vulnerability to seduction and, because of the incest-like nature of their interaction, the likelihood of negative consequences as well.

This view is shared by most but not all healers. Martin Shepard wrote *The Love Treatment* in 1971, a book that extols the virtues of sex between patient and psychotherapist.[2] Though his case is presented with great style, I find his conclusion unconvincing. I remain of the opinion that sex with patients benefits only the physician.

And that leads us to another limitation, the use of touch as an *instrument of power*. So commonly is touch associated with closeness and intimacy that its use as a social distancer seems unlikely; as an implement of subordination, even more so. But novelist Joseph Heller recognized this reality when he wrote about life in the corridors of power in *Good as Gold*:

> There are men who place their hand on the shoulder of another in friendly greeting. There are others who do so to assert possession over whoever or whatever comes within their grasp. On instant of contact Gold recognized the unmistakable intent of one of the

latter, and he turned with a tremor to discover who was claiming him captive.[3]

Social scientist Nancy Henley has explored the power aspects of touch in an article, "The Politics of Touch,"[4] and in her book, *Body Politics*.[5] It is she more than anyone else who has charted the geography of touch as a status differentiator. Henley's thesis is that when it is reciprocal touch is a sign of solidarity, but when nonreciprocal, it indicates status differences. This makes physical contact a tactile equivalent of first-naming. If we call each other by first names, that is a mark of closeness and equality, but if you call me by my first name while I address you by title (Doctor, Mister, Duchess) and last name, that difference reflects and reinforces a difference in our status.

Henley uses as example an incident at the university where she works. Wanting to speak to her after a meeting, the vice chancellor took her upper arms in his hands and continued holding them as he spoke to her at some length. When he finished, Henley took hold of *his* arms, and, now keeping him captive, described her observations about status and nonreciprocal touch. Just as he was beginning to get the picture, the chancellor—the one man on campus with higher status than he—came along, began to talk to the vice chancellor and, as he did so, *took him by the arm.*

Henley takes her case a step further and argues that nonreciprocal touch is a subtle physical threat, a small reminder that power lies in the hands of the toucher. To support her argument, she asks the reader

> . . . to picture who would be more likely to touch the other e.g., putting an arm around the shoulder, hand on the back, tapping the chest, holding the wrist, etc.): teacher and student, master and servant, policeman and accused, doctor and patient, minister and parishioner, advisor and advisee, foreman and worker, businessman and secretary. If you have had the usual enculturation, I think you will find the typical picture to be that of the superior-status person touching the inferior-status one.[6]

Unfortunately, this reinforcing of status differences frequently accompanies the use of touch in healing relationships. The doctor's touch, particularly, is often a paternalistic one—a pat on the head for

the good patient, a playful smack on the behind for the naughty one.
But it need not be so. There are two ways reciprocity can be achieved
in helping relationships: allowing the patient to touch the healer, and
responding to the patient's wishes not to be touched.

I saw a nice example of the former in the far north of New Zealand.
Bruce Gregory, now the Member of Parliament for the Northern
Maori electorate but then a country general practitioner, took me on
his weekly Land Rover rounds to visit his most rural and isolated
patients. One of our first stops was at the simple farmhouse of a *kuia*,
an old and respected Maori woman, and in this case one who was
blind as well. No sooner had we entered her home than she took
Bruce's hand in hers, and, holding it tightly, told him of a dream she
had had the night before. First she described the content (which had
to do with his mother, who had been dead for many years), then the
interpretation (he was drifting into trouble and needed a friend), and
finally the instructions (he was to come visit her more often). The
entire conversation was in Maori, and the whole time she kept his
hand tightly clasped in her own. He made no move to release himself
and was as attentive to her as she later was to him, when his turn
came to diagnose and treat her ailments.

The second way to achieve reciprocity is to respond to the patient's
wishes not to be touched. An example of putting this principle to
work comes from the practice of a young family doctor. Both well
trained and widely read, the doctor was keenly aware that a doctor
should speak frankly with dying patients about their condition, and
realistically, about their limited chances of survival. And that was
his intention when he paid a home visit to Paul, a World War II
veteran who was dying of cancer. The doctor spoke to Paul's wife in
the living room and confirmed that she recognized the seriousness of
her husband's condition. He then walked quietly into the bedroom
where Paul lay in bed, propped up with pillows. The doctor sat on the
bed next to him and placed a hand firmly on his shoulder, saying,
"Well, Paul, what do you think's wrong with you?"

The patient looked at him suspiciously for a moment, then rolled
over and faced the wall, effectively removing his body from under
the doctor's hand. "Buggered if I know," he replied.

Whether because of his training or despite it, the doctor had the
good sense not to replace his hand and not to further pursue the
subject. He mumbled a few comforting generalities and departed.
Later, Paul's wife confirmed what he already suspected: "He's been

that way since the war, Doctor. If there's anything unpleasant, he doesn't want to know about it. He's lived that way, and I guess he's gonna die that way."

Paul did die that way—untold, untouched, and, at least on the surface, unknowing. That may not be good medicine, but it is the way he chose to go out, and his doctor—I think, wisely—acceded to his unspoken wishes.

Reciprocal touch leads to closeness, but closeness is not always desirable in the healing relationship. Sometimes it poses a threat to the healer: a comforting hand on the arm of a psychiatric patient in the midst of a homosexual panic may result in unexpected and unwanted contact between his fist and the therapist's teeth. More often, it can threaten the patient: the counsellor's reassuring embrace may feel smothering to a teenage girl who is desperately trying to extricate herself from an all-enveloping mother. Too friendly a touch may evoke distrust in the sexually exploited child, and too quick a touch may elicit fear in the child who has been beaten. Appropriate touch becomes inappropriate when given at the wrong time, in the wrong dose, or to the wrong person.

With very few exceptions, touch is an adjunct to—not a substitute for—talking and listening. I say this for the benefit of psychoanalysts. Almost every time I speak on the subject of touch before a psychiatric group, a psychoanalyst leaps to his feet and says accusingly, "You're trying to do away with language! You want to eliminate talk in therapy!"

I reply, "No I'm not. I think talking and listening are the basic ingredients of psychotherapy. Touch is an adjunct, useful at some times, to be avoided at others. In my own work I'm a listener and talker at least 90 percent of the time, a toucher maybe 10 percent."

Sometimes that clarification is sufficient, but more often the analyst is back on his feet before I finish, shouting, "You're trying to do away with language! You want to eliminate talk . . ."

And I growl back, "No I'm not. I think talking and listening are the basic . . ."

And that's the end of useful dialogue for *that* day. Touching does not preclude talking.

A more serious criticism, and one also raised by analysts, is that physical contact can be used to *avoid feelings.* Some patients act out their impulses as a defense against experiencing the tensions and conflicts that underlie them. Therapists who indiscriminately comply with every patient's desire to be touched may be entering a collusion against awareness. This limitation of touch should be borne in mind by all healers although it most especially applies to psychotherapists. An example of when not to touch is offered by a Canadian analyst treating a middle-aged woman. She frequently wanted to be held, and she both requested and demanded that he gratify her wish. The analyst consistently declined, always returning her to her own feelings. In time she got in touch with overwhelming feelings of deprivation rooted in childhood memories of an ungiving, untouching family. In this case, not-touching accomplished more than touching would have.

While the purpose of this chapter is to remind readers that not all uses of touch are good ones, neither is all criticism of therapeutic touch valid. Throughout the book we have looked at traditional indifference, hostility and ignorance about the healing uses of touch, but there has been a new attack recently, and this may be the best place to deal with it. The criticism comes from Paul Vitz, a man who manages to combine hard-nosed laboratory psychology with conservative fundamentalist Christianity. He has written an interesting critique of American ego psychology (post-Freudian schools of therapy usually associated with Harry Stack Sullivan, Karen Horney, and Carl Rogers) called *Psychology As Religion: The Cult of Self-Worship*. In it he says:

> The emphasis on empathy and identification with others (for instance, the touching and feeling encouraged in encounter groups) has led to an over-reaction against reason and objectivity. One result has been a cultivation of the irrational in therapy, the rejection of reason, and a lowering of perfectly legitimate standards for training psychotherapists.[7]

Like a number of other statements in the book, this one gets things a bit twisted. Touching is a singularly earthy activity; after all, the traditional test for contact with reality is "Pinch me to see if I'm dreaming." Touch does not automatically lead to "cultivation of the irrational," "rejection of reason," or "overreaction against objectivity." The encounter movement, including its use of touch, was a reaction against sterile, intellectual, orthodox analysis in much the same way that the charismatic movement was a reaction against those same tendencies in Christianity. Vitz himself acknowledges this elsewhere in the book. As for "lowering standards," I hope no reader who has come this far can still believe it. If I'm wrong, the next chapter is my last chance at persuasion.

Let me conclude this brief treatise on the limits of touch with a piece of advice. It is this: In tactility, as in so much else in this world, common sense is more often than not a reasonable guard against bad behavior. Do nothing that is outright silly. Avoid, for example, the sort of enthusiastic obsession of Professor Kirk of Edinburgh and his son, Edward Bruce Kirk. In 1899 the latter condensed his doctor-father's eleven volume *Papers on Health* into one, and in doing so brought into even brighter light the core of their shared belief. Both maintained that massaging with the lather of a soap made from the ash of the Barilla plant could cure nearly all the ills that befall humankind. M'Clinton's soap, a brand of Irish manufacture, was the only one that would do—accept no substitutes: "Take care you are not cheated by a wrong substance."

And indeed you should, for the *right* substance, good ol' M'Clinton's, when worked into a lather and massaged into the proper area of the body, cures abscesses, asthma and angina pectoris; cancer, carbuncles and the common cold; palpitation, paralysis, and purple spots on the skin, not to mention stammering, stomach ulcers, and St. Vitus' Dance. It is also just the thing for measles and mental illness.[8]

The history of massage is like a pattern of waves. A swelling of enthusiasm grows until it becomes a great crest; then it crashes down upon itself, unable to sustain the weight of overstated claims. After the trough, the swelling begins again.

Such rough seas are not limited to massage. Medicine, nursing, psychotherapy, and counseling may be about to sail out of a touchless trough. Will we rise to the frothy foam of another wave only to sink once again under the weight of false promises and imitation miracles?

This time let us break the pattern. As we—doctors and patients, scientists and clinicians, writers and readers—return touch to its rightful place in the art of healing, let us do so without hype, without mystification, without silliness. If our crests are less inflated, our troughs need not be so deep. Smooth sailing.

## 15

# Teaching Touching

No sooner is touch trained than it becomes the teacher of the other senses. It is from touch that the eyes, which by themselves would only have sensations of light and color, learn to estimate sizes, forms, and distances; and they are trained so quickly that they seem to see without having learned.

—Condillac

How do you teach touch to health workers?

This is a question with many answers, for touching, like spelling and reading, can be taught in a number of ways. The method chosen will be determined by the characteristics of the teacher, the needs of the students, and the demands of the setting. But whatever the method, the first step is always the same and always the most important. Without it there will be no teaching, and with it any method will work . . .

Not long ago I canoed down the Barton River in the Northeast Kingdom of Vermont. With me was my neighbor, John Morley, a man who has fished those waters and hunted the surrounding woods all his life. He has lived among the Yankee hunters of Vermont and the Cree Indian trappers across the border in Canada. As we paddled and fished, John pointed out the animal signs along the banks.

"There's a popple [a tree non-Vermonters mistakenly insist on calling a poplar] that a beaver tried to build his nest with this winter.

He got it down, but it got hung up in those cedars when he tried to slide it over the snow, and there he left it. Here's a beaver slide now, and up there, a crane's nest. Listen! You can hear the chicks. And look at this mud. A raccoon, a couple of beavers, a deer and a coy-dog crossed the river here. The coy-dog's tracks follow the deer's . . ."

A year earlier I was on the other side of the globe. Near the New Zealand city of Napier, my friend Denis O'Reilly and I stood looking at a green, pastured hillside. "When you look at that hill," he said, "you see a couple of cows, a little pond, and a clump of manuka trees. Right?"

Since that was exactly what I saw (and seemed to be all there was to see), I answered yes, right.

"When I look at it," he went on, "I see more. I see the remains of a *pa* [a Maori fortification], the place they guarded the water supply, the gardens where they raised *kumeras* . . ."

As he talked and pointed, I saw it all. The raised outlines of the fortifications, the indentations of an old path leading to the spring, the terracing of the *kumera* fields—it was all there for me once I knew what to look for. Once they were pointed out, I became conscious of the meanings of a smooth indentation in a Vermont river bank and the irregular sculpturing of a New Zealand hillside.

It is the same with touch. When you watched *An Unmarried Woman,* you saw a film about marriage and divorce in New York City. I saw the way a woman comforts a friend by lightly stroking her cheek with the back of her fingers. When you went to *Rachel Rachel* you saw a movie about two lonely women in the Midwest. I saw a revivalist minister lift a woman out of her self (and out of her seat) by spreading his palms and fingers along her jaw line. When you observe a general practitioner at work you're thinking about diagnoses, drugs, and outcomes. I think of those things, too, but my attention is directed to the way he relates to the young woman with the injured knee; first telling her that he is going to touch her leg, then explaining what he's looking for while he's touching it, and finally telling her when the touching is about to end. In a psychotherapy session you listen for the interpretations. While I'm listening I watch the small, back and forth movements of the therapist's hands and trunk which tell me that he is resisting an impulse to touch.

*The first and most important step in teaching touching is to create awareness of touch.*

How to create this awareness? The options are limited only by lack of imagination. Films, books, lectures, field observations and, of course, hands-on experience are all ways of conveying touch consciousness. Which you choose depends in large measure on whom you are teaching. I have taught therapeutic touch a number of ways in a number of settings: graduate school lectures, hospital Grand Rounds, convention (medical, osteopathic, psychological) presentations, an all-day university extension workshop, and a holistic health conference seminar. The time involved has ranged from a one-hour lecture to a seminar that met three hours a week for five weeks.

Once you're aware of touch, you'll start to see it everywhere. Use what you see. Plays and movies that have specific touch content can be recommended to students, or, better still, you can build a videotape library of touch in action. Not all the tapes need come from the cinema; some can be made in your own office or in your institution's studios.

Readings for a course on therapeutic touch should be varied according to the needs of the students. *The Massage Book*[1] is likely to be of more interest to masseurs than audiologists, and *Maternal-infant Bonding*[2] will have more relevance to obstetricians than to chiropractors. The bibliography of this book should provide a basis for reading lists in a number of specific areas of healing.

In addition, there are books that are important for any health worker. First among them is Ashley Montagu's *Touching.*[3] Another is Desmond Morris's *Manwatching.*[4] A third is Sidney Jourard's *The Transparent Self,*[5] a book of particular importance to social scientists.

Field observation is an important means of learning and one that is often neglected in university courses. Students can unobtrusively observe touch or the absence of touch in social settings like cafés, elevators, and airports, then move on to settings specifically concerned with health. The doctor's office, the hospital ward, the all-important waiting room—all are good places to observe the way people touch or do not touch each other.

Student observation can go beyond recording the number of times skin meets skin. Who touches whom, and who does not? Which part of the body is used to make contact, and which is the part contacted? Are there untouchable people and untouchable parts? Are the touches fleeting or prolonged, tender or businesslike, mediated through rubber gloves or in the flesh? Are there male-female or young-old differences in touching? What messages are conveyed through the fingers? Does physical appearance or seriousness of condition affect the number of times a patient is touched?

Observation is a great teacher, but supervised experience is an even better one. In the end, no matter how many contacts you have recorded, no matter how many films you have seen or books you have read, the art of touching cannot be taught without touching. Hands-on experience is the best teacher, but that experience must be structured in such a way that it is both conducive to student experimentation and so safe that no harm will come to patients through early ineptitude or awkwardness. Role-playing is a method that meets these criteria. Some of the role-play situations that follow come from the work of other teacher-healers (people like masseuse Julie McLane); others are from my own seminars and from the ongoing Workshop on Emotions that I've run at Otago University. We'll start with the ability to say No.

Saying No may seem an unusual way to begin a touch exercise, but the No and the touch are closely related. Fear of rejection—fear of the No—is a major inhibitor of touch. Many is the healer who has stifled a touch when this thought flashed through her mind: "Maybe my patient doesn't want to be touched—or worse, maybe he doesn't want *me* to touch him!" That very real possibility is not the end of the world, but students have to experience that for themselves. To allow them to do so, I have the class divide itself into pairs. One member of each pair is instructed to offer touch and the other to refuse it. I paired off with a young masseur at a seminar, and our conversation went like this:

"Would you like a massage, John?"

"No, Jules, I wouldn't."

"How's that arm? May I touch it gently?"

"No."

"You look like you have a headache. It might help if I massaged your temples."

"I'd rather have the headache."

This exercise is followed by a role reversal, and that is followed by discussion of the feelings aroused in both the offerer and the refuser. It's important to allow plenty of time for exploration of these feelings.

In addition to teaching that one can cope with rejection, this exercise allows the student to experience another touch-related problem, how hard it is to say No when you don't want to be touched. Julie McLane emphasizes the importance of the No right from the beginning. She tells her students, "If you don't want to be touched, say so! It's your body, your space. Besides, if you really don't want me to touch you, you're not going to let me in when I do."

Any exercise that involves body movement should be helpful in learning to use the body to make contact with another person. In the Workshop on Emotions, one session is devoted to charades. It was here that I first discovered *body illiteracy*. I learned about it from Giles. Giles was a medical student who had been in the group every week for nearly half a year, and in that time I had noticed nothing unusual about him. But when his turn came in charades, it quickly became clear that Giles portrayed horse the same way he portrayed woman, and woman was identical to spider, which was the same as parachute. He had passed three years of medical school with no problem, but when it came to expressing himself with his body, Giles would have flunked kindergarten.

I was so amazed at this somatic ineptitude that I scheduled a special session the next week. Each of the group brought a favorite cassette and each danced expressively to the music. Then we all danced together. By the end of an energetic two hours, Giles' movements were smoother, and he even danced in time to the rhythm of the song, more or less. Well, less. But he was a lot better than he had been at the beginning.

To increase awareness of touch as a mode of communication, all forms of communicating should be brought into consciousness. One way of accomplishing this is through a game I have used with a number of groups. Instruct the students to sit in pairs and talk to each other. Then, one at a time, take away their modes of communication. The first to go is verbal language; they can still grunt and laugh, but words are forbidden. After a few more minutes, all sound is outlawed, and they have to find other means of contact. Then they are instructed to close their eyes; it is at this point that most of them try touching each other for the first time. In a few more minutes, take away touch and see how many of them can figure out ways to keep up some form of communication. Some can—and I don't mean by telepathy.

It's a good rule that healers should have some experience of what it's like to be a patient. This applies to touching just as much as to other forms of healing. Role-play can give this experience. In order for students to get a sense of the isolation of the hospitalized patient, I divide them once again into pairs. The "patients" lie on the floor, eyes closed, arms and legs spread. Making neither physical nor auditory contact with anyone else, they stay in that position for up to ten minutes. Then the "healers" approach them. It is a slow process, a rough equivalent of pausing at the door, smiling, making eye contact, and asking permission to come in. The healers let their presence be felt, then gently come into the patients' space. Each kneels next to a patient without touching him for some moments, then gently places a hand on his shoulder. After the roles are reversed, the group reforms to discuss and examine the feelings elicited by the exercise.

Another paired experience is designed to create awareness of the subtleties of touch. One partner is the receiver; the other, the toucher. The receiver closes his eyes and instructs his partner, "Touch me as if I'm a——" The next word defines the type of touch that will follow. The phrase is repeated and the touch experienced a number of times. Here is a sample series:

"Touch me as if I'm a . . . porcupine
jellyfish
bowl of Jello
orchid
broken bone
old lady crossing the street
crying child
someone you love"

The parameters to be aware of are the amount of contact involved (fingertips, whole hand, entire body), the fragility or solidity of the object, the amount of pressure in the touch, and the message the touch is meant to convey.

It is important to know how clearly the message is being received. A simple feedback exercise is for the touchers to practice different kinds of touch and the receivers to give their immediate response to them. A tentative touch will bring on different feelings than one that is authoritative; an intentioned touch may be experienced more forcibly than a distracted one. Sometimes the feedback is of a more mundane nature. In a session involving foot massage, the university administrator on whose feet I was working gave me the simple but useful advice to take off my watch—the band was scratching her. Switching partners in this exercise allows comparative feedback. If two or three receivers tell you you're too rough, it is a good idea to ease up.

Because of the taboos associated with touch, I try always to move slowly and to encourage open airing of feelings along the way. In my seminar for Otago medical students, for example, I use a progression of touches that begins with very limited contact and moves in the direction of greater intimacy. At the end of our first session the students massage each other's shoulders through their clothing. Since this involves neither skin nor eye contact, they all handle it without much difficulty. Even in this exercise (which is identical to that which I use with high-risk mothers) they start small, working from fingertip contact to use of the whole hand. We begin with *snowflakes*, the lightest possible drumming of individual fingers on the shoulders. Next is *raindrops*, a heavier version of snowflakes but with all fingers hitting at the same time. This is followed by *gliding*, the heels of the palm working in tandem over areas of the shoulder and upper back. Then comes *horsehooves*, cupped-palm slapping of the same area. We end with *whirlpools*, gripping fingers and slowly rotating thumbs. Then the receivers are asked which one they liked best and are given another dose of that before places are exchanged.

In the second session we practice hand and finger massage. Baby oil is used to reduce friction, and the focus is on attending to every part of the hand. At the third meeting we extend contact up the arms, and before the fourth, students go out and practice massage on friends or classmates.

For the final session we meet with an experienced masseuse; in our case it is Sheena Inglis, director of the Physiotherapy Clinic. She demonstrates therapeutic shoulder massage, this time with the receiver lying down and without a shirt. Much of the preceding session is spent discussing this state of shirtlessness and airing student (particularly female student) feelings about it. I always leave the option of not participating though no one has yet used it.

This talking-it-out is of greatest importance when teaching therapeutic touch, and especially so when teaching students whose experience as a doctor, nurse, or therapist is either limited or nil. Discussion of sexuality and intimacy must be thorough and should be undertaken early in the course. Embarrassment is to be expected, accepted, and brought into the open.

There are more mundane details to be taught as well. Clean fingernails and a clean body are essential for the healer who works close enough to touch. Oils and powders are worth trying as a soothing adjunct to massage. Keeping the knees bent and the back straight preserves the masseuse's energy and prevents her from developing the same back complaints as her clients.

The ideas and exercises in this chapter were developed in the classroom, but almost all can be adapted for use with patients or among family members. They are good ways to stay in touch.

### A Final (Disquieting) Word

In the years spent researching this topic, I have come across a myriad of theories that seek to explain why touch works as a healing agent. Some of the theories have been mystical; others, scientific. A few have sought to unite mysticism and science. What they all have in common is that none are convincing explanations of the power of human touch. I have not found one that persuades me that its author has significantly added to our understanding of how touch heals.

Have I, during these years of research, contrived a theory of my own that fills this explanatory gap? Regrettably, I have not. I know the down-to-earth healing properties of touch from my own experience as a psychotherapist, child care worker, and nurse's aide. My awareness has been expanded by the experience of the doctors, nurses, ministers, physiotherapists, and other healers with whom I have consulted. Some of them have spoken from the pages of this book, and many, many others have influenced its development though they were not quoted here. I have learned still more about touch from books and articles that explore various aspects of the subject. But despite all this study, I still do not really understand how human touch works as it does. As always, More Research Is Needed.

To build a theory of touch, clinicians and researchers need to work together with a cooperative spirit that has not always characterized their relationship in the past. If they are to achieve this relationship, they are going to need a climate in which experimentation with touch is encouraged, not punished; a climate in which uses of touch are openly discussed in case conferences, not hidden in a guilty corner of the mind; in which therapeutic touch is subjected to scientific scrutiny, not consigned to darkness by unexamined taboo.

# Notes

## 1. Touching and Healing

1. *Steadman's Medical Dictionary*, Twenty-third edition (Baltimore, 1976).
2. Jerome, Frank, *Persuasion and Healing*, Revised edition (New York, 1974), pp. 60–61.
3. Sidney Simon, *Caring, Feeling, Touching* (Niles, Illinois, 1976), p. 23.

## 2. Touching and Birthing

1. Desmond Morris, *Intimate Behaviour* (London, 1971), p. 14.
2. Ashley Montagu, *Touching* (New York, 1971).
3. Marshall Klaus and John Kennell, *Maternal-Infant Bonding* (St. Louis, 1976), p. 22.
4. John Money and Robert Athanasiou, "Pornography: Review and Bibliographic Annotations," *American Journal of Obstetrics and Gynaecology* 115 (1973), p. 141.
5. Gail Peterson, Lewis Mehl, and Herbert Leiderman, "The Role of Some Birth-Related Variables in Father Attachment," *American Journal of Orthopsychiatry* 49 (1979), pp. 330–38.
6. *Ibid.*, p. 337.
7. Klaus and Kennell, *op. cit.*, p. 59.
8. Roberto Sosa *et al.*, "The Effect of Mother-Infant Contact on Breastfeeding Infection and Growth," *Ciba Symposium #45 on Breastfeeding and the Mother*, pp. 179–93.

9. Betsy Lozoff *et al.*, "The Mother-Newborn Relationship: Limits of Adaptability," *Journal of Pediatrics* 91 (1977), p. 5.
10. T.B. Brazelton, in Klaus and Kennell, *op. cit.*, p. 62.
11. Montagu, *op. cit.*, p. 66.
12. John Bowlby, *Attachment* (New York, 1969).
13. Reva Rubin, "Maternal Touch," *Nursing Outlook* (1963), p. 830.
14. *Ibid.*, p. 831.

### 3. Bringing Touch to Birth

1. Eric Cassell, *The Healer's Art: A New Approach to the Doctor-Patient Relationship* (Philadelphia, 1976).
2. Fernand Lamaze, *Painless Childbirth: The Lamaze Method* (Chicago, 1970).
3. Karen Penny, "Postpartum Perceptions of Touch Received During Labor," *Research in Nursing and Health* 2 (1979), p. 16.
4. Frederick Leboyer, *Birth Without Violence* (New York, 1975).
5. J.H. Weekley, "Dr. Leboyer Sells His Concept of Delivery While Plugging Book," *Obstetrics and Gynecology News* 1 (August 1, 1975).
6. *Medical World News*, "Taking the Violence out of Birth (May 19, 1975).
7. Nancy Nelson *et al.*, "A Randomized Clinical Trial of the Leboyer Approach to Childbirth," *New England Journal of Medicine* 302 (1980), pp. 655–60.
8. *Ibid.*, p. 5.
9. Ina May Gaskin, *Spiritual Midwifery*, Revised edition (Summertown, Tennessee, 1978), p. 136.
10. *Ibid.*, p. 123.
11. Marshall Klaus and Avroy Fanaroff, *Care of the High-Risk Neonate* (Philadelphia, 1973).
12. Arnold Rudolph, "Anticipation, Recognition, and Transitional Care of the High-Risk Infant," in Klaus and Fanaroff, pp. 31–32.
13. Marion Blondis and Barbara Jackson, *Nonverbal Communication with Patients* (New York, 1977), p. 39.
14. *Ibid.*, p. 40.
15. Sheldon Korones, *High-Risk Newborn Infants* (St. Louis, 1972), pp. 116–17.
16. Elizabeth Kübler-Ross, *On Death and Dying* (New York and London, 1969).
17. R.W. Beard *et al.*, "Help for Parents After Stillbirth," *British Medical Journal* 1 (1978), p. 172.

18. Hugh Jolly, "Family Reactions to Child Bereavement," *Proceedings of the Royal Society of Medicine* 69 (1976), pp. 835–37.

19. Stanford Bourne, "Stillbirth, Grief, and Medical Education," *British Medical Journal* 1 (1977), p. 1157.

20. _____, "The Psychological Effects of Stillbirths on Women and their Doctors," *Journal of the Royal College of General Practitioners* 16 (1968), pp. 103–12.

21. Jolly, *op. cit.*, p. 836.

22. *Ibid.*, p. 837.

23. Hugh Jolly, in Beard *et al.*, p. 172.

24. Klaus and Kennell, *op. cit.*, p. 212.

### 4. Touch Gone Wrong

1. *Otago Daily Times*, "Mothers of Sick Children 'Nuisance'" (March 26, 1975), p. 13.

2. *Ibid.*, p. 13.

3. Carol Hardgrove and Rosemary Dawson, *Parents and Children in Hospital* (Boston, 1972), pp. v–vii.

4. H.R. Leiderman *et al.*, "African Infant Precocity and some Social Influences during the First Year," *Nature* 242 (1973), pp. 247–49.

5. Seymour Levine, "Stimulation in Infancy," *Scientific American* (May 1960), Reprint 436.

6. P.A. Russell, "'Infantile Stimulation' in Rodents, A Consideration of Possible Mechanisms," *Psychological Bulletin* 75 (1971), p. 196.

7. Montagu, *op. cit.*, pp. 77–78.

8. James Ross, "The Middleclass Child in Urban Italy," in deMause, Lloyd, editor, *A History of Childhood* (New York, 1975), p. 203.

9. Quoted in Morton Schatzman's *Soul Murder: Persecution in the Family* (London, 1973), p. 61.

10. Montagu, *op. cit.*, p. 78.

11. *Ibid.*, p. 79.

12. René Spitz, "Hospitalism," *Psychoanalytic Study of the Child* 1 (1945), pp. 53–74.

13. *Ibid.*, p. 68.

14. Arthur Janov, *The Primal Scream* (New York, 1979).

15. John Money and June Werlwas, "Folie à Deux in the Parents of Psychosocial Dwarfs: Two Cases," *Bulletin of the American Academy of Psychiatry and the Law* 4 (1976), pp. 351–62.

16. Georg Wolff and John Money, "Relationship between Sleep and Growth with Reversible Somatotropin Deficiency (Psychological Dwarfism)," *Psychological Medicine* 3 (1973), pp. 18–27.

17. Derek Goodwin, "GCRC Research Teams Study Link Between Psychosocial Dwarfism and Child Abuse," *Research Resources Report* 2 (1978), pp. 1–6.

18. Spitz, *op. cit.*, p. 54.

19. Klaus and Kennell, *op. cit.*

20. John B. Watson, *Psychological Care of Infant and Child* (New York, 1928).

21. *Ibid.*, p. 14.

22. *Ibid.*, p. 44.

23. *Ibid.*, p. 80.

24. *Ibid.*, p. 81.

25. H. Durfee and K. Wolf, "Anstaltspflege und Entwicklung im ersten Lebensjahr," *Zeitschrift für Kinderforschung* 42 (1933).

26. Lauretta Bender and H. Yarnell, "An Observation Nursery: A Study of 250 children in the Psychiatric Division of Bellevue Hospital," *American Journal of Psychiatry* 97 (1941), pp. 1158–74.

27. Spitz, *op. cit.*, p. 68.

28. *Ibid.*, p. 70.

29. Wayne Dennis, *Children of the Crèche* (New York, 1973).

30. James Prescott, "Somatosensory Deprivation and Its Relationship to the Blind," in *The Effects of Blindness and Other Impairments on Early Development*, Zofja Jastrzembska, editor (New York, 1976), pp. 65–121.

31. Harry Harlow, *Learning to Love* (San Francisco, 1971).

32. Charles Kaufman, "Learning What Comes Naturally: The Role of Life Experience in the Establishment of Species-Typical Behaviour," *Ethos* 3 (1975), pp. 129–42.

33. Gary Mitchell, "What Monkeys Tell Us About Human Violence," *The Futurist* 9 (1975), p. 77.

34. James Prescott, "Sensory Pleasure: the Therapy of Choice for Those Who Abuse Children," *San Francisco Child Abuse Council News* 2 (1976), p. 7.

35. John Money, personal communication.

36. Jean Goodwin *et al.*, "Hysterical Seizures: A Sequel to Incest," *American Journal of Orthopsychiatry* 49 (1979), pp. 698–703.

37. Meir Gross, "Incestuous Rape: A Cause for Hysterical Seizures

in Four Adolescent Girls," *American Journal of Orthopsychiatry* 49 (1979), pp. 704-8.

38. Goodwin *et al., op. cit.,* p. 698.
39. *Time* magazine, "Attacking the Last Taboo" (April 19, 1980), p. 46.
40. *Ibid.,* p. 46.
41. *Ibid.,* p. 46.
42. Patrick Dunn, "'That Enemy Is the Baby': Childhood in Imperial Russia," in deMause, p. 393.
43. Samuel Radbill, "A History of Child Abuse and Infanticide," in *The Battered Child,* Second edition, Ray Helfer and Henry Kempe, editors.
44. *Ibid.,* p. 6.
45. *Ibid.,* p. 6.
46. Derek Goodwin, "Child Abuse—Our Silent Epidemic," *Parade* (September 16, 1979).
47. Brandt Steele, "Parental Abuse of Infants and Small Children," in *Parenthood, Its Psychology and Psychopathology,* E. James Anthony and Therese Benedek, editors (Boston, 1979), pp. 449-77.

## 5. The Restoring Touch

1. Helfer and Kempe, editors, *The Battered Child* (Chicago, 1974).
2. Ray Helfer, "The Responsibility and Role of the Physician," in *ibid.,* pp. 25-39.
3. Elizabeth Davoren, "The Role of the Social Worker," in *ibid.,* pp. 135-50.
4. Jack Collins, "The Role of the Law Enforcement Agency," in *ibid.,* pp. 179-86.
5. Brandt Steele and C.B. Pollack, "A Psychiatric Study of Parents Who Abuse Infants and Small Children," in *ibid.,* pp. 25-39.
6. *Ibid.,* p. 140.
7. *Child Abuse and Neglect, Volume One: An Overview of the Problem.* U.S. Department of Health, Education and Welfare (1976).
   _____, *Working with Abusive Parents from a Psychiatric Point of View.* U.S. Department of Health, Education and Welfare (1976).
   _____, *The Diagnostic Process and Treatment Programs.* U.S. Department of Health, Education and Welfare (1976).
8. D.C. Geddis, *Child Abuse* (New Zealand, 1979).

9. Mary McCracken, *A Circle of Children* (New York, 1975), p. 23.
10. *Ibid.*, p. 23.
11. *Ibid.*, *p. 23.*
12. Prescott, *op. cit.*, p. 9.
13. *Ibid.*, p. 9.
14. Harlan Lane, *The Wild Boy of Aveyron* (London, 1977).
15. *Ibid.*, p. 7–8.
16. *Ibid.*, p. 18.
17. *Ibid.*, p. 43.
18. *Ibid.*, p. 110.
19. Barry Kaufman, *Son Rise* (New York, 1976).
20. Lane, *op. cit.*, p. 270.
21. Esther Rothman, *The Angel Inside Went Sour* (New York, 1972), pp. 21–22.
22. *Ibid.*, p. 84.
23. *Ibid.*, p. 23.

## 6. Massage

1. Julius Althaus, "The Risks of 'Massage,'" *British Medical Journal* (July 23, 1883), p. 1223.
2. Ilza Veith, *The Yellow Emperor's Classic of Internal Medicine*, new edition (Berkeley, 1966).
3. Herman Kamenetz, "History of Massage," in *Massage, Manipulation and Traction*, Sidney Licht, editor (New Haven, 1960).
4. *Ibid.*
5. Ilza Veith, *Hysteria: The History of a Disease* (Chicago, 1975), p. 5.
6. Kamenetz, *op. cit.*, p. 10.
7. *Ibid.*, p. 13.
8. Fleetwood Churchill, *A Manual for Midwives and Monthly Nurses*, third edition (Dublin, 1872).
9. Kamenetz, *op. cit.*, p. 18.
10. *Ibid.*, p. 21.
11. *Ibid.*, p. 21.
12. Te Rangi Tiroa (Sir Peter Buck), *The Coming of the Maori* (Wellington, 1952), p. 355.
13. K.R. Beals, "Clubfoot in the Maori: A Genetic Study of 50 Kindreds," *New Zealand Medical Journal* 88 (1978), p. 144.
14. Christina Johnston, personal communication.

15. Donald Sandner, "Navaho Indian Medicine and Medicine Men," in David Sobel's *Ways of Health* (New York, 1979), pp. 117-46.
16. Lydia Carbrera, *El Monte* (Miami, 1968), p. 296.
17. Tala Ta'avao, "Traditional Samoan Medicine," Unpublished behavioral science manuscript, Otago Medical School (Dunedin, New Zealand, 1978), p. 16.
18. E. Fuller Torrey, *The Mind Game: Witchdoctors and Psychiatrists* (New York, 1972), p. 33.
19. Diana Anker, "Keep It Healthy," *19* (February 1971), pp. 72-73.
20. Khalil Wakim, "Physiologic Effects of Massage," in Licht, *op. cit.*, p. 38.
21. Irmgard Bischof and Ginette Elmiger, "Connective Tissue Massage," in Licht, pp. 57-85.
22. James Cyriax, "Clinical Applications of Massage," in Licht, pp. 122-44.
23. Charles Bryson, *Health and How To Get It* (Racine, Wisconsin, 1912).
24. Kamenetz, *op. cit.*, p. 8.
25. *Ibid.*, p. 10.
26. *Ibid.*, pp. 19-20.
27. Françon François, "Classical Massage Techniques," in Licht, p. 45.
28. Cyriax, *op. cit.*
29. George Downing, *The Massage Book* (New York, 1972), p. 1.
30. Bischof and Elmiger, *op. cit.*, p. 69.
31. Downing, *op. cit.*, p. 108.
32. C.B. Truax and R.R. Carkhuff, *Toward Effective Counseling and Psychotherapy: Training and Practice* (Chicago, 1967).
33. Morris Parloff, Irene Washkow, and Barry Wolfe, "Research on Therapist Variables in Relation to Process and Outcome," in Sol Garfield and Allen Bergin, *Handbook of Psychotherapy and Behavior Change: An Empirical Analysis*, Second edition (New York, 1978), pp. 233-82.
34. Jerome Frank, *op. cit.*
35. E.M. Prosser, *Manual of Massage and Movements* (Philadelphia, 1951). Quoted in Kamenetz, *op. cit.*
36. Sidney Simon, *op. cit.*
37. Gay Luce, *Your Second Life* (New York, 1979), p. 122.
38. *Ibid.*, p. 93.
39. *Ibid.*, p. 140.

40. *Ibid.*, p. 281–82.

### 7. Holistic Healing

1. Hobertha Wreagh, editor, *Vermont Holistic Healing Directory* (1979).
2. Tom Huth, "Dances, Massages and Healing Thyself," *Washington Post* (September 16, 1979), p. B1.
3. *Many Hands* (Fall 1979).
4. Donal Gould, "Spirits, Doctors and Disease," *New Scientist,* 70 (May 27, 1976), p. 475.
5. Mary Coddington, *In Search of the Healing Energy* (New York, 1978), p. 124.
6. John Thie, *Touch for Health* (Los Angeles, 1973), p. 17.
7. George Downing, *op. cit.*, p. 150.
8. Ivan Illich, *Medical Nemesis* (New York, 1976).
9. James Lynch, *The Broken Heart: The Medical Consequences of Loneliness* (New York, 1977).
10. Downing, *op. cit.*, p. 137.

### 8. Miracle of Miracles

1. Francis MacNutt, *Healing* (New York, 1977), p. 304.
2. Jerome Frank, *op. cit.*
3. E. Fuller Torrey, *op. cit.*
4. Jules Older, *The Pakeha Papers* (Dunedin, New Zealand, 1978), p. 78.
5. William Nolen, *Healing: A Doctor in Search of a Miracle* (New York, 1974), p. 292.
6. *New Testament,* Acts 5:15.
7. *Ibid.*, Acts 19:12.
8. *Ibid.*, Acts 9:18.
9. *Ibid.*, Acts 28:8.
10. *Ibid.*, Mark 7:33.
11. *Ibid.*, John 9:6.
12. *Ibid.*, Mark 8:23.
13. *Ibid.*, Matthew 9:20.
14. MacNutt, *op. cit.*, p. 255.
15. Barbara Schlemon, Dennis Linn, and Matthew Linn, *To Heal as Jesus Healed* (Notre Dame, Indiana, 1978), p. 23.
16. Leslie Weatherhead, *Psychology, Religion, and Healing,* revised edition (New York, 1952), p. 100.

17. Oskar Somner, editor, *The Vulgate Version of the Arthurian Romances* (Washington, D.C., 1910), v. IV, p. 100.
18. *Ibid.*, v. III, p. 417.
19. Marc Bloch, *The Royal Touch: Sacred Monarchy and Scrofula in England and France* (London, 1973).
20. William Shakespeare, *Macbeth* 4:3.
21. Bloch, *op. cit.*, p. 51.
22. *Ibid.*, p. 236.
23. *Ibid.*, p. 243.
24. Charles Mackay, *Memoirs of Extraordinary Popular Delusions and the Madness of Crowds* (Boston, 1932).
25. *Ibid.*, p. 312.
26. Valentine Greatrakes, *A Brief Account of Mr V. Greatrakes, And Divers of the Strange Cures By Him Lately Performed* (London 1666). Quoted in Bryan Laver's "Miracles No Wonder! The Mesmeric Phenomena and Organic Cures of Valentine Greatrakes," *Journal of the History of Medicine and Allied Sciences* 33 (1978), p. 37.
27. Laver, *ibid.*, p. 37.
28. Mackay, *op. cit.*, p. 314.
29. Duncan Bennett *et al.*, *Trager Psychophysical Integration* (undated information sheet).
30. Mackay, *op. cit.*, pp. 324–25.
31. *Ibid.*, pp. 322–23.
32. Sigmund Freud, *The Interpretation of Dreams* (London, 1953), p. 151.
33. Quoted in Mackay, *op. cit.*, pp. 315–16.
34. G.B. Leonard, *The Silent Pulse: A Search for the Perfect Rhythm that Exists in Each of Us* (New York, 1978).
35. Kenneth Pelletier, *Mind as Healer, Mind as Slayer: A Holistic Approach to Preventing Stress Disorders* (New York, 1977).
36. Kate Seredy, *The Chestry Oak* (New York, 1948), p. 233.

## 9. The Age of Miracles Hasn't Passed

1. Donald Gropman, "Thursday Morning at St. Johns," *Yankee* (February 1979), p. 184.
2. *Ibid.*, p. 78.
3. Nolen, *op. cit.*, p. 65.
4. Weatherhead, *op. cit.*, pp. 197–98.
5. *Ibid.*, pp. 197–98.

6. Gropman, *op. cit.*, p. 78.
7. William Reed, *A Doctor's Thoughts on Healing* (St. Paul, Illinois, 1961).
8. _____, *Surgery of the Soul* (Old Tappan, New Jersey, 1969).
9. Kübler-Ross, *op. cit.*
10. Karen Jackovitch, "Sex, Visitors from the Grave, Psychic Healings: Kübler-Ross Is a Public Storm Center Again," *People* (October 29 1979), p. 28.
11. *Ibid.*, p. 28.
12. Dolores Krieger, *The Therapeutic Touch* (Englewood Cliffs, New Jersey, 1979).
13. Carla Fine, "New: Nurse Healers," *Woman's Day* (June 26, 1979), p. 42.
14. Clive Johnson, "Touch for Health: An Interview with John Thie, D.C.," *Science of Mind* (September 1977).
15. Bernard Grad, "The Biological Effects of the 'Laying on of Hands' on Animals and Plants: Implications for Biology," in *Parapsychology: Its Relation to Physics, Biology, Psychology and Psychiatry.* Gertrude Schmeidler, editor (Metuchen, New Jersey, 1976), pp. 76–89.
16. _____, "The 'Laying on of Hands': Implications for Psychotherapy, Gentling, and the Placebo Effect," *Journal of the American Society for Psychical Research*, 61 (1967), pp. 286–305.
17. *Ibid.*, p. 296.
18. Elie Schneour, "The Faith Healer and the Bacterium," *The Skeptical Inquirer* (Spring 1980), pp 7–8.
19. Bernard Korman, with Bernhardt Hurwood, *Hands—The Power of Hand Awareness* (New York, 1978).
20. Krieger, *op. cit.*, p. 17.

### 10. Touching and Doctoring

1. P.N.K. Heylings, "The No Touching Epidemic—An English Disease," *British Medical Journal* (April 14, 1973), p. 111.
2. Sidney Jourard, *The Transparent Self*, revised edition (New York, 1971).
3. Heylings, *op. cit.*, p. 111.
4. Desmond Morris, *The Naked Ape* (London, 1967).
5. Lynn Carmichael, *What Is Family Practice?* Unpublished manuscript, Department of Family Medicine, University of Miami School of Medicine (1978), p. 5.

6. Lynn and Joan Carmichael, *The Relational Model in Family Practice*, Unpublished manuscript, Department of Family Medicine, University of Miami School of Medicine (1977), p. 9.

7. A.S. Kraus and A.M. Lillienfeld, "Some Epidemiological Aspects of the High Mortality Rate in the Young Widowed Group," *Journal of Chronic Diseases* 10 (1959), pp. 207-17.

8. H. Carter and P.C. Glick, *Marriage and Divorce: A Social and Economic Study* (Harvard, 1970).

9. J.H. Medalie, "Factors Associated with the First Myocardial Infarction: 5 Years Observations on 10,000 Adult Males," cited in *Life, Stress and Illness*, E.K. Gunderson and R.H. Rahe, editors (Springfield, Illinois, 1974).

10. Lynch, *op. cit.*

11. J.E.O. Newton and W.H. Erlich, "The History of a Catatonic Dog," *Conditional Reflex*, 3 (1968), pp. 45-61.

12. W.H. Gantt *et al.*, "Effect of Person," *Conditional Reflex*, 4 (1966), pp. 18-35.

13. Lynch, *op. cit.*

14. Lynch, *et al.*, "Effects of Human Contact on the Heart Activity of Curarized Patients in a Shock-Trauma Unit," *American Heart Journal* 88 (1974), pp. 160-69.

15. _____, "The Effects of Human Contact on Cardiac Arrhythmia in Coronary Care Patients," *Journal of Nervous and Mental Disease* 158 (1974), pp. 83-99.

16. Mary Mills *et al.*, "Effect of Pulse Palpation on Cardiac Arrhythmia in Coronary Care Patients," *Nursing Research* 25 (1976), pp. 378-82.

17. Lynch *et al.*, "Human Contact and Cardiac Arrhythmia in a Coronary Care Unit," *Psychosomatic Medicine* 39 (1977), p. 191.

18. _____, "Psychological Aspects of Cardiac Arrhythmia," *American Heart Journal* 93 (1977), p. 652.

19. Judith Perry, "Physicians' Erotic and Nonerotic Physical Involvement with Patients," *American Journal of Psychiatry* 133 (1976), p. 840.

20. H. Musaph, "The Skin as an Organ of Communication," *Hexagon* 1 (1978), p. 11.

21. Warren Johnson, "A Personal Experience with Scleroderma," *British Journal of Sexual Medicine* (June 1978), pp. 46-50.

22. *Ibid.*, p. 48.

23. *Ibid.*, p. 50.
24. Alan Bennett, *Habeas Corpus* (London, 1974), p. 27.

### 11. R.N., P.T., O.T., M.D.—Touch in Hospital

1. Jane De Augustinis *et al.*, "Ward Study: The Meaning of Touch in Interpersonal Communication," in *Some Clinical Approaches to Psychiatric Nursing*, Shirley Burd and Margaret Marshall, editors (New York, 1963).
2. Leah Cashar and Barbara Dixson, "The Therapeutic Use of Touch," *Journal of Psychiatric Nursing* (September–October 1967), pp. 443–44.
3. Joy Huss, "Touch with Care or a Caring Touch?" *American Journal of Occupational Therapy* 31 (1977), pp. 11–18.
4. John Bruhn, "The Doctor's Touch: Tactile Communication in the Doctor-Patient Relationship," *Southern Medical Journal* 171 (1978), p. 1469.
5. Kathryn Barnett, "A Survey of the Current Utilization of Touch by Health Team Personnel with Hospitalized Patients," *International Journal of Nursing Studies* 9 (1972), pp. 195–209.
6. Virginia Henderson and Gladys Nite, *Principles and Practice of Nursing*, sixth edition (New York, 1978).
7. Susie Meredith, "The Importance of Touch in Patient Care," *Imprint*, 25 (1978), p. 66.
8. *Ibid.*, p. 74.
9. Ruth McCorkle, "Effects of Touch on Seriously Ill Patients," *Nursing Research*, 23 (1974), pp. 125–32.
10. Donna Aguilera, "Relationship between Physical Contact and Verbal Interaction between Nurses and Patients," *Journal of Psychiatric Nursing*, (January–February 1967), pp. 5–21.
11. Sheryle Whitcher and Jeffrey Fisher, "Multidimensional Reaction to Therapeutic Touch in a Hospital Setting," *Journal of Personality and Social Psychology* 37 (1979), pp. 87–96.
12. Richard Selzer, *Mortal Lessons* (New York, 1974), p. 34.
13. Nancy Jean Amacher, "Touch is a Way of Caring," *Nursing* (May 1973), p. 854.
14. June Triplett and Sara Arneson, "The Use of Verbal and Tactile Comfort to Alleviate Distress in Young Hospitalized Children," *Research in Nursing and Health*, 2 (1979), p. 22.
15. Jean Hardy, "The Importance of Touch for Patient and Nurse," *Journal of Practical Nursing* 25 (1975), p. 26.

16. *Ibid.*, p. 26.

## 12. Touch in Psychotherapy

1. Erica Jong, *How To Save Your Own Life* (New York, 1977), p. 31.
2. Ernest Jones, *The Life and Work of Sigmund Freud* (New York, 1957), p. 165.
3. Karl Menninger, *The Theory of Psychiatric Technique* (New York, 1973), p. 40.
4. Lewis Wolberg, *The Technique of Psychotherapy*, second edition (New York, 1967), p. 606.
5. Abraham Kardener, William Sheldon, Marielle Fuller and Ivan Mensh, "A Survey of Physicians' Attitudes and Practices Regarding Erotic and Nonerotic Contact with Patients," *American Journal of Psychiatry* 130 (1973), pp. 1077-81.
6. Virginia Davidson, "Psychiatry's Problem with No Name: Therapist-Patient Sex," *American Journal of Psychoanalysis* 37 (1977), p. 46.
7. Jill Bourdais de Charbonnière, "An Exploration of Interpersonal Physical Contact and its Application in Psychotherapy," Unpublished manuscript, Goddard College, Plainfield, Vermont (1979).
8. Elizabeth Mintz, "Touch and the Psychoanalytic Tradition," *Psychoanalytic Review* 56 (1969), p. 367.
9. Sigmund Freud, *Standard Edition of the Complete Psychological Works. Volume 2, Studies in Hysteria (1893-95).* Josef Breuer and Sigmund Freud (London 1955). Chapter II, "Case Histories . . . (3) Miss Lucy R. (Freud) [pp. 106-24] "(5) Fraulein Elisabeth von R. (Freud) [pp. 131-81]."
10. *Ibid.*, pp. 110-111.
11. *Ibid.*, p. 111.
12. Elizabeth Mintz, "On the Rationale of Touch in Psychotherapy," *Psychotherapy: Theory, Research and Practice* 6 (1969), pp. 232-34.
13. Malcolm Brown, "The New Body Psychotherapies," *Psychotherapy: Theory, Research and Practice* 10 (1973), p. 113.
14. Michael Argyle, *Bodily Communication* (New York, 1975), p. 52.
15. Melitta Schmideberg, "A Note on Transference," *International Journal of Psychoanalysis* 34 (1953), p. 199.
16. Jerome Frank, "How Psychotherapy Heals," *Henry Ford Hospital Medical Journal* 122 (1974), pp. 71-80.

17. Truax and Carkhuff, *op. cit.*

18. J.C. Whitehorn and B.J. Betz, "A Study of Psychotherapeutic Relationships between Physicians and Schizophrenic Patients," *American Journal of Psychiatry* III (1954), pp. 321-31.

19. Sol L. Garfield and Allen E. Bergin, editors, *Handbook of Psychotherapy and Behavior Change*. Sixth edition (New York, 1978).

20. Allen E. Bergin and Michael J. Lambert, "The Evaluation of *Therapeutic Outcomes*," in *ibid.*, p. 180.

21. Jules Older, "Four Taboos That May Limit the Success of Psychotherapy," *Psychiatry* 40 (1977), pp. 197-204.

22. James Linden, "On Expressing Physical Affection to a Patient," *Voices* (Summer 1968), p. 36.

23. Carl Christensen, "Discussion," *Voices* (Summer 1968), p. 36.

24. Vin Rosenthal, "Holding: A Way Through the Looking Glass?" *Voices* (Spring 1975), pp 2-7.

25. *Ibid.*, p. 3.

26. Jules Older, "Interpersonal Testing and Pseudotesting in Counseling and Therapy," *Journal of Counseling Psychology* 19 (1972), pp. 374-81.

27. Althea Horner, "To Touch or Not to Touch," *Voices* (Summer 1968), p. 27.

28. *Ibid.*, p. 27.

29. *Ibid.*, p. 27.

30. O. Ivar Lovaas and James Q. Simmons, "Manipulation of Self-Destruction in Three Retarded Children," *Journal of Applied Behavior Analysis* 2 (1969), pp. 143-57.

31. Mackay, *op. cit.*, pp. 318-19.

### 13. The Body Therapies

1. Wilhelm Reich, *Character Analysis* (New York, 1972).

2. _____, *The Function of the Orgasm* (New York, 1961).

3. Ilse Ollendorff Reich, *Wilhelm Reich: A Personal Biography* (New York, 1969).

4. Nic Waal, in *Wilhelm Reich: The Evolution of His Work*, by David Boadella (Chicago, 1974), p. 356.

5. *Ibid.*, p. 361.

6. *Ibid.*, p. 364.

7. David Boadella, *Wilhelm Reich: The Evolution of his Work* (Chicago, 1974), pp. 119-210.

8. _____, personal communication (1981).

9. Charles Rycroft, *Reich* (London, 1971), p. 76.

10. Alexander Lowen, *The Language of the Body* (New York, 1958).

11. *Ibid.*, p. 139.

12. *Ibid.*, p. 47.

13. *Ibid.*, p. 135.

14. *Ibid.*, p. 113-14.

15. Brown, *op. cit.*, p. 105.

16. Hendrik Ruitenbeek, *The New Group Therapies* (New York, 1970).

17. *Ibid.*, p. 161.

18. *Ibid.*, p. 164.

19. Jane Howard, *Please Touch* (New York, 1970), p. 4.

20. *Ibid.*, p. 29.

21. Jules Older, "Improving the Introductory Psychology Course," *Teaching of Psychology* 6 (1979), pp. 75-77.

22. Gwen Davis, *Touching* (Garden City, New York, 1971).

23. David Arnold, "Hugging Costs a Man His Job," *Boston Globe* (January 28, 1981), pp. 17-20.

24. Robert Edward Brown, "Sex Surrogates," *Playgirl* (April 1977), p. 57.

25. Barbara Roberts, "Experiencing Intimacy to Expanded Sexuality," Unpublished monograph, Center for Social and Sensory Learning (Los Angeles), p. 2.

26. Robert Edward Brown, "Sex Surrogates," *Playgirl* (March 1977), p. 37.

### 14. Limits to Touch

1. Abraham Kardener, William Sheldon, Marielle Fuller and Ivan Mensh, "Characteristics of 'Erotic' Practitioners," *American Journal of Psychiatry* 133 (1976), p. 1324.

2. Martin Shepard, *The Love Treatment* (New York, 1971).

3. Joseph Heller, *Good as Gold* (New York, 1979).

4. Nancy Henley, "The Politics of Touch," in *Radical Psychology*, Phil Brow, editor (New York, 1973).

5. _____, *Body Politics* (Englewood Cliffs, New Jersey, 1977).

6. *Ibid.*, p. 424.

7. Paul Vitz, *Psychology As Religion: The Cult of Self-Worship* (Grand Rapids Michigan, 1977), p. 116.

8. Edward Kirk, *Papers on Health* (London, 1899).

### 15. Teaching Touching

1. George Downing, *op. cit.*
2. Klaus and Kennell, *op. cit.*
3. Montagu, *op. cit.*
4. Desmond Morris, *Manwatching* (London, 1977).
5. Jourard, *op. cit.*

# Opinionated Bibliography

## 1. Touching and Healing

Frank, Jerome. *Persuasion and Healing.* Revised edition. New York, 1974.

Vital reading for psychotherapists; helpful to other healers. A thorough updating of his original edition, the book which placed psychotherapy in the context of world healing practices.

Simon, Sidney. *Caring, Feeling, Touching.* Niles, Illinois, 1976.
Underweight, oversweet, appropriately short.

*Steadman's Medical Dictionary.* Twenty-third edition. Baltimore, 1976.

## 2. Touching and Birthing

Bowlby, John. *Attachment.* New York, 1969.
A pioneering, exhaustive, and enormously influential work of theory and observation of the maternal-infant relationship.

Gaskin, Ina May. *Spiritual Midwifery.* Revised edition. Sumnertown, Tenn., 1978.
Spiritual and earthy, reverential and clinical, it gives mother, mate, and midwife equal time.

Klaus, Marshall, and John Kennell. *Maternal-infant bonding.* St. Louis, 1976.

If your obstetrician hasn't read this, tell him about it. If by your next appointment he still hasn't read it, change obstetricians.

Lozoff, Betsy, *et al.* "The Mother-newborn Relationship: Limits of Adaptability," *Journal of Pediatrics*, 1977, pp 1-12.

Money, John, and Robert Athanasiou. "Pornography: Review and Bibliographic Annotations," *American Journal of Obstetrics and Gynecology* 115, 1973, pp. 130-146.
A fascinating article which effectively challenges many firmly held beliefs about pornography and its effects.

Montagu, Ashley. *Touching*, New York, 1971.
The father and mother of all books on touch written since, this one included.

Morris, Desmond. *Intimate Behaviour*, London, 1971.

Peterson, Gail, Lewis Mehl, and Herbert Leiderman. "The Role of some Birth-Related Variables in Father Attachment," *American Journal of Orthopsychiatry* 49, 1979, pp. 330-338.

Rubin, Reva. "Maternal Touch," *Nursing Outlook*, 1963, pp. 828-831.

Sosa, Roberto *et al.* "The Effect of Mother-Infant Contact on Breast-Feeding, Infection and Growth," *Ciba Symposium #45 on Breast-Feeding and the Mother*, pp. 179-193.

### 3. Bringing Touch to Birth

Beard, R.W., *et al.* "Help for Parents After Stillbirth," *British Medical Journal* 1, 1978, p. 172.

Blondis, Marion, and Barbara Jackson. *Nonverbal Communication with Patients*. New York, 1977.
A book for nurses. A bit too general for the working nurse but with its heart in the right place. Contains the sentence "She should, whenever possible, extend the same accommodation when the patient's significant other is visiting."

Bourne, Stanford. "The Psychological Effects of Stillbirths on Women and Their Doctors," *Journal of the Royal College of General Practitioners* 16, 1968, pp. 103-112.

This is the article most responsible for improving the treatment of parents of stillborn children.

_____ "Stillbirth, Grief, and Medical Education," (letter) *British Medical Journal* 1, 1977, p. 1157.

Cassell, Eric. *The Healer's Art: a New Approach to the Doctor-Patient Relationship.* Philadelphia, 1976.
A wise book, of particular interest to doctors and doctors-in-training.

Jolly, Hugh. "Family Reactions to Child Bereavement," *Proceedings of the Royal Society of Medicine* 69, 1976, pp. 835–837.

Klaus, Marshall and Avroy Fanaroff. *Care of the High-Risk Neonate.* Philadelphia. 1973.
Primarily of interest to specialists.

Korones, Sheldon. *High-Risk Newborn Infants.* St. Louis, 1972.

Kübler-Ross, Elizabeth. *On Death and Dying.* New York and London, 1969.
The book which broke open the floodgates of denial about the care of the dying patient. Worthy of a Nobel prize.

Lamaze, Fernand. *Painless Childbirth: The Lamaze Method.* Chicago, 1970.
A book which changed the American way of birth.

Leboyer, Frederick. *Birth Without Violence.* New York, 1975.
The book that's changing it again. A visual and poetic treat, it brings reverence to birth in hospital.

*Medical World News.* "Taking the Violence out of Birth," May 19, 1975.

Nelson, Nancy *et al.* "A Randomized Clinical Trial of the Leboyer Approach to Childbirth," *New England Journal of Medicine,* 1980, pp. 302, 655–60.

Penny, Karen. "Postpartum Perceptions of Touch Received during Labor," *Research in Nursing and Health,* 1979, pp. 9–16.
A nice piece of research which should stimulate more scientific study of the role of touch in the birth process.

Weekley, J.H. "Dr. Leboyer Sells His Concept of Delivery While Plugging Book," *Obstetrics and Gynecology News*, August 1, 1975.

#### 4. Touch Gone Wrong

Anthony, E. James, and Therese Benedek, editors. *Parenthood, Its Psychology and Psychopathology.* Boston, 1970.

Bender, Lauretta, and H. Yarnell. "An Observation Nursery: A Study of 250 Children in the Psychiatric Division of Bellevue Hospital," *American Journal of Psychiatry* 7, 1941, pp. 1158-1174.

Chapin, Henry. "A Plea for Accurate Statistics in Infants' Institutions," *Archives of Pediatrics.* October, 1915.

deMause, Lloyd, editor. *The History of Childhood.* New York, 1975.
A thoroughly frightening study of childhood from early barbarism to very recent barbarism. Reading it puts current practices and widespread attitudes toward children in historical perspective.

Dennis, Wayne. *Children of the Crèche.* New York, 1973.

Dunn, Patrick. " 'That Enemy Is the Baby': Childhood in Imperial Russia," in deMause, pp. 383-405.

Durfee, H., and K. Wolf. "Anstaltspflege und Entwicklung im ersten Lebensjahr," *Zeitschrift für Kinderforschung* 2, 1933.

Goodwin, Derek. "GCRC Research Teams Study Link Between Psychosocial Dwarfism and Child Abuse," *Research Resources Report* 2, 1978, pp. 1-6.

———. "Child Abuse—Our 'Silent Epidemic,'" *Parade*, September 16, 1979.

Goodwin, Jean, Mary Simms, and Robert Bergman. "Hysterical Seizures: A Sequel to Incest," *American Journal of Orthopsychiatry* 49, 1979, pp. 698-703.

Gross, Meir. "Incestuous Rape: A Cause for Hysterical Seizures in Four Adolescent Girls," *American Journal of Orthopsychiatry* 49, 1979, pp. 704-708.

Hardgrove, Carol, and Rosemary Dawson. *Parents and Children in Hospital.* Boston, 1972.
A most useful book for those concerned with improving the way

hospitals relate to children and their families. Important reading for administrator, health provider, and consumer.

Harlow, Harry. *Learning to Love.* San Francisco, 1971.
Harlow and his associates have influenced a host of other researchers studying the effects of lack of stimulation and lack of maternal love in monkeys.

Helfer, Ray, and Henry Kempe, editors. *The Battered Child.* Second edition. Chicago, 1974.

Janov, Arthur. *The Primal Scream.* New York, 1970.
A book with enormous implications for the practice of psychotherapy. Its insights of lasting value may go unrecognized because:
  (a) the book, when published, enjoyed a sudden, enormous, and brief flood of popular attention, and
  (b) Janov disparages all therapies other than his own and fails to document his own failures.

Jastrzembska, Zofja, editor. *The Effects of Blindness and Other Impairments on Early Development.* American Foundation for the Blind. New York, 1976.

Kaufman, Charles. "Learning What Comes Naturally: The Role of Life Experience in the Establishment of Species-Typical Behavior," *Ethos* 3, 1975, pp. 129–42.

Leiderman, H.P., B. Babic, J. Kagia, H. Kramer, and G. Leiderman. "African Infant Precocioty and Some Influences During the First Year," *Nature* 242, 1973, pp. 247–249.

Levine, Seymour. "Stimulation in Infancy," *Scientific American,* May, 1960. Reprint 436.

Mitchell, Gary. "What Monkeys Can Tell Us About Human Violence," *The Futurist,* 1975, pp. 75–80.

Money, John. Personal communication. March 25, 1979.

Money, John, Charles Annecillo, and June Werlwas. "Hormonal and Behavioral Reversals in Hyposomatotropic Dwarfism," in *Hormones, Behavior, and Psychopathology.* Edited by Edward Sacher. New York, 1976.

Money, John, and June Werlwas. *"Folie à Deux* in the Parents of

Psychosocial Dwarfs: Two Cases," *Bulletin of the American Academy of Psychiatry and the Law* 4, 1976, pp. 351–362.

Money, John, Georg Wolff, and Charles Annecillo. "Pain Agnosia in the Syndrome of Reversible Somatotropin Deficiency (Psychosocial Dwarfism)," *Journal of Autism and Childhood Schizophrenia* 2, 1972, pp. 127–139.

"Mothers of Sick Children 'Nuisance,'" *Otago Daily Times*, March 26, 1975, p. 13.

Prescott, James. "Body Pleasure and the Origins of Violence," *The Futurist* 9, 1975, pp. 64–74.

_____. "Somatosensory Deprivation and Its Relationship to the Blind," in Jastrzembska, pp. 65–121.

_____. "Sensory Pleasure: the Therapy of Choice for Those Who Abuse Children," *San Francisco Child Abuse Council News* 2, 1976, pp. 7–10.

Radbill, Samuel. "A History of Child Abuse and Infanticide," in Helfer and Kempe, pp. 3–21.

Robertson, James. Film: John, 17 months: Nine days in a residential nursery. New York University Film Library. 1969.

Robertson, James and Joyce Robertson. Film: Young Children in Brief Separation. No. 1: "Kate, aged 2 years 5 months, in foster care for 27 days." New York University Film Library. 1967.

Ross, James. "The Middleclass Child in Urban Italy," in deMause, pp. 183–228.

Russell, P.A. "'Infantile Stimulation' in Rodents, a Consideration of Possible Mechanisms," *Psychological Bulletin* 75, 1971, pp. 192–202.

Schatzman, Morton. *Soul Murder: Persecution in the Family.* London, 1973.

Schlossman, A. "Zur Frage der Sauglingssterblichkeit," *Münchner Med. Wochenschrift*, 1920, p. 67.

Spitz, René. "Hospitalism," *Psychoanalytic Study of the Child* 1, 1945, pp. 53–74.

A pioneering, comprehensive, and extremely important chapter in the history of children in institutions. To be read with gratitude.

Steele, Brandt. "Parental Abuse of Infants and Small Children," in Anthony and Benedek, pp. 449-477.
Basic reading for those concerned with child abuse.

Steele, Brandt, and C.B. Pollack. "A Psychiatric Study of Parents Who Abuse Infants and Small Children," in Helfer and Kempe, pp. 89-133.
More basic reading in child abuse.

"Attacking the Last Taboo," *Time*, April 19, 1980, p. 46.

Watson, John B. *Psychological Care of Infant and Child.* New York, 1928.
One of the most influential and destructive books of the twentieth century on the subject of child rearing. Thank God for Dr. Spock.

Wolff, Georg, and John Money. "Relationship Between Sleep and Growth with Reversible Somatotropin Deficiency (Psychological Dwarfism)," *Psychological Medicine* 3, 1973, pp. 18-27.

## 5. The Restoring Touch

Bettelheim, Bruno. *Love Is Not Enough—The Treatment of Emotionally Disturbed Children.* New York, 1955.
All of Bettelheim's books are important; this one is a classic in the field.

Bettelheim, Bruno. *The Empty Fortress—Infantile Autism and the Birth of the Self.* New York, 1972. (Copyright, 1967.)

Collins, J.G. "The Role of the Law Enforcement Agency," in Helfer and Kempe, pp. 179-186.

Davoren, Elizabeth. "The Role of the Social Worker," in Helfer and Kempe, pp. 135-150.

Geddis, D.C. *Child Abuse.* National Children's Health Research Foundation. New Zealand, 1979.

Helfer, Ray. "The Responsibility and Role of the Physician," in Helfer and Kempe, pp. 25-39.

Kaufman, Barry. *Son Rise.* New York, 1976.

Lane, Harlan. *The Wild Boy of Aveyron.* London, 1977.
Searching through rotting records, discovering discarded documents and retrieving lost letters, this tireless researcher has saved a vital chapter in the history of education from oblivion. We owe him thanks.

MacCracken, Mary. *A Circle of Children.* New York, 1975.
If you're thinking of working with emotionally disturbed children, read this book. The trials and joys of the job are lovingly and honestly described.

Rothman, Esther. *The Angel Inside Went Sour.* New York, 1972. Copyright 1970.
Tough, insightful, loving—wonderful! Ya' wanna work with toughies? You couldn't pick a better place to start. By the time I finished reading it, Esther Rothman had climbed to the top of my Heroes of Education list.

Steele, Brandt, and C.B. Pollack. "A Psychiatric Study of Parents Who Abuse Infants and Small Children," in Helfer and Kempe. pp. 89–133.

*Child Abuse and Neglect. Volume One: An Overview of the Problem.* U.S. Department of Health, Education, and Welfare, 1976.
The first of a useful series of booklets on the subject of child abuse. All are sold by the Superintendent of Documents, U.S. Government Printing Office, Washington, D.C. 20402.

*Child Abuse and Neglect. Working with Abusive Parents from a Psychiatric Point of View.* U.S. Department of Health, Education, and Welfare, 1976.

*Child Abuse and Neglect. The Diagnostic Process and Treatment Programs.* U.S. Department of Health, Education, and Welfare, 1976.

### 6. Massage

Althaus, Julius. "The Risks of 'Massage,'" *British Medical Journal,* July 23, 1883, pp. 1223–1224.

Anker, Diana. "Keep It Healthy," *19*, February 1971, pp. 71–73.

Beals, K.R. "Clubfoot in the Maori: A Genetic Study of 50 Kindreds," *New Zealand Medical Journal* 88, 1978, pp. 144–146.

Bischof, Irmgard, and Ginette Elmiger. "Connective Tissue Massage," in Licht, pp. 57–85.

Bryson, Charles. *Health and How to Get It.* Racine, Wisconsin, 1912.

Carbrera, Lydia. *El Monte.* Miami, 1968.

Churchill, Fleetwood. *A Manual for Midwives and Monthly Nurses.* Third edition. Dublin, 1872.
A lovely little book which nicely captures the attitudes of medical men of that day toward midwives. Contains the information, ". . . I have endeavoured to teach as much as a midwife in Great Britain need know, considering the limitation in her practise; without giving an amount of information which must lead to mischief, by tempting her to interfere in cases for which she is not competent." (p. viii)

Cyriax, James. "Clinical Applications of Massage," in Licht, pp. 122–144.

Downing, George. *The Massage Book.* New York, 1972.
A helpful, optimistic how-to book on massage, well-deserving of its immense popularity.

Françon, François. "Classical Massage Technique," in Licht, pp. 44–56.

Hiroa, Te Rangi (Sir Peter Buck). *The Coming of the Maori.* Wellington, New Zealand, 1952.
An anthropologist's treasure chest written so plainly that everyone can take home a prize.

Johnston, Christina. East Calais, Vermont. Personal communication.

Kamenetz, Herman. "History of Massage," in Licht, pp. 3–37.
The best scholarly historical overview of massage available.

Leboyer, Frederick. *Loving Hands: The Traditional Indian Art of Baby Massage.* New York, 1976.

Licht, Sidney. *Massage, Manipulation and Traction.* New Haven, 1960.
Massage from a medical viewpoint. Worth tracking down—it's not widely available—for the serious massage practitioner.

Luce, Gay. *Your Second Life.* New York, 1979.
A somewhat mystical, very enthusiastic, and most significant work on the possibilities and excitements of old age. Should have a major effect on gerontology and could have an even greater effect on general perceptions of aging.

Muramoto, Naboru. *Healing Ourselves.* Edited by Michael Abehsera. New York, 1973.

Parloff, Morris, Irene Washkow, and Barry Wolfe. "Research on Therapist Variables in Relation to Process and Outcome," in Garfield, Sol, and Allen Bergin. *Handbook of Psychotherapy and Behavior Change: An Empirical Analysis.* (Second edition) New York, 1978, pp. 233–282.

Pilmer, Gordon. *Chronic Prostatitis.* Norwich, New York, 1962.

Prosser, E.M. *Manual of Massage and Movements.* Philadelphia, 1951. Quoted in Kamenetz, *op. cit.*

Sander, Donald. "Navaho Indian Medicine and Medicine Men," in Sobel, pp. 117–146.

Simon. *Op. cit.*

Sobel, David, editor. *Ways of Health.* New York, 1979.
Well-chosen essays on holistic, ancient, and unorthodox approaches to health. Damned by some medical journal reviewers for reasons that escape me.

Ta'avao, Tala. "Traditional Samoan Medicine," unpublished Behavioral Science manuscript. Otago Medical School. Dunedin, New Zealand, 1978.

Torrey, E. Fuller. *The Mind Game: Witchdoctors and Psychiatrists.* New York, 1972.
A most interesting comparison of indigenous healers and psychia-

trists, written by a most interesting psychiatrist. A good companion-piece to Jerome Frank's *Persuasion and Healing.*

Truax, C.B., and R.R. Carkhuff. *Toward Effective Counseling and Psychotherapy: Training and Practice.* Chicago, 1967.

Veith, Ilza. *Hysteria: The History of a Disease.* Chicago, 1975.

_____. *The Yellow Emperor's Classic of Internal Medicine.* New edition. Berkeley, 1966.
Both this and *Hysteria* set standards of excellence in the field of medical history.

Wakim, Khalil. "Physiologic Effects of Massage," in Licht, pp. 38–43.

Wolbarst, Abraham. "An Apparatus for Pneumo-vibratory Massage of the Prostate," *Journal of Urology* 25, 1931, pp. 519–523.

### 7. Holistic Healing

Coddington, Mary. *In Search of the Healing Energy.* New York, 1978.
"A startling probe into the secret of a strange, curative force that has baffled humankind for centuries!" says the cover. It's not startling, and it doesn't reveal secrets, but it is an interesting overview of beliefs that have influenced the holistic movement. An unfortunate tendency to accept *everything,* but useful nonetheless.

Gould, Donal. "Spirits, Doctors and Disease," *New Scientist* 70, May 27, 1976, pp. 474–475.

Huth, Tom. "Dances, Massages and Healing Thyself," *Washington Post,* September 16, 1979, p. B1.

Illich, Ivan. *Medical Nemesis.* New York, 1976.
One of the most controversial books about medicine ever published. While I disagree with its conclusions, I strongly recommend it both to doctors and to others interested in sickness and its treatment. The book is required reading in my medical school course.

Lynch, James. *The Broken Heart: The Medical Consequences of Loneliness.* New York, 1977.
A well-written and thought-provoking work of particular use to those involved with preventive aspects of health care.

*Many Hands.* Fall, 1979.

Thie, John. *Touch for Health.* Los Angeles, 1973.

Wreagh, Hobertha, editor. *Vermont Holistic Healing Directory,* 1979.

### 8. Miracle of Miracles

Bennett, Duncan, Betty Fuller and Sheila Johnson. "Trager Psychophysical Integration." Undated information sheet (mimeo.).

Bloch, Marc. *The Royal Touch: Sacred Monarchy and Scrofula in England and France.* London, 1973.
A brilliantly written, extensively researched history of healings by the hands that hold the scepter.

Freud, Sigmund. *The Interpretation of Dreams.* London, 1900 and 1953.

Laver, A. Bryan. "Miracles No Wonder! The Mesmeric Phenomena and Organic Cures of Valentine Greatrakes," *Journal of the History of Medicine and Allied Sciences,* 33, 1978, pp. 35–46.

Leonard, G.B. *The Silent Pulse; A Search for the Perfect Rhythm that Exists in Each of Us.* New York, 1978.

Mackay, Charles. *Memoirs of Extraordinary Popular Delusions and the Madness of Crowds.* Second edition. Boston, 1932. Originally published, London, 1892.
Bernard Baruch's favorite book; it has lost nothing over the years.

MacNutt, Francis. *Healing.* New York, 1977. (Hard cover edition, Notre Dame, Indiana, 1974.)
Enthusiastic and popular perspective on Christian healing by a Catholic priest-healer. Allows as how God just may fill teeth.
———. *The Power to Heal.* Notre Dame, Indiana, 1977.
More personal and more to my liking than *Healing.* Both are of interest to non-Catholics involved with healing.

*New Testament.* I have used the American Bible Society's 1849 edition, regularly checking it against later translations. A useful supplement has been *Gospel Parallels,* edited by Burton Throckmorton, Jr., and published in Nashville.

Nolen, William. *Healing: A Doctor in Search of a Miracle.* New York, 1974.

A breath of fresh air blown through the miracle market by a surgeon who writes like an investigative reporter. Recommended to all true believers; required for all miraculous healers. This book is hated by more promoters of miracles than any other one I know.

Older, Jules. *The Pakeha Papers.* Dunedin, New Zealand, 1978.

About race, medicine, and psychology in contemporary New Zealand, it received decidedly mixed reviews there. I liked it.

Pelletier, Kenneth. *Mind as Healer, Mind as Slayer; A Holistic Approach to Preventing Stress Disorders.* New York, 1977.

Sandner, Donald. "Navaho Indian Medicine and Medicine Men," in Sobel, pp. 117–146.

Schlemon, Barbara, Dennis Linn, and Matthew Linn. *To Heal as Jesus Healed.* Notre Dame, Indiana, 1978.

A pleasantly written little book which is probably of most interest to Catholics involved in healing.

Seredy, Kate. *The Chestry Oak.* New York, 1948.

An exciting, idealistic, postwar children's story which managed to engross me 30 years later.

Sommer, Oskar, editor. *The Vulgate Version of the Arthurian Romances.* Washington, D.C., 1910.

Weatherhead, Leslie. *Psychology, Religion and Healing.* Revised edition. New York, 1952.

A carefully considered blend of the three elements in the title.

**9. The Age of Miracles Hasn't Passed**

Fine, Carla. "New: Nurse healers," *Woman's Day.* June 26, 1979, pp. 40–44.

Grad, Bernard. "The Biological Effects of the 'Laying on of Hands' on Animals and Plants: Implications for Biology," in *Parapsychology: Its Relation to Physics, Biology, Psychology, and Psychiatry.* Gertrude Schmeidler, editor. Metuchen, New Jersey, 1976, pp. 76–89.

_____. "The 'Laying on of Hands': Implications for Psycho-
therapy, Gentling, and the Placebo Effects," *Journal of the American Society for Psychical Research* 61, 1967, pp. 286–305.

Gropman, Donald. "Thursday Morning at St. Johns," *Yankee*,
February, 1979.

Jackovitch, Karen. "Sex, Visitors from the Grave, Psychic Healing: Kübler-Ross Is a Public Storm Center Again," *People*, October
29, 1979, pp. 28–29.

Johnson, Clive. "Touch for Health: An Interview with John Thie,
D.C.," *Science of Mind*, September, 1977.

Korman, Bernard, with Bernhardt Hurwood. *Hands—The Power
of Hand Awareness*. New York, 1978.
Full of enthusiasm but not much more. Somehow your knowledge
of hand lore (including palmistry) is going to give you power over
others. Swell.

Krieger, Dolores. *The Therapeutic Touch*. Englewood Cliffs, New
Jersey, 1979.
A loosely written, shockingly edited book featuring a number of
indifferent photographs without captions. Contains the words:

> ... as the person playing the role of the healer scans the healee
> and tries to make sense of the garnered information, in his or her
> mind he or she uses the healee—that is, his or her impressions of
> the healee—as a model. He or she then tries to replicate this
> model: that is, in his or her attempt to understand how he or she
> can best help the healee, he or she (perhaps unconsciously) tries
> to attune him- or herself to the differences which he or she
> becomes aware of as he or she scans the healee. In some such
> manner as this, he or she begins to understand the healee in
> relation to him- or herself. (p. 71)

Reed, William. *A Doctor's Thoughts on Healing*. St. Paul, Illinois,
1961.
Nasty, brutish, and short-sighted. A religious tract written by a
surgeon who has apparently never heard of a Jewish doctor. For
tranquilizers it prescribes, "... the only true solution ... is Shiloh, the

Tranquilizer of the world, the Son of God, the Prince of Peace, Jesus Christ." (p. 12)

_____. *Surgery of the Soul.* Old Tappan, New Jersey, 1969.

Eight years later, Reed is less One Way, Jesus and more insightful into the human condition, though apparently still uncomfortable with it: "It is my position at this point to state that our patient cannot become whole without Jesus Christ." (p. 28). A little hard on Hindu patients, eh, doctor?

Shneour, Elie. "The Faith Healer and the Bacterium," *The Skeptical Inquirer.* Spring, 1980, pp. 7–8.

## 10. Touching and Doctoring

Bennett, Alan. *Habeas Corpus.* London, 1974.

A devilish and delightful look at medics and mores in an English setting. Loses nothing in translation to North American.

Carmichael Lynn. "What is Family Practice?" Unpublished manuscript. Department of Family Medicine, University of Miami School of Medicine. 1978.

Carmichael, Lynn, and Joan Carmichael. "The Relational Model in Family Practice," Unpublished manuscript. Department of Family Medicine, University of Miami School of Medicine. 1977.

Carter, H., and P.C. Glick. *Marriage and Divorce: A Social and Economic Study.* American Public Health Association, *Vital & Health Statistics Monograph.* Harvard, 1970.

Cousins, Norman. "The Doctor as Artist and Philosopher," *Saturday Review,* July 22, 1978, p. 56.

Freeling, Paul. Personal communication. May 2, 1979.

Heylings, P.N.K. "The No Touching Epidemic—An English Disease," *British Medical Journal,* April 14, 1973, p. 111.

Johnson, Warren. "A Personal Experience with Scleroderma," *British Journal of Sexual Medicine,* June, 1978, pp. 46–50.

Jourard, Sidney. *The Transparent Self.* Revised edition. New York, 1971.

Kraus, A.S., A.M. Lillienfeld. "Some Epidemiologic Aspects of the High Mortality Rate in the Young Widowed Group," *Journal of Chronic Diseases* 10, 1959, pp. 207-217.

Lynch, James, L. Flaherty, C. Emrich, M. Mills, and A. Katcher. "Effects of Human Contact on the Heart Activity of Curarized Patients in a Shock-trauma Unit," *American Heart Journal* 88, 1974, pp. 160-169.

Lynch, James, D. Paskewitz, K. Gimbel, and S. Thomas. "Psychological Aspects of Cardiac Arrhythmia," *American Heart Journal* 93, 1977, pp. 645-657.

Lynch, James, S. Thomas, M. Mills, K. Malinow, and A. Katcher. "The Effects of Human Contact on Cardiac Arrhythmia in Coronary Care Patients," *Journal of Nervous and Mental Disease* 58, 1974, pp. 88-99.

Lynch, James, S. Thomas, D. Paskewitz, A. Katcher, and L. Weir. "Human Contact and Cardiac Arrhythmia in a Coronary Care Unit, *Psychosomatic Medicine* 39, 1977, pp. 188-192.

Medalie, J.H. "Factors Associated with the First Myocardial Infarction: 5 Years Observation of 10,000 Adult Males." Presented at the Symposium on Epidemiology and Prevention of Coronary Heart Disease, Helsinki, 1972. Cited in *Life, Stress and Illness.* Editors E.K. Gunderson and R.H. Rahe. Springfield, Illinois, 1974, p. 91.

Mills, Mary, S. Thomas, J. Lynch, and A. Katcher. "Effect of Pulse Palpation on Cardiac Arrhythmia in Coronary Care Patients," *Nursing Research* 25, 1976, pp. 378-382.

Morris, Desmond. *The Naked Ape.* London, 1967.
A speculative, sexist, entertaining, enriching dissertation on the human species. For best results it should be taken with a half gram of sodium chloride and followed immediately by Elaine Morgan's *The Descent of Woman* (New York, 1972).

Musaph, H. "The Skin as an Organ of Communication," *Hexagon* 1, 1978, pp. 8-13.

Newton, J.E.O. and W.W. Ehrlich. "The History of a Catatonic Dog," *Conditional Reflex* 3, 1968, pp. 45-61. See also, Gantt, W.H. *et al.* "Effect of Person," *Conditional Reflex* 4, 1966, pp. 18-35.

Perry, Judith. "Physicians' Erotic and Nonerotic Physical Involvement with Patients," *American Journal of Psychiatry* 133, 1976, pp. 838–840.

Spitz, René. *The First Year of Life.* New York, 1965.

St. George, Ian. Personal communication. 1979.

### 11. R.N., P.T., O.T., M.D.—Touch in Hospital
Aguilera, Donna. "Relationship Between Physical Contact and Verbal Interaction Between Nurses and Patients," *Journal of Psychiatric Nursing,* Jan.-Feb. 1967, pp. 5–21.

Amacher, Nancy. "Touch Is a Way of Caring," *American Journal of Nursing,* May 1973, pp. 852–854.

Barnett, Kathryn. "A Survey of the Current Utilization of Touch by Health Team Personnel with Hospitalized Patients," *International Journal of Nursing Studies* 9, 1972, pp. 195–209.

Bruhn, John. "The Doctor's Touch: Tactile Communication in the Doctor-Patient Relationship," *Southern Medical Journal* 71, 1978, pp. 1469–1473.

Cashar, Leah, and Barbara Dixson. "The Therapeutic Use of Touch," *Journal of Psychiatric Nursing,* Sept.-Oct. 1967, pp. 442–451.

DeAugustinis, Jane, Rebecca S. Isani, and Fern R. Kumler. "Ward Study: The Meaning of Touch in Interpersonal Communication," in Burd, Shirley F., and Margaret A. Marshall, *Some Clinical Approaches to Psychiatric Nursing.* New York, 1963.

Fisher, Jeffrey, Marvin Rytting, and Richard Heslin. "Hands Touching Hands: Affective and Evaluative Effects of an Interpersonal Touch," *Sociometry* 39, 1976, pp. 416–421.

Hardy, Jean. "The Importance of Touch for Patient and Nurse," *Journal of Practical Nursing* 25, 1975, pp. 26–27.

Henderson, Virginia, and Gladys Nite. *Principles and Practice of Nursing.* Sixth edition. New York, 1978.
An attempt to include most of the world's knowledge in a nursing textbook. Beyond all odds, the attempt is successful.

Huss, A. Joy. "Touch with Care or a Caring Touch?" *American Journal of Occupational Therapy* 31, 1977, pp. 11–18.

Kübler-Ross. *Op. cit.*

McCorkle, Ruth. "Effects of Touch on Seriously Ill Patients," *Nursing Research* 23, 1974, pp. 125–132.

Meredith, Susie. "The Importance of Touch in Patient Care," *Imprint* 25, 1978, pp. 66–76.

Selzer, Richard. *Mortal Lessons.* New York, 1974.
A book that transforms falling dandruff, enlarged livers, splotchy skins, scaly growths, and blood-drenched scalpels into the purest of poetic prose. A breathtaking success.

Triplett, June, and Sara Arneson. "The Use of Verbal and Tactile Comfort to Alleviate Distress in Young Hospitalized Children," *Research in Nursing and Health* 2, 1979, pp. 17–23.

Whitcher, Sheryle, and Jeffrey Fisher. "Multidimensional Reaction to Therapeutic Touch in a Hospital Setting," *Journal of Personality and Social Psychology* 37, 1979, pp. 87–96.

## 12. Touch and Psychotherapy

Argyle, Michael. *Bodily Communication.* New York, 1975.
Interesting, useful, and well-written.

Bergin, Allen E., and Michael J. Lambert. "The Evaluation of Therapeutic Outcomes," in Sol L. Garfield and Allen E. Bergin (Eds.) *Handbook of Psychotherapy and Behavior Change*, Sixth edition, New York, 1978.
This entire volume is exhaustively researched, conservative in its conclusions, and surprisingly lively in its writing. This book should be on the desk of anyone who is serious about psychotherapy research.

Bourdais de Charbonnière, Jill. "An Exploration of Interpersonal Physical Contact and Its Application in Psychotherapy," Unpublished manuscript, Goddard College, Plainfield, Vermont, 1979.
An unusually literate and insightful Master's thesis.

Brown, Malcolm. "The New Body Psychotherapies," *Psychotherapy: Theory, Research and Practice* 10, 1973, pp. 98–116.

A critical exploration of four forms of therapy: Reichian, Bioenergetics, Gestalt and primal therapy. Unfortunately, the article is thoroughly mined and undermined by sentences like: "There is the barest recognition of the principle of higher spiritual centering which states that the more evolved and integrated a person becomes the more the person's energy economy becomes stabilized and internalized with a core region of energy flow whose surface or outward manifestations are characterized by a maximum continuity and harmonization." (p. 111)

Christensen, Carl. "Discussion," *Voices*, Summer 1968, pp. 37-38.

Davidson, Virginia. "Psychiatry's Problem with No Name: Therapist–Patient Sex," *American Journal of Psychoanalysis* 37, 1977, pp. 43-50.

Frank, Jerome. "How Psychotherapy Heals," *Henry Ford Hospital Medical Journal* 22, 1974, pp. 71-80.
Another important contribution from one of psychotherapy's most important thinkers. I strongly disagree with his final conclusion that great therapists can read minds.

Freud, Sigmund. *Standard Edition of the Complete Psychological Works. Volume 2, Studies in Hysteria (1893-95).* Josef Breuer and Sigmund Freud. London, 1955. Chapter II, "Case Histories . . . (3) Miss Lucy R. (Freud) [pp. 106-124] "(5) Fräulein Elisabeth von R. (Freud) [pp. 135-181]."

Horner, Althea. "To Touch or Not to Touch," *Voices*, Summer 1968, pp. 26-28.

Jones, Ernest. *The Life and Work of Sigmund Freud.* New York, 1957.

Jong, Erica. *How to Save Your Own Life.* New York, 1977.
Oh, how I wish Ms. Jong had left well alone. Loved her first book (*Fear of Flying*); hated this one. Where *Flying* was spontaneous and open, this one is merely impulsive and embarrassing. High hopes she'll fly again.

Kardener, Abraham, William Sheldon, Marielle Fuller, and Ivan Mensh. "A Survey of Physicians' Attitudes and Practices Regarding Erotic and Non-erotic Contact with Patients," *American Journal of Psychiatry* 130, 1973, pp. 1077-81.

Linden, James. "On Expressing Physical Affection to a Patient," *Voices*, Summer, 1968, pp. 34–37.

Lovaas, O. Ivar, and James Q. Simmons. "Manipulation of Self-destruction in Three Retarded Children," *Journal of Applied Behavior Analysis* 2, 1969, pp. 143–157.

> Also see:  Lovaas, O. Ivar, Benson Schaeffer, and James Simmons. "Building Social Behavior in Autistic Children by Use of Electric Shock," *Journal of Experimental Research in Personality* 1, 1965, pp. 99–109.
>
> Lovaas, O. Ivar, Gilbert Freitag, Vivian Gold, and Irene Kassorla. "Experimental Studies in Childhood Schizophrenia: Analysis of Self-destructive Behavior," *Journal of Experimental Child Psychology* 2, 1965, pp. 67–84.

Menninger, Karl. *The Theory of Psychiatric Technique.* London and New York, 1958 and 1973.
Despite his Cotton Mather approach to touch, Menninger's book contains much practical advice for psychotherapists.

Mintz, Elizabeth. "Touch and the Psychoanalytic Tradition," *Psychoanalytic Review* 56, 1969, pp. 365–376. 1969.

_____. "On the Rationale of Touch in Psychotherapy," *Psychotherapy: Theory, Research and Practice* 6, 1976, pp. 232–234.
The Mintz articles deserve considerably more attention than they have received. They are the product of careful research, considerable personal experience, and a synthesizing mind. Highly recommended.

Older, Jules. "Interpersonal Testing and Pseudotesting in Counseling and Therapy," *Journal of Counseling Psychology* 19, 1972, pp. 374–381.

_____. "Four Taboos That May Limit the Success of Psychotherapy," *Psychiatry* 40, 1977, pp. 197–204.

Rosenthal, Vin. "Holding: A Way Through the Looking Glass?" *Voices*, Spring, 1975, pp. 2–7.

Schmideberg, Melitta. "A Note on Transference," *International Journal of Psycho-Analysis* 34, 1953, pp. 199–201.

Truax, C.B., and R.R. Carkhuff, *Toward Effective Counseling and Psychotherapy: Training and Practice.* Chicago, 1967.

Whitehorn, J.C., and B.J. Betz. "A Study of Psychotherapeutic Relationships Between Physicians and Schizophrenic Patients," *American Journal of Psychiatry* III, 1954, pp. 321-331.

Wolberg, Lewis. *The Technique of Psychotherapy.* Second edition. New York, 1967.

## 13. The Body Therapies
Arnold, David. "Hugging Costs a Man His Job," *Boston Globe,* January 28, 1981, pp. 17-20.

Boadella, David. *Wilhelm Reich. The Evolution of His Work.* Chicago, 1974.

_____, Personal communication, 1981.

Brown, Robert Edward. "Sex Surrogates," *Playgirl,* March, 1977, pp. 33-39.

_____, "Sex Surrogates," *Playgirl,* April, 1977, pp. 55-62.

Davis, Gwen. *Touching.* Garden City, New York, 1971.
A good novel, but not a great novel. Goes well with Jane Howard's book. Serve at body temperature.

Howard, Jane. *Please Touch.* New York, 1970.
One critic called this book "insightful, funny and enormously fair . . ." It is all that and more. To understand the human potential movement, read this book.

Lowen, Alexander. *The Language of the Body.* New York, 1958.
The cover describes it as "a bold, innovative breakthrough to new health, happiness, vigor for the victims of crippling tension, anxiety, and neurosis." I found it a dry mixture of fact and fiction dressed up in scientific clothes.

Older, Jules. "Improving the Introductory Psychology Course," *Teaching of Psychology* 6, 1979, pp. 75-77.

Reich, Ilse Ollendorff. *Wilhelm Reich: A Personal Biography.* New York and London, 1969.

A biography of Reich by his third wife. It is at the same time brave and generous, frank and kind. Well worth reading.

Reich, Wilhelm. *Character Analysis*. New York, 1949. Republished, New York, 1972. *The Function of the Orgasm*. New York, 1961.

Roberts, Barbara. "Experiencing Intimacy to Expanded Sexuality," unpublished monograph.
The clearest description I've seen of the issues involved in the use of sexual surrogates is also by Roberts. It's an unpublished manuscript available from the Center for Social and Sensory Learning entitled "The Use of Surrogate Partners in Sex Therapy."

Robinson, Paul A. *The Freudian Left: Wilhelm Reich, Geza Roheim, Herbert Marcuse*. New York, 1969.
A lively though sometimes too flippant intellectual biography of three men who combined psychoanalysis and radicalism.

Ruitenbeek, Hendrik. *The New Group Therapies*. New York, 1970.
An appropriately conservative guide to the human potential movement, it finds a middle path between the outrageous claims of some encounter freaks and the plaster-cast orthodoxy of psychoanalysis.

Rycroft, Charles. *Reich*. London, 1971 and New York, 1972.
Concise, meaty, fulfilling.

### 14. Limits to Touch

Heller, Joseph. *Good as Gold*. New York, 1979.
The venting of a spleen—even an artist's spleen—does not a novel make. [For another literary example of touch as an agent of power, see Marilyn French, *The Bleeding Heart*, London, 1980, pp. 286–88.]

Henley, Nancy. "The Politics of Touch," in *Radical Psychology*. Phil Brown, editor. New York, 1973.

———, *Body Politics*. Englewood Cliffs, New Jersey, 1977.
A radical feminist perspective on the power aspects of everyday events, including a chapter on touch. An interesting exercise is to compare it with Paul Vitz' (below) conservative tract. I think both overstate their case, but for scholarship and analysis it's Henley, hands down.

Kardener, Abraham, William Sheldon, Marielle Fuller, and Ivan Mensh. "Characteristics of 'Erotic' Practitioners," *American Journal of Psychiatry* 133, 1976, pp. 1324–25.

Kirk, Edward. *Papers on Health.* London, 1899.
A home-remedy compendium based almost entirely on belief in olive oil, hot water, and M'Clinton's soap. Mercifully lost to history.

Shepard, Martin. *The Love Treatment.* New York, 1971.
A fascinating defense of sex between therapist and patient. Presents a series of encounters whose consequences range from indifferent to disastrous, then concludes that sex with patients might just be a good thing. Lively and challenging despite the canyon between evidence and conclusions.

Vitz, Paul. *Psychology as Religion: The Cult of Self-Worship.* Grand Rapids, Michigan, 1977.
While much of this short book does not stand up to close analysis, its conservative Christian viewpoint is so different from most psychological perspectives that it is well worth reading.

### 15. Teaching Touching
Morris, Desmond. *Manwatching.* London, 1977.

# Index